Window on my Heart

Window on my Heart

The Autobiography of Olave,
Lady Baden-Powell, G.B.E.

as told to Mary Drewery

HODDER AND STOUGHTON
LONDON SYDNEY AUCKLAND TORONTO

Contents

Illustrations

CHAPTER ONE

Victorian Childhood

Years: 1889 – 1898

The big jets stream out overhead, one every two minutes, from Heathrow. There are three coaches drawn off the road outside the Palace gates; the car park is full. Sightseers from all parts of the country, tourists from abroad, school-children in straggling columns, little groups of earnest foreigners with guidebooks and cameras: visitors in their thousands crunch down the gravelled drive, past the Queen's Beasts and under the arch into Base Court.

Sometimes, perhaps, as they pause to survey the history all around them, they may – if there is a lull between the jets – wonder to hear the clatter of my typewriter from an open window on the first floor.

Even at eighty-three, I cannot claim as great antiquity as Hampton Court Palace where I have my home, but my beginnings were in an age that is now history.

February 22nd, 1889.

Queen Victoria had been twenty-eight years a widow, withdrawn in her sorrow to the privacy of Osborne. I can sympathise with her grief, having myself suffered an even longer separation from a dearly-loved husband. I can understand her desire to shut herself away and nurse her unhappiness in seclusion, as I myself was tempted to do in 1941 when my darling Robin died. What a wealth of happiness I should have missed, had I not felt it was his wish that I should carry on the work he started.

1889. There was a lull in the African wars. My future husband, at that time no more than Captain Baden-Powell, Acting Military Secretary to General Smyth in South Africa, was spending a short leave hunting elephants.

At home in England, Lord Salisbury was Conservative Prime Minister.

9

One of his many beautiful residences, Cranborne Manor, would become my home only a few years later. The Labour Party was still in its birth throes and it would be eleven years before its first two members were elected to Parliament. That prominent Socialist, George Bernard Shaw, was publishing his *Fabian Essays* but had not yet had a play produced. J. M. Barrie's first book, *A Window in Thrums*, was going through the press. Beatrix Potter had not yet even begun to write her delightful *Tales*. The standard rate of Income Tax was sixpence in the pound. A first-class cook could be obtained for £50 a year and domestic servants for as little as £16. There were as yet no motor-cars in this country and only a few abroad. There were no motor-cycles, no aeroplanes, no vacuum cleaners, no cinemas. It would be another nine years before Marconi sent and received his first wireless signals across the Channel, but there had been a revolutionary style of newspaper in existence for over two years; it was Lord Northcliffe's *Daily Mail* which cost a halfpenny.

It was a leisured age when educated people read more and wrote more, than they do today. I myself have kept a diary daily since the first day of this century.

This is what happened to Olave St. Clair Soames in 1900 at Cranborne Manor, Nr. Salisbury [I wrote self-consciously on 1st January, 1900]. Mother woke us at twelve last night to hear the church bells ring out the old and ring in the new century and year. Muffled peal is most impressive.

I was not quite eleven years old and I smile now to turn the gilt-edged pages of the tiny diary, only some two and a half inches by two, with 'Olave' embossed in gold letters on the red leather binding. The hand-writing is cramped and unformed, recording such, to me, important events as:

January 15 — Two baby pigeons born.
February 8 — I cannot do the double-through at skipping.
March 14 — Drawing lesson. I *hate* it . . .
March 23 — Elocution. Recited 'The Little Quaker Sinner' — quite a long poem — also 'A Smack in School'. I like doing it very much.

However, although I can turn to these childish jottings to refresh my memory of events and places and emotions, I must turn to my mother's journal to see in proper perspective those early years and the ones that went before.

Mother's Book is a massive volume, handwritten on thick deckle-edged paper and bound in limp morocco leather. It is a work of love, lavishly illustrated with photographs and with attractive little water-colours painted by my father. Mother copied it all out three times, once for my sister Auriol, once for my brother Arthur and once for me. With all the condescension of a teenager, I wrote in 1904: 'Mother has been writing her life all this summer. So lovely, funny and pathetic.' Yet I am grateful now that my mother did make this book for her children for it throws much light on her character and, consequently, on my own life and upbringing.

My mother (or 'Muz', as I always called her) was born Katharine Hill — though she preferred to spell her name 'Kath'rine' in order to be different. She could trace her ancestry back to a late fifteenth-century Crichton of Ruthven whose great-grandson, George, was created first Earl of Kinnoul by King Charles I in 1633. The great-granddaughter of the 7th Earl, Amelia Auriol Hay Drummond, married one Archdeacon Wilkins of Nottingham. *Their* granddaughter was my mother. Hence my sister's name, Auriol.

Mother was extremely beautiful and, being conscious of the fact, was very affected. I remember that even if she were only going to speak to one of the gardeners, she would put on a picture hat and gloves to walk in the garden. She had one style of dress and stuck to it all her life, still wearing graceful flowing late-Victorian-style clothes up to the time of her death in 1932. All her shoes came from Pinet in Bond Street — elegant shoes with Louis heels — and she always wore 'Gainsborough' hats. She was quite famous for them. Sometimes I wonder that I am her child, we have proved so different in temperament and outlook.

Her gift for self-dramatisation is evident throughout her book. Her father's business had something to do with Russia. In about 1880 he had the misfortune to lose all his money and, as he had the usual large family of the mid-Victorian period, it became necessary for my mother and her sisters to earn their living. There were few opportunities in those days for a girl of gentle birth, apart from a position as companion or governess. Gertrude (my godmother) became an art teacher at Bilton Grange, the prep. school for Rugby; Annette taught art at Rugby School itself; Constance started a girls' school at Halliwick in Hertford-shire; Marion was fortunate enough to marry. My mother, after a short period as a governess in Switzerland, became a 'companion' in a somewhat Bohemian family in Harley Street. There were four children in this family. Dora and Wilfred were of school age but a son 'Chris' and a daughter 'Jewel' were grown up. My mother records how, in February 1883, Chris brings home a friend:

> ... whom he had met cruising for a cutlet in Bond St ... I recog-nise him as brother to Reginald Soames whom I had met some years ago ... This man was very bright and genial and made a pleasant addition to our luncheon party ...

'The friend' was Harold Soames, my father. Some months later, my mother's employers were leaving to take up residence in Malta. The two younger children were sent to boarding school and my mother was faced with the problem of finding a fresh appointment. Her em-ployers gave a farewell dinner to which Harold Soames was invited and the following morning he proposed marriage.

I have often wondered how much my mother actually loved my father. He adored her but she always seemed to me to make very little effort to share his interests. Perhaps part of the attraction was the security offered by marriage to him, even though her journal denies this:

> Not as a way out of difficulties or fearful of fighting single-handed a hard future – which after all might prove less hard than a life linked with a nature so complex as this man's, who asks me to go to him ... But as tired eyes ever seek the shade – I give – with a longing for peace – my storm-tossed heart into the keeping of one who will, I know, give out of the abundance of his own.

My father was, indeed, a complex character.

On the border-land of genius (was how my mother described him). Cynical — exacting — pessimistic and keenly critical — mitigated by an intellect of singular brilliance.

He had a wide knowledge of art and literature and was no mean painter.

His mental culture, his sense of beauty — his love of nature — his power of giving out from a richly-stored mind that is equally willing to take in, makes him a companion of peculiar charm and interest.

It also made him a father of peculiar charm and originality — but more of that later.

When mother first met my father he was a brewer. That sounds dreadful for a man I have described as artistic and sensitive. It was dreadful for him, too. When he finished his studies at Cambridge, his father (who was a maltster) gave him a brewery business in Chesterfield and told him 'to get on with it'. It was known as the Brampton Brewery Company in those days but has since been taken over by one of the big companies. You can imagine that running a brewery was the very last thing my father wanted to do; it was much too mundane. He was ethereal-minded; he would far rather watch the sunlight on dew-drops than do business. He was a poet — he actually met and talked with Browning once. Nevertheless, he applied himself vigorously to the task his father had set him and worked up the business. After ten years, when he was still in his early thirties, he sold it and never did another stroke of work for the rest of his life. It seems strange that he should have so wasted his years after he gave up the brewery. He just drifted along, spending his money, making beautiful gardens, moving rest-lessly from one lovely house to another. He never did any form of public service, never served on any committees. Indeed, the only 'public' thing I ever remember him doing was when he started the Lawn Tennis Club at Parkstone. He lived the luxurious life of a very rich man until he died in 1918, so he must have put the ten years in the brewery to good effect.

When my mother married him on December 20th, 1883, however, the business was only moderately successful. He was twenty-nine, she was thirty-two. Their first home was Stubbing Court, near Chester-field. Even today, it enjoys as peaceful a setting as it did when my mother went there as a bride. It is a square, grey Georgian manor house, overlooking parkland that slopes gently down to a large lake. My father must have lived there in some seclusion prior to his marriage for my mother describes how she opened up to fresh air 'rooms long closed – gasping for sunshine', of how only one old man and one old woman were in charge of 'the big gloomy house' and its grounds. A young girl was engaged as an additional servant, the neglected garden was taken in hand and soon 'ladies of high and low degree trickle out from C'field, and beyond it, to see what manner of woman this is who has disturbed the hermit of Stubbing.'

It was five miles from Stubbing to the brewery in Chesterfield – a long distance in an age when the only form of travel was on foot or on horseback. It must have been lonely and isolated for a young wife who, on her doctor's advice, had to spend six months, including a 'long, snowbound winter', on a sofa. Whether this was the beginning of the heart weakness that troubled her all her life or whether it was the normal treatment in the eighteen-eighties when a woman was expect-ing a child, I do not know. My sister, Edith Auriol, was born there on September 26th, 1885 and my brother, Arthur Granville, on October 11th, 1886.

For a woman who has survived to my great age, my own birth appears to have been decidedly unpromising. Mother describes the event with a wealth of dramatic detail:

> 1889. January. Coming home late one afternoon over Bole Hill – to avoid a long way round I attack a Derbyshire stile – with woeful results . . . anxiety culminates in grave forebodings for the safety of my coming babe, and of my own life . . .
>
> February. It hangs in the balance through a night of darkness – and as I cling in terror to the thread that binds me to life, and to my children – I send a speechless Farewell in spirit to my little ones peacefully sleeping in the room over the briar garden, and I say 'good night' to my husband and all the house is still – save nurse and doctor and myself – If they can only save me!
>
> February 22nd. The dawn breaks – on a new little life – nearly

extinct — and I am saved to love and welcome my tiny babe, Olave. My heart goes out to this little daughter — the token of a life spared, of dead hopes revived. If I can rear her — if this tiny frail creature, with all loving care, survives the dangers of her birth, and her presence be linked ever with the 'heaviness that endured for a night', may the clear course of her after life be associated with the 'joy that came in the morning'.

I did survive. For the next few months in the Journal, the only reference to me is that 'Baby sleeps always, like a little dormouse, wrapped in flannel.'

In April 1889, I was taken to Buxted in Sussex to be shown to my mother's family and to be christened by my mother's eldest brother who was curate of the parish church. I was given the names 'Olave St. Clair' — 'St. Clair' after my godmother, Gertrude St. Clair Hill; 'Olave' because my father loved the stirring Norse sagas and, had I been a boy, had planned to call me 'Olaf'.

I cannot remember anything of Stubbing Court for I was only fourteen months old when we moved from there to Chesterfield — the first of many, many moves. It could have been that Stubbing Court was too far from Chesterfield for my father to manage his business conveniently. More likely, it was a question of retrenchment for his partner had left what he called 'a sinking ship' and my father had to cope single-handed with what was for him the 'sordid struggle of a commercial world.'

West House, Chesterfield, my second home, was on the edge of the town, not far from the brewery. If the tram-lines passed the door on one side, at least on the other there was a view over distant moors and 'the white road that winds away to Chatsworth'. It was quite a commodious house with a broad staircase and Adam fireplaces. There were hothouses, and a walled garden and an orchard where we could play. Even so, these must have been difficult times for my parents, for mother writes:

'The sinking ship, with cautious guidance, rights itself — and we are encouraged to branch out in luxuries hitherto eschewed. A daily paper — a subscription to the library — a whole housemaid . . . ' This is probably a slight exaggeration for we children had a succession of nurses at that time. We also acquired a parlourmaid and a groom. The latter was probably of the most interest to me for I have always loved animals and I remember as children we used to be taken as a treat to see and stroke the big dray horses at the brewery. As the business prospered, our trap was exchanged for a carriage and my father joined a local hunt. I was evidently taken to a meet at the age of three and given the brush as being 'the youngest lady at the death'. The Master was Sir Lancelot Rolleston, later County Commissioner for Scouts for Nottinghamshire. Oddly enough, he was our first host at a Scout Rally in Nottingham within a month of my marriage to Robin. I cannot imagine myself enjoying hunting at the tender age of three; I was far happier helping mother with her poultry—an enterprise which Auriol and I were later to take entirely into our own hands.

Auriol and Arthur, of course, were both having lessons from a governess by now. Berthe 'reached the end of her tether' with them and was replaced by Louise. She in her turn left, to be succeeded by a Miss Wilson who had been 'run to ground' in the High School at Mansfield. 'Wissie', as she became known, was dark and attractive, with a pointed elfin face. She was evidently more to my brother and sister's liking than her two predecessors for she stayed with us for two and a half years. Indeed, when my parents went away to stay with friends in Yorkshire for grouse-shooting, we three children were left in Wissie's complete charge and she took us on holidays to Filey and Whitby. I kept in close touch with her until her death two years ago.

It was understandable that as soon as the business was prospering, my father would wish to return to a more gracious style of living. In 1895, we moved again, this time leasing Renishaw Hall from Sir George Sitwell who, as restless as my father, had decided to spend a few months at his house in Scarborough, which constituency he represented in Parliament.

Renishaw is, I know, a show-place famed for its gardens and furniture, its pictures and its Brussels tapestries, but again, all I can remember of our stay there is an occasion when three horses strayed into the entrance hall! I can remember the to-do there was shooing them out. There must have been even more to-do the day I fell over the banisters at Renishaw. We had been playing upstairs and terrified screams brought my mother rushing to what she describes as 'a sickening scene'. I was hanging upside-down, unconscious, with a gash in my head, only prevented from falling to certain death on the stone floor below by Auriol's presence of mind in grabbing my legs as I fell over the banisters. This, of course, *would* happen just as we were due to vacate the house for a short time to allow the Sitwells to return with a large house-party! However, they were kindness itself and allowed my mother and me to stay on for another ten days until I was fit to be moved. The shock should have taught me a lesson – but within a year I was caught red-handed climbing the same staircase on the *outside* of the banisters! After this, my mother writes: 'Olave is allowed to play with me – to make sure that the little head is in working order, before she is told to think what is twice one – which, in even her more brilliant moments, she is not quite sure of!'

So the rest of the summer was spent in the open-air, and lessons, to my delight, were temporarily abandoned.

At the end of 1895 our beloved Wissie left and was replaced by a more 'advanced' teacher, a Miss Heap, who was a strict disciplinarian. My brother Arthur (known affectionately as 'Boogie') must have been relieved to escape to Bilton Grange where Aunt Ger. was teaching. Mother, of course, was terribly distressed for she always doted on Arthur and spoiled him outrageously. 'My little Sonnie', she called him. 'My dear Sonnie', 'our little redhead'.

'With aching heart I prepare and pack the little school outfit for him who will be known as "Soames". For him – a babe still – the Home life is over.' Lucky Arthur! Auriol and I remained at home to suffer under Miss Heap.

'Toughened by a sense of duty, as practised by ladies of broad feet and narrow "views", she neither seeks nor inspires aught save a school-room attitude in her pupils . . . ' Fortunately, her reign was a short one and we spent another blissful summer at Renishaw, attended everywhere by our beloved grey and white collie, Bonnie, who had been with us since Stubbing. We learned to handle boats on the lake, we ran our own secret society, *The Bungalow Club*, in the grounds, and at night we listened from our beds to the distant harmonies of our parents' musical evenings. We changed houses with the Sitwells for the month of August and occupied their place in Scarborough, returning once again to Renishaw until the summer of 1897.

Before we left Derbyshire, however, two events of significance were to take place.

Thanks to my father's efforts, the affairs of the Brampton Brewery continued to prosper to such an extent that he decided to turn it into a company. He handed over to others the day-to-day running of the business he found so distasteful and thereafter devoted the whole of his life to the activities that gave him pleasure: shooting, painting, gardening, travel.

My mother wrote: 'From henceforth H(arold) has no work, only the pleasure of living and enjoying the things he loves best—No task, but of his own choosing—No cares, but of his own making.' Thus he was able to leave 'a climate ill-suited to an already shaken constitution' and, with an ample fortune at his disposal, to move around the country perpetually seeking his 'Earthly Paradise'. It was a quest that was to take him eleven years and that was to take us to seven more country mansions and innumerable London houses and flats before he finally bought the property at Lilliput in Dorset that was to become his permanent home.

The other event of significance was the appointment as governess to Auriol and me of Friede Dentzelmann. She was a German woman of uncertain age and stern demeanour, the latter accentuated by rimless pince-nez worn on a cord. Her hair was drawn back severely from her face and screwed into a bun. She was a strict disciplinarian—quite a martinet at times—but was a kindly soul withal and extremely sentimental about her Fatherland. She had a picture of the Kaiser on the wall of her room. Friede had an enormous influence on me during my early, formative years and she remained a life-long friend until her death in 1929.

In June 1897, we moved to Bryerswood, a charming house overlooking Lake Windermere. Whatever regret we children may have had at leaving the now dear familiarity of Renishaw, it was soon swept away in the delight of exploring our new surroundings. Friede gave us our lessons out of doors on the moors so that learning became a positive pleasure. There were picnics and expeditions and sailing on the lake. It was the first of many carefree summers, for now my parents were free to move around the country as their fancy took them. Lessons were never the problem they are for the modern family for Auriol and

I never went to school. We never sat a public examination, either. Friede was our governess, travelling around with the household wherever we happened to be. After she left our service when I was twelve, I had no more schooling—only spasmodic coaching in music or French or German as the need arose. Obviously, this form of education, however casual-seeming, was planned for Auriol and me by our parents. My mother described us as:

> . . . untrammelled by any laid down system of education. Not *made* to learn—but made to *wish* to learn in wider spheres of self-taught interests—they await their life-work equipped with a strange mixture of depth and simplicity—of quaint shrewdness and the freshness of earliest childhood . . .

When I say that my education was haphazard, I do not mean that I did not have regular lessons. Indeed, Friede kept us to a strict routine and our 'terms' approximated to school terms. We did an hour's work before breakfast which was at 9 o'clock. Then we always had a walk from 10 o'clock to 11, followed by lessons till 1 o'clock. After lunch, work was resumed from 2 till 4 o'clock. Tea was at 4.30 and dinner at 7.0. That was my day. I had history lessons on Mondays and Thursdays, Geography on Tuesdays and Fridays, sums—'which I positively loathe'—on Wednesdays and Saturdays. But there was no Science, no Latin, and languages only intermittently. What I did learn was thoroughly taught—but I would be the first to admit that there are large gaps in my knowledge.

In 1889, the year I was born, my mother visited an exhibition of paintings in London where she fell in love with a portrait 'by the new great painter Shannon'. It was a companion picture to a portrait of Ellen Terry as Lady Macbeth and depicted, full length in a white gown, a beautiful girl with a sweet, thoughtful face. Mother had thought many times during the years about this picture. Imagine her surprise one day in 1897 when, invited over from Bryerswood to Grasmere to lunch with Mr. and Mrs. Graham, who should walk into the room but the girl in the portrait! She was the Graham's daughter, Jean. She became a great friend of my parents and had a big influence on my life as a child. She died in 1953.

By the autumn of 1897 my father had decided that his Earthly Paradise was not to be found in the Lake District. He moved us all to 18, St. James's Place, London and went off himself to Italy to paint. We were not happy that winter. London was not the place for us. Auriol and I had a spell of illnesses—whooping cough, diphtheria, influenza, mumps—and when father returned from Italy, he swept us off again to yet another home, Pixton Park, in Somerset. It was a big, three-storeyed house with a balustraded parapet round the roof and a pillared portico in classical style. It was tucked into a hillside above Dulverton and surrounded by beechwoods. Father had leased this property and the 9,000 acres of shooting that went with it from Lord Carnarvon. There was a heronry, there was fishing in three rivers, and there were the wild stretches of Exmoor on our doorstep. We girls enjoyed it. Friede was a fresh-air enthusiast and, as at Bryerswood, we had our lessons out of doors. We would climb up through the beechwoods on to the edge of the moor, taking our books and a picnic tea. In addition, we learned new skills. The introduction of the safety bicycle with pneumatic tyres had started a craze for cycling, and it was a sport that gave new freedom to women and girls. Auriol and I had our own bicycles and could enjoy a freedom of exploration unknown to youngsters on today's crowded roads. We also had our first pony-rides—the beginning of perhaps our favourite sport, with tennis, over the next fifteen years.

Unfortunately, Pixton did not suit mother. It was 'wrapped in mist above, below, around' and she was not well during the nine months we spent there. So once again we packed our belongings and moved to an hotel in Bournemouth for eight weeks until such time as we could take possession of the next house my father had leased, Cranborne Manor, near Salisbury.

The move from Pixton caused me to experience my first grief—that comes often with such heart-rending sorrow to those who have dogs. Poor Bonnie, who had been with us for thirteen years, was too old to face yet another move and had to be put down. It was as well that I had plenty to distract me in connection with the move to the new house.

CHAPTER TWO

A New Century

Years: 1899–1903

Lord Salisbury was midway through his third term as Prime Minister when he leased Cranborne to my father – 'this desolate and beautiful old Manor – isolated from modern times in the wild down country of Dorset'.

On January 24th, 1899, mother and I went ahead from Bournemouth by road with the servants to prepare the house. Father and Auriol followed some days later. The coachman drove us in the brougham complete with hamper of food and drink, with the butler also on board to serve it. It was a complete expedition – all of twenty miles!

Looking back, our rootless existence must have tried mother's patience sorely. The endless packing and unpacking – even with a staff of servants to take over the more arduous part of the work – must in itself have been fatiguing. No sooner was she settled in a neighbourhood and established in the social life of the locality than we were on the move again. We children, on the other hand, found the constant change exciting and stimulating.

On this day in 1899 I was an excited almost-ten-year-old, rather small and thin for my age, with dark hair cut short like a boy's, and brown brandy-ball eyes eagerly watching for the first glimpse of Cranborne through the cold mist. The brougham, piled high with packages, spun along the Wimborne Road till we reached the Manor gates. From here a beech-lined drive – like a dark tunnel to my childish imagining – led to a gatehouse and so to the Manor itself.

I have never been particularly interested in the study of history or architecture – maybe my erratic education missed out on these subjects – but I have always appreciated beautiful surroundings and this appreciation must surely have been developed subconsciously from the gracious and lovely houses I lived in as a child. Cranborne was quite the most beautiful of them all. It was an enchanting and, to me, enchanted place. There had been a home on the site for nearly a thousand years, from the reign of Athelstane, but the house I knew and loved dated from Elizabethan times. It was quite small as manor houses go but graceful in design and built of mellow golden stone. There were tiny, lead-roofed turrets with stiff little metal pennants atop them; moss-grown grey tiles rising behind a battlemented parapet; tall mullioned windows wreathed in crimson Virginia Creeper. There was a little gatehouse made of brick, creeper-clad like the manor itself. We used to play all kinds of games on the winding outside stairs that led off left and right of the main gate. Between the gatehouse and the manor was a walled courtyard, and beyond the house and to the side of it, formal gardens with high hedges and alleys and set-pieces in clipped yew, laid out, I understand, in the early seventeenth century by John Tradescant the Elder who later became gardener to Queen Henrietta Maria.

I loved moving around from house to house and was in my element packing and unpacking. Mother wrote of me at this time:

> Olave, who is equal to three charwomen in work, and to the whole char race in wits, hurls all her sweet energy and thought into every corner, and masters at once intricacies of staircase and passage from dungeon to garret.

Cranborne was a wonderful place for playing Hide-and-Seek. I remember a young man called Uvedale Tristram coming to stay. He had been a partner of my father's in the brewery but had gone off to the Boer War and been wounded; he had the most awful headaches in consequence. We played Hide-and-Seek with him up and down the winding stairs and I eventually tracked him down to his own bed! Was he hiding, I wonder, or had he taken to his bed to gain relief from a blinding headache?

My father loved flowers. 'In each garden as we move,' my mother wrote, 'we plant flowers from each home—and with loving care our Stubbing gentians—thus keeping ever with us living tokens of each happy period of our roving life'. There was an old-world garden at Cranborne where father planted splendid herbaceous borders, all carefully planned as to colour grouping. Auriol and I were expected to help keep the beds in order and we soon 'knew the name and nature of each flower'. It was a delightful way to learn about nature and was typical of my somewhat haphazard education. It was always very much a case of 'learning by doing'.

For example, at Cranborne Auriol and I took over the care of the poultry from my mother. We did everything ourselves: bought the corn, looked after the birds, set the eggs, and hatched out the chicks. We supplied the house with eggs and sent in a bill to mother each week. Auriol kept the money in a leather bag with the initials 'C.P.F.' on it for 'Cranborne Poultry Farm'. We did the same later at Purley Hall, near Pangbourne, except that there the initials had to be altered to 'P.P.F.' It was an excellent way of learning arithmetic — a subject which I loathed in the classroom.

I loved those hens and knew them all by name. An entry in my diary for Easter Day, 1900 reads: 'Pulley, our dear darling tame black Leghorn hen had six babies. We had her at Pixton in 1898 and we love her. She sits in the swing with us.' Photographs taken at this time show me in the inevitable sunbonnet, long-sleeved cotton frock and black stockings, usually with either a hen cradled in my arms or a dove sitting on my head. I adored my doves even more than the hens. I used to let them fly free and they all had their own pet names. They would coo us drowsy on summer afternoons, and they would flutter down to my hand when I called them. I liked to bury my nose in their soft neck feathers; doves smell so sweet. I kept doves right up to the time of my marriage.

I loved all my animals and spent hours and hours playing with them when I should have been doing something useful.

Father bought us our first pony that April: a nice bay cob called Peggy. Auriol and I took it in turns to ride her but she could be very frisky. In June I was thrown and concussed so badly that I was unconscious for two hours. My diary for the following year is full of references to the times I fell off her. There is even an entry 'Peg so fresh that A(uriol) couldn't ride her' so maybe it was not entirely my lack of skill. She was sold by auction at Wimborne at the end of 1901 when we left Cranborne for Purley. A blacksmith bought her. I hope he was kind.

Arthur, of course, was away at prep. school still and in September of 1899, following his father's pattern of education, he went to Eton. Mother was shattered at her little redhead's being launched into the big world and was even more overcome when he returned at the end of the first term considerably matured and—the inevitable result of Public School—much less disposed to be demonstrative towards her than he had been formerly.

On the whole, we children got on well together at this time, though we were all happier when Arthur was away at school. It always happens when there are three at home that they tend to divide into two against one—the two eldest against the youngest, the two girls against the boy, and so on. Actually, I was usually the 'runty' one who got pushed out because I was much smaller than they were. They were in every way superior to me; I was the dunce of the family. But when Arthur was away at school, Auriol and I played happily together and when he returned home for the holidays, it was exciting to see him again and to hear about all his doings.

On the whole, I was a happy child though I am afraid that sometimes I used to sulk. When this happened, Friede would say 'Oh, Susannah is with us today. Now then, Olave, take Susannah out of the room and *leave* her there.'

I took part in my first concert that autumn of 1899. It was held in our barn. The proceeds from the concert were to be used to buy books for the village library. I recited, I remember. I used to like to recite and faithfully recorded the titles of the pieces I performed. 'I Have a Little Shadow' by Robert Louis Stevenson is one that I noted in my diary. Later on, Auriol would play the piano and I the violin. Apparently the first time I played the fiddle in public, I insisted on doing it with my back to the audience, to give myself confidence! Auriol and I also used to dance. We had one or two special numbers. I did a sabot dance; also a song and dance called 'Chinese Dolly'.

Dressing up and making one's own entertainment was very much a part of life at the turn of the century and, indeed, for many years after that. My parents also had frequent musical evenings.

Towards the end of January 1900, father went off, as had become his custom, to spend the winter months in a warmer climate. He could not stand the cold and wet, even in the gentler climate of Dorset, so he took his youngest brother, Reggie, and a painter friend, Ainslie Bean, on a painting holiday to Italy. It must have been lonely for mother at Cranborne, and in any case she loved a busy social round, so we took a house—Talbot Leigh—in Bournemouth for two months. Mother and I drove the twenty miles there in the victoria; Auriol and Friede followed on bicycles and the servants went by train.

Auriol and I were growing up. She was fourteen and a half, I was nearly eleven. So Bournemouth, this time, was fun. We went to concerts at the Winter Gardens where I heard the great Clara Butt for the first time ('so coarse, but has a glorious voice' I recorded). I saw my first Shakespeare play, *A Midsummer Night's Dream*, which 'I liked but did not understand'. We had dancing lessons twice a week in the big ballroom of the Grand Hotel where, in an attempt to give myself a figure, I left undone the top button of my stays! We had elocution lessons from the headmistress of the High School ('she is so nice and *so* hideous') and went to gymnasium classes run by a 'Mr. Mugford near Beale's shop'. 'Great fun' was how I described them. It was all very exciting for a young child but I was glad to return to Cranborne at the end of March to 'our dear dovies and pigeons and chicks which have been well looked after by Mrs. Loveless the gardener's wife'.

How much was I aware at this time of the big events that were taking place in the outside world? Occasionally in my diary I record some incident that must have impinged on my consciousness: 'July 29th, 1900—To church. Very hot. King Humbert I of Italy assassinated —awful.' More often I record just the trivialities of existence: 'Small garden party here.' 'Blackberry party on Partridge Down.' 'Dad shot a snipe.' I wish, with the benefit of hindsight, that I could say I had recorded the Relief of Mafeking on 17th May, 1900 – but I did not. I *can* remember the church bells ringing but the only reference to the Boer War in my diary is a vague entry on June 2nd, 1900, 'Heard Pretoria had fallen but it was really only Johannesburg that was taken. Great excitement tho'.' Of course, we children wore Boer War buttonhole badges of the generals. We bought them at the village shop. Auriol wore Lord Roberts, Arthur had Lord Kitchener and I like to think it was prophetic that I wore a buttonhole badge of B.-P. When the Boer War finally came to an end in May of 1903, I did actually record the event.

Thus the secure, happy months of the first year of the century passed by in a seemingly endless progression of summer days, of parties and picnics, of cycling and driving, of birds and horses and dogs. Gradually my horizons widened. Mother took me to stay in London just before Christmas and I recorded the excitement of seeing Albert Chevalier at the Little Queen's Hall and of going to Daly's Theatre to see *San Toy*. We went down to Eton to see Arthur and had tea with him in his little room at Heygate's House; but soon I was back at Cranborne and the dear familiar routine once more enveloped me.

January 1901 seems to have passed in the same quiet way: 'Morning —played with hoops. Afternoon rather wet, made camphor bags. Evening—practised, read, wrote out poetry . . .' and so on, each successive day. Even the end of an era rates no more than a laconic: 'Jan. 22. Played about. Went to Mrs. Budden. The Queen died.' In a way, it was the end of an era for me, too—the end of my child-hood—for a few days later I went abroad for the first time.

We spent the night before leaving England at the Charing Cross Hotel. I can still remember how gloomy London looked, all in mourning for Queen Victoria. Some shop windows were shuttered and others were draped down the sides with black curtains. I was bought a little grey velvet elephant at Debenham's; I christened him 'Tweets'. I can still remember the agony when my father said: 'You can't take Tweets away with you. There is absolutely no room in the luggage.' But somehow I managed to smuggle him abroad and he became my inseparable companion. He is still around somewhere after all these years.

We travelled with the usual entourage of governess and servants via Boulogne and Paris to Mentone. I think it was the only occasion on which mother accompanied father abroad. She did not enjoy travel and wrote with some asperity: 'The coffee . . . is the only thing worth having come all this way for! What compensation can the Riviera offer for the trouble of getting there!'

The compensation to me was not just the excitement of a new country and new customs; it lay in the acquisition of my very first violin.

A very dear friend of ours, Sybil Mounsey-Heysham (whose

father owned a very lovely house, Branksome Park, in Bournemouth) had been urging my father to let me study the fiddle. She herself was a most competent performer. Now at last, I had my 'first little squeaker', as mother called it. I was taught by a Herr Graf and I must be grateful that he endured the pain of my first efforts without discouraging me, for my fiddle was to become a constant source of pleasure throughout my girlhood and until the early years of my marriage. I practised every day with great enthusiasm while I was in Mentone. I was also required to read French daily, though I fear I never became fluent.

May saw us back at Cranborne again but by now my mother was feeling it too isolated. She longed to be nearer London, particularly as Auriol was almost ready to be 'launched' into Society – and it would not be so far to visit her beloved Boogie at Eton.

This time my father leased Purley Hall at Pangbourne in Berkshire. We moved there at the beginning of December 1901. I found it very ugly after the beauty and antiquity and peace of Cranborne. I was very unhappy, also, that Friede had departed from our service, my parents feeling that Auriol had by now 'outstripped her teacher in intelligence'. So when Auriol's schooling stopped, mine stopped also – or virtually so. I wrote: 'Having given up all book work I have more leisure for Tompy, for Doogy, and the rest of my pets.' Tompy was a Welsh pony who lived rough. I used to follow the hounds on him occasionally that winter, though not with the passionate dedication I showed later on in Suffolk. Doogy – 'my own brown angel' – was a liver and white English springer spaniel given to me by Willie Arkwright. He had been a friend of my father's in Derbyshire; I think he bred spaniels.

Our beloved Jean Graham came to stay with us for three months and gave me a little schooling, but Purley stands out in my memory particularly on account of my progress with the fiddle.

Mr. Stephen V. Shea became my violin teacher. He had a Stradivarius, I remember. I can see myself now bicycling into Reading from Purley, with my violin on my back, to have my music lesson. It was five miles from Pangbourne to Reading so I needed to be keen. I had by now acquired a full-sized fiddle which I christened 'The Nightingale'. I heard Jan Kubelik play the violin in Reading. It was the first real recital I had ever been to and I was rapt. It was too lovely for words. I had never heard anyone play like him before. I felt I *must* practise my own fiddle-playing. One day, perhaps, *I* might become a concert violinist.

'Who knows?' I thought to myself. 'One day I might even have *my* name on a programme!'

Of course, life at Purley was not all music. I have always thrown myself with enthusiasm into whatever activities my surroundings have offered. The greatest joy of Purley was the river. We had already learned to handle boats at Renishaw but that did not compare with the bliss of canoeing or punting or rowing on the Thames, toiling slowly upstream to Goring, or drifting down with tea to Mapledurham. There were regattas at Goring. I even won a prize for coxing.

We also had a farm, so there was hay-making and playing on the ricks, and helping with the herd of Jersey cows. My father taught me tennis and squash (we had our own squash court) and my diary records endless parties and tournaments. In particular, one S. W. Spooner seems to have been over almost daily. He was, I think, a nephew of Dean Spooner of the 'isms' and was madly in love with Auriol.

I was still leggy and thin with, by now, long dark hair. Auriol, on the other hand, had developed into a great beauty — tall and elegant, with a mass of auburn hair. It was time for her 'coming out' for she was turned seventeen. We had a big house party over the New Year, and Tuesday, 6th January was *the* day. I noted — very discreetly for not-quite-fourteen: 'A's coming-out dance. A great to-do. About 150 people. I stayed up till three. Great success. A cotillion is such fun.' I say 'discreetly' for this was the beginning of my first shy romance.

Arthur had invited some of his Eton friends to stay with us for the ball, among them a young man of fifteen called Roley N. I think we went altogether to nine dances in ten days but Auriol's dance is the one I remember the best. I had my hair tied back with a big bow of ribbon. Roley kissed me and snatched my bow and took it back to Eton with him the next term. Even today, between the pages of mid-April in my diary for 1903 there is a faded four-leaved clover that Roley gave me. There are shy references to him during the ensuing weeks; then, sadly, in August: 'R. rather stand-offish . . . so concluded he didn't care any more.' Two days later: 'Roley explained matters behind the stables.' By the following December, however, I quoted in full in my diary:

> Pale hands I loved
> Beside the Shalimar,
> Where are you now, etc., etc.
> I am quite off Roley N. It is odd. I thought
> I loved him so much!

Dear Roley! I lost touch with him completely in later years but shall always remember him with affection as my 'first love'.

That romantic episode was typical of me in my 'teens. Right up to meeting Robin, I was so impressionable, falling in and out of love with one young man after another, yet never being wholly satisfied, never being *sure* that this time it was the real thing. Three times I received proposals of marriage and three times I refused. Always I was saying to myself 'Surely this cannot be the love I dream of.' Yet I need not have suffered the agonising doubts I confided to my diary over the years. When at last I met Robin, we both knew immediately that we were right for each other. How grateful I am that God saved my darling for me, and me for him.

CHAPTER THREE

Edwardian Idyll

Years: 1902—1905

Looking back over my long life, I realise now what a happy, sheltered, but utterly useless existence I enjoyed up to the time of my marriage. Certainly it was scant preparation for the life I was to lead from the First World War onwards. Today, young people of conscience throw their energies into Scouting and Guiding and other forms of voluntary service. They are alive to the needs of the homeless, the old and the physically handicapped, and they feel deeply and passionately the sufferings of the world. By their critical standards, the activities of my early years were not so much frivolous as futile. In explanation, if not in extenuation, I can only plead that during the late Victorian and the Edwardian period, girls of my age and class very rarely did do anything useful with their lives. The system condemned us to remain in our homes until matrimony brought us release.

Not that it was an unenjoyable prison.

We were part of a class-conscious society. I remember my mother saying: 'The criterion of a good housemaid is that she is never *seen*.' It was a secure and prosperous time for the country – at least for well-to-do people like my parents. If I had been a labourer's daughter, the times might have appeared less secure and less prosperous.

In the summer of 1901, for example, when we went on a week's tour of the New Forest, mother and I travelled in the carriage, driven by a groom in breeches, frock coat and top hat. Father, Auriol and Arthur accompanied us, as was the craze at the time, on their bicycles.

When mother took Auriol to London for a week in May 1903, they had to take with them Lizzie (one of the maids) and the butler.

When my father rented a moor in Scotland for two months later that year, the entire household moved north—family, staff, dogs, horses. It was rather like the medieval 'progression' from castle to castle. Such a style of living is unimaginable nowadays. We kept a household of nine permanent servants who travelled with us, complete with their own families, from house to house. Not only did they travel, but also our entire complement of sheets, blankets, household linen, silver, china, kitchen utensils and various pieces of personal furniture such as a grand piano, garden ornaments, etc. My parents felt the 'restriction' of only having nine servants, for there was always the problem of only being able to have up to twelve guests at any one time to stay. Any more would have necessitated a considerable increase in staff.

It would appear from my diaries for this period—particularly when I had given up lessons—that my days were spent in an endless round, according to the time of the year, of tennis, riding, swimming, skating, boating, picnics, garden parties, luncheons, dinners and house-parties. There was a constant stream of guests through our houses. I can still remember the lavish meals, particularly the breakfasts: porridge with cream; eggs, poached and boiled; finnan haddock, kippers, kidneys; and always on the sideboard cold ham, tongue or grouse, if it was in season.

I liked food. I still do. I have always been 'a good doer'. Father, on the other hand, was very fussy and complaining about his food. If there was even a minute speck of core or peel in the stewed apple, he would send it back. It is true that he was a martyr to dyspepsia but he was also a bit of a hypochondriac. For all that, I adored him. He and I were great companions, though he treated me like a favourite toy. Mother was more concerned with Auriol, her 'flower', who was the beauty of the family. Mother hoped she would make a good match and always liked to whisk her off to London for 'the Season'.

Of course, my parents were not 'in the swim' of High Society. They were not aristocracy, rather country gentry; so there was no question of taking a big London house and entertaining for Auriol. That aspect of the Season was little more than a marriage market. If a girl was not engaged by the end of her first season, she dare not do a second. Arthur was more a part of that sort of Society life. When he was in the Guards, he was very much in demand by designing mothers who wanted eligible young men as escorts for their daughters.

However, Auriol 'did the Season' in that she was taken around to a certain number of dances, dinners, theatres and so on.

I was too young—and, in any event, was not yet 'out'—to enjoy a season. I much preferred the country and the company of my horses, dogs and birds. Father and I often stayed behind when mother and Auriol went up to Town. We cycled and rode together, and I would partner him at tennis. I used to love to accompany him out shooting. I would be with the beaters, with Doogy I, my spaniel, close by me. I loved trampling through the turnips, putting up a covey of partridges. Doogy would crouch by my side, quivering with excitement. I used solemnly to record the day's bag in my diary: 'Friday, October 31st, 1902. 25 rabbits, 7 pheasants, 1 partridge, 1 pigeon.'

Mother was not interested in sport and never played a game in her life. She was not interested in painting or any of my father's hobbies, either, though she used to do beautiful sewing and embroidery. It irritated her if people sat with idle hands. I remember her trying to teach my friend, Sie Bower, to crochet. 'It will give you inner peace,' she told her; but Sie could never master crocheting and used to leave her work lying around. If anyone asked what it was, mother would say 'That's Sie's inner peace.' Ever since then I have always called any piece of needlework 'my inner peace'.

My parents had not many tastes in common. They shared a loving— if, at times, distant—concern for their children, though this love was not equally divided between us three. They also both enjoyed enter- taining but there must have been a constant tug of will between them for my father loved the countryside, whereas mother adored London. As soon as father went abroad for the winter, she would close up the house and move to Town. She was a woman of forceful character, for all her frail health. She wrote once: 'Man is what God makes him, but Woman must put the finishing touches. If his instincts are evil, a wife can crush them—If good, she can crush them also.'

I notice an entry in my diary here for June 1st: 'Captain and Mrs. Towse and friends to lunch and tennis. He *felt* Dad's pot. He was wonderful.' 'Dad's pot' was a beautiful and enormous classical well- head in terra-cotta, with very scantily-dressed Greek gods around it. Father had brought it home from his last visit to Italy. My grandson, Robert, has it now in his garden at Ripley. Captain Towse (later Sir

Olave, aged 10, with (above) her parents,
Harold and Katharine Soames;
(below) Stubbing Court, near
Chesterfield, where Olave was born.
(Photo: John Pugh-Smith)

Olave, at the time of her engagement, wearing the
Scout Thanks Badge B.-P. gave her.

Beechcroft Towse, V.C.) 'felt' the pot because he was blind. I was at once shocked and fascinated by his disability. He had lost the sight of both eyes in the Boer War and had to be led about everywhere. He was awarded the V.C. and later founded an Institute for the Blind in London.

Later in this summer of 1903 there was the 'progression' to Scotland. It took us a week to get there. On our way we called at Huntingstyle, the Graham's home at Grasmere. I admired Jean Graham more than I can say. She was beautiful and well-read. She sang and was full of the best, nicest music. She was gay, friendly, cheerful, and always sweet to me. She helped me so much and encouraged me in my music, playing the piano to accompany me on the violin (which must have been absolute agony for her). She was utterly charming. In fact, as far as indoor pursuits and manners were concerned, she was everything I wanted to be.

From Grasmere, we went on to Castletown, near Carlisle, to stay at the country home of the Mounsey-Heyshams. Sybil (or 'Ba', as she was always known to us) was as much a model for me in outdoor pursuits as Jean was in indoor. Ba shared my love of animals; she could fish and sail; she rode superbly. Together we tramped over the moors, explored the life of the wilds – and played the violin.

Both these women were to me then what a Guider should be today to her Guides – an example and an inspiration. They fostered in me a sense of beauty and a love of the out-of-doors. They gave me ideals, set me on fire with a desire to achieve something in life.

Many years later, just before my husband died and I was in need of money, Ba Heysham bought from me the beautiful violin my father gave me when he realised I was serious in my musical studies. It was a copy of a Stradivarius, made by Messrs. Hill for the Paris Exhibition. I called it 'Diana'. Ba presented this violin to the Girl Guides Association together with one of her own. They are loaned to promising young violinists in the Association to use during their studies.

We arrived at Kirkdale in Kirkcudbrightshire on August 1st, 1903 and stayed there until the beginning of October. It was yet another enormous house and father filled it with guests for the shooting. Then back we all came to Purley for the autumn.

I started hunting again on my rough little horse, Tompy. I was learning to ride side-saddle now, as became a young lady of nearly fifteen, and had to wear a riding-habit. Before this I had ridden bareback and astride. Auriol had a pony called Lento 'because he is very slow'.

I was also making progress with my music. I noted on November 22nd, 1903: 'I can play *Salut d'Amour* by E. Elgar on the fiddle.' And in December: '(Mr. Shea and I) played Purcell Sonatas together.'

After Christmas, Father took No. 51, Great Cumberland Place, London for two months. I had my fifteenth birthday there and on this visit I seem to have thoroughly enjoyed the experience of London. We went to several of 'Mr. Henry Wood's' concerts at the Queen's Hall; I heard Kreisler play ('He beats the others into fits. Quite splendid in everything and very fascinating'). Later, a friend obtained Kreisler's autograph for me, which I treasured. I had a good collection, including the autographs of such notables as George Meredith, the novelist.

It seems ironical to me now that I should have taken part in this childish craze. Little did I dream what I myself was going to suffer from it in later years. I have at least one request a week for my autograph, often from complete strangers and from people who have nothing to do with Scouting or Guiding—and only very rarely do the people remember to enclose a stamped addressed envelope. Whatever do people want autographs for? What do they do with them when they have obtained them? Do they use them to crow over their friends or to indicate that they have met the person? It seems to me a completely time-wasting exercise, both for the givers and the getters.

I was also introduced to the Variety Theatre on this visit to London. This was not like the Variety of today; it was a mixture of circus, music-hall and straight musical recital—though obviously, the animal acts held the most interest for me.

1904. Feb. 14 . . . All to Hippodrome. Lovely. Elephants go down chute into water.

March 12th. To 'Palace' music hall with Dad. Great fun. Performing bears were sweet.

March 26th. Dad, Muz and I to Hippodrome. Houdini, handcuff King. Too extraordinary for words. Unlocks the handcuffs. Little man, like Kubelik. Plunging elephants again.

We also witnessed the funeral procession of the Duke of Cambridge on March 22nd. 'Dozens of regiments. His coffin on a gun carriage and his charger being led behind with his big boots reversed. Very impressive.' The Duke, apart from the Grand Duchess Augusta of Mecklenburg-Strelitz, had been the last surviving grandchild of King George III and the last surviving cousin of Queen Victoria. Thus another figure from the Victorian age passed from the stage of history. In the same week I was introduced to one of the wonders of the new century and age: I travelled by Underground for the first time. London's first Tube Railways, from the City to the Elephant and 'The Twopenny Tube' from Bank to Shepherd's Bush, had only been opened in 1890 — during my short lifetime. They were still a novel form of transport. It was very smoky and smelly with the steam engine.

Once again, my father was finding the English winter trying so he departed for a cruise in the Eastern Mediterranean while the rest of the family returned to Pangbourne — but only for a brief while. Father had not really settled at Purley Hall; he felt the atmosphere was too suburban and he wanted more shooting. Thus, by the middle of May 1904, we were on the move yet again. This time my father took Luscombe Castle, near Dawlish in Devon. He leased it for a year from Mr. Peter Hoare, the banker.

Luscombe was a 'Victorian Gothic' castle, rather pretentious with crenellated battlements and pointed windows with elaborate tracery. It had a private chapel, too. But the situation was lovely, set in a sheltered hollow below wooded hills. Mother wrote: 'Flowers and shrubs grow in rich luxuriance. Palms live out of doors. Pampas grow like weeds.' It was another splendid home and the first weeks were spent in eager exploration of the surrounding woods and the moors behind. On Whit Monday there was a fête in our park. People were allowed to go round our gardens and chapel. It struck me as being very funny. Being so near the coast, we bathed almost every day.

Remained in the sea a whole hour as the water was almost hot. July 9th. I can really swim at last.

In these days, when children can swim like fishes at an early age, it may seem odd that I was unable to swim until I was nearly fifteen.

There were, however, very few opportunities for swimming; few people had private pools and there were not many public swimming baths. When we lived at Purley Hall, we used to go occasionally to a pool at Sulham, built for the local children by the vicar, a go-ahead man called Wilder. That was where I began to learn to swim, though I did not do much as mother disapproved of such activity. I had a lovely bathing costume, dark blue with white piping round the edges. It came up round my neck, and down to my knees, and had sleeves.

We bought a pair of chestnut horses and christened them 'Bryant and May' ('because they are a safety match'); I went ratting; I learned to play billiards; I went prawning in the sea at Dawlish. I had my portrait painted by Lionel Baird and the following year had the excitement of seeing it on display in a London gallery. Arthur left Eton and went to Sandhurst. These events punctuate the summer like exclamation marks; but otherwise, the weeks slipped by in uneventful fashion. I was growing up, not only physically—though I noted on May 24th: 'I am 5 foot 4 inches and weigh 6 stone 8 lbs.' I had become really dedicated to my violin and practised assiduously each day, recording each lesson I had, each new piece of music I learned.

In addition, I was confirmed.

Religion had not occupied any great place in our family life. Unlike many households of that period, we did not have family prayers. Indeed, my father was not a religious man at all. He worshipped beauty of thought and mind, of music and nature, but had no specific Christian belief. Mother went part of the way with him in his views:

> In lavishing upon my children all that goes to make life beautiful in things temporal [she wrote] I have tried also to impress upon them the need of things Eternal.
>
> Young plants require delicate handling—and a child's teaching, to take root, should be laid lightly, not a forcing in of rules, a dreary systematic routine of church-going. It is a good thing to establish in their hearts from the first gleam of intelligence, an open-air Te Deum—a love of scenery—of flowers—of animals—of wild winds and gentle rain.

Nevertheless, we did follow 'the systematic routine of church-going'.

Mother, Auriol and I went, fairly regularly, to church, in hats and gloves as convention dictated.

> On the way to church we linger on the bridge to watch the stream, and we reluctantly leave the warm service of God's creation for man's chill rendering of the Hymns of Praise!

That is my mother speaking. For myself, I was for the first time beginning to think seriously about my role in life. My confirmation on December 7th by the Bishop of Crediton at St. Gregory's Church, Dawlish, filled me with awe and, in my usual 'summing up' of the year at the end of 1904, I wrote: 'I am a beast not to think more of religion.'

In January 1905 father left to spend the winter in Egypt and, as would be expected, mother immediately moved us all to a maisonette in London at 10, Eccleston Street. We had the usual hectic round of concerts and theatres and I had an operation on my throat.

> 1905. February 4th. Saturday. Mr. Milsom Rees cut my adanoids (*sic*) out at 8.45. I was put on a table for it. Great fun. First time I had eether (*sic*). Stayed in bed.

I was glad to be back at Luscombe again at the end of March and was immediately happy with my horses and dogs. 'Doogy is celestial. Exquisite ride through the woods and on to the moor.' We did not stay at Luscombe much longer, however. My mother found the place enervating and depressing, and wrote: 'I long to get away from this closed in Castle and its dark, depressing rooms—the overwhelming *silence* of the beautiful valley.' Once again, she and father set out in search of their Earthly Paradise. This time they leased Bradfield, near Cullompton in Devon. I think this was my favourite among the many homes I lived in before my marriage.

It was a rather splendid E-shaped Elizabethan mansion, approached from the south by a long drive lined with cedars. On the eastern side of the house was a formal, sunken garden with clipped yews or 'bollops' as I called them. The dining-room at the back of the house overlooked a large lake which presumbly had been used to stock fish for the household table in days gone by. We kept a pair of swans on the lake. We christened them 'Lohengrin' and 'Elsa'. For the rest, there were wide acres of park and woodland, smooth lawns and rhodo-dendron groves. We moved there on May 10th, 1905.

At the same time as taking Bradfield, my father had also taken a London flat in Kensington Court. Mother and Auriol went there for a round of dances and theatres and stayed in Town till July. Meantime, my father and I settled our possessions into Bradfield. I had to take charge.

'It is such fun and a business managing Dad's meals,' I wrote in my diary. I may say that, apart from an occasional period such as this when I was nominally running the household (though in fact every-thing was probably done by the servants according to my mother's prescribed routine) I was never given any responsibility. I really had no preparation for life at all. I never went into the kitchen or learned the first thing about housework or cooking or sewing. When I married, I had no idea even how to make a rice pudding. Sometimes I wonder how on earth I ever managed to run a home and bring up a family — certainly not from knowledge or experience! One thing I was expert in, though, and it has stood me in good stead throughout my travels all over the world: the ability to settle into new surroundings and 'make a home' wherever I have been.

1905. May 24th. Our furniture came which had been stored in Reading for a year. Great fun and a business arranging and planning.

May 25th. More furniture and dozens of cases with china, etc. of all sorts. I unpacked about 50 cases with the maids and managed the arranging of other things as well. Such a business. Dad and I got very tired.

At sixteen, I was on a constant see-saw between childhood and young womanhood. My diary records wild elation over my dancing partners or frequent bouts of depression about nothing in particular and everything in general. In the next entry I am playing cricket or messing about on our lake in 'corricles' (*sic*).

Auriol and I had found a new use for the flat saucer-shaped tin baths that were the standard equipment of each bedroom at Bradfield. We discovered that they made surprisingly effective boats and we would paddle them across the lake with our hands, one person to each bath. The idea of our game of 'bath polo' was to try to catch hold of one of the other baths and tip out the occupant into the water. (The lake was only about four feet deep so it was quite safe.) The unseated (or unbathed) player had to empty the water out of his or her bath and climb in again before he could continue the game. It was really most undignified for a twenty-year-old and a sixteen-year-old (as Auriol and I then were) but it was great fun. One afternoon, we were having a hilarious time with one of our friends when Lord Waleran called unexpectedly. As he was the owner of the house and they were his tin baths we were using, it could have been embarrassing, but he was very nice about it and said he 'never knew what the baths were meant for before'.

There was good shooting at Bradfield so that my father entertained a good deal during the autumn. 'September 24th, 1905. This is a topping shoot. We've got over 100 brace already.' I was trying to teach my little black pup, Dinah, to retrieve as Doogy did but had to report: 'She retrieves a hanky but wants to eat a partridge.'

My brother was by now commissioned in the 3rd Battalion, Coldstream Guards so, of course, we just had to go to London to see him on parade. '1905. November 5th. Friday. Went to see Arthur change guard at St. James's Palace. He carried the colour and looks sweet in his hairy hat.' Mother, with her gift for the dramatic, describes the event: 'Arthur "guarding" the Palace. I take Olave to London to peer through rails and lurk round corners and wait in cutting winds to see our red boy change guard, and march about full of fire and ferocity.'

While I was in Town, I went to see an early version of the cinema at the Polytechnic. 'Animated photographs', it was called. How strange it seems that the cinema was a novelty in my lifetime. That same week, I see that I was fitted for a ball gown at Liberty's and also made the harrowing entry: 'Sybil Dyson Laurie had an eye damaged looking at the eclipse and may have to have it out. Astley Corbett's son's eye shot out too.' This refers to the total eclipse of the sun which I had witnessed on August 30th from Bradfield.

However, despite the theatres and the glamour of a brother in the Guards, I was glad to return with my father to Bradfield. There was snow in Devon although it was only November – and perhaps the snow had turned my thoughts to other lands of snow for, in one of my rare references to outside events, I record: 'The revolutions in Russia are as bad as ever. People being killed by 1000s by Cossacks.'

Secure in my comfortable home, I was unaware that these were the opening skirmishes in the revolution that was to sweep away the old order in Russia in October 1917; that Germany was already arming for another war; that everywhere throughout Europe there were stirrings of unrest that would in time challenge our privileged way of living, our wealth and the luxury it brought us. These ideas were unimaginable in that quiet November of 1905 when I spent my days walking through the snow with my father and the dogs, and my evenings playing the violin to him.

So Christmas came, and Auriol and I drove round the estate delivering presents to the gardeners and keepers and their families. On the surface all was serene and gracious, but deep down inside me there were restless stirrings, a vague dissatisfaction with the butterfly role of 'daughter of the Big House'. I wrote on Christmas Day, 1905: 'Oh dear. Another year nearly gone. *Wasted*!'

CHAPTER FOUR

A Young Lady Comes Out

Years: 1906–1908

There was a General Election in January 1906 that resulted in a great Liberal landslide. Looking back, one can see that this election was as important in its way as the great Whig victory of 1832 or, to come to the present day, the overwhelming Labour vote after the Second World War. However, with my limited instruction in history, I could hardly have been expected to recognise the significance of the election at the time. I merely noted that I walked into Verbeer on January 17th to accompany my father to the polls. Unlike today, when North Devon is one of the last bastions of Liberalism, in 1906 the Conservative candidate was elected.

It mattered far more to me that I had to leave my beloved Doogy behind in Devon while I went up to the flat for two months. My father was taking Auriol abroad with him this winter and I, at seventeen (though still, I recorded, 'looking like fourteen') was old enough to be a companion to my mother.

What an intensive course in culture I had in those two months! There were lessons in German and music from one Fraulein Ulmer. There were visits to museums and galleries. We went to two or three concerts each week. I heard Wilhelm Backhaus at the Albert Hall. The composer, Roger Quilter, took me to one of the Broadwood concerts. He would have been twenty-nine at the time. Later, in 1911, he was to compose the music for the children's fairy play, *Where the Rainbow Ends*, which was produced by Charles Hawtrey at the Savoy Theatre as the Christmas entertainment that year. Probably the most memorable concert was a performance of a relatively new work by Sir Edward Elgar, *The Dream of Gerontius*, with Gervase Elwes singing the title role.

It is thrilling to look back and remember that many of the concert performers and actors I saw in my 'teens have since become household names. *Peter Pan*, for example, is a regular part of the contemporary London scene at Christmas-time, but I saw one of the very early performances with my beloved Gerald du Maurier as Captain Hook. I say 'beloved' because I was to make a point of seeing every play in which he appeared and even went to the extreme of seeing him seven times in *Raffles*. Maskelyne and Devant, the illusionists, were baffling audiences with their magical entertainments. I found them 'wonderfully mystifying'. Mr. and Mrs. Beerbohm Tree and Constance Collier were playing in *Nero* at His Majesty's Theatre. 'The burning of Rome *was marvellous*,' I noted.

Mother and I had shopping expeditions and tea parties almost daily. I recall that Buzzards in Oxford Street was a great favourite, and Stewarts on the corner of Bond Street and Piccadilly—both, now, long since demolished. Searcys in Sloane Street was a favourite place for lunch.

I even, on this visit to London, travelled on a motor bus—an event so outstanding and memorable that it warrants a special entry in my diary.

It seems amazing, too, that when I recorded the terrible earthquake in San Francisco, it was necessary for me to add 'California' in brackets after the name to remind me of where it was! Vesuvius was also in eruption at the time and I morbidly recorded the number of people killed in San Francisco and Naples. 'Damned uncomfortable things earthquakes,' I commented, greatly daring.

But these excitements were as nothing compared with the joy of returning to Bradfield and of being reunited with my beloved spaniel, Doogy, and with the other dogs. It was a glorious March, warm as summer, and I would be out before seven in the morning gathering wild daffodils beyond Arkill, or picking primroses, or riding out with Holloway, our groom, and with the dogs. For all that I was growing up, I was still very much a tomboy. I used to enjoy going out with the Culmstock Otter hounds and frequently came home soaked to the waist.

Our own dogs occupied much of our time. I was never so proud as when I entered Doogy for the Taunton Dog Show. I had washed and brushed and anointed him and in my eyes he was the most beautiful dog of all the fifty-five entries. Alas, he was beaten into third place by a dreadful doormat with a long tail. Being a true spaniel, he would sniff the ground all the time he was in the ring instead of standing proudly to show off his best points. Fired by this small success at Taunton, I entered him for Yeovil and Chard Dog Shows as well, but he was unplaced in both competitions.

Dear Doogy! I was overflowing with a capacity for love and, for lack of any suitable human, lavished all on him. He went with me everywhere at Bradfield and once followed me into church. It was Harvest Thanksgiving. He trotted down the aisle during the sermon and right up the chancel to where Auriol and I were sitting in the choir! Later that year he became sick with Mange. I nursed him devotedly and confided to my diary: 'With luck he won't die until I have something better to love.' Alas, he had only another year to live. He became progressively more sick and on April 10th, 1907, had to be destroyed. My grief spread over pages of my diary:

The most miserable day in my life. Rained. The sky and I weep in unison. Doogy the Divine, my own darling and precious dog had to be shot. He was much worse. It was Red Mange and incurable . . . I told Holloway to take him up to the keeper in the evening. At 20 minutes past seven I heard the shot from my bedroom. As the fatal shot rang out, Sweep sitting in his kennel moaned dismally. Did he know? It was too awful . . . In theory it is right to have a diseased pet shot but in practice it is dreadful. I tried to be philosophical and think it was alright and I didn't mind but I had no control over myself. He was so angelic. I had worshipped and adored him for so long. I am reminded of him always. He always slept with me here and no soft nose cuddles under my chin any more.

I remember I wept for three whole days and it was a long, long time before I could speak of him dry-eyed. Even a year later, if I was sad, I would howl at the remembrance of my darling dog.

Whenever one went away for a weekend in those days, one always took one's violin, one's music and one's tennis racquet. Tennis was becoming increasingly enjoyable as my own game improved. That summer of 1906 at a house-party I had the experience of partnering a Miss Bronfield, a Wimbledon lawn-tennis player. I was very impressed with her style and skill. I had never met a woman who played right up to the net and volleyed so strongly. I myself was never brilliant at tennis and never learned to serve overarm, but I enjoyed it and used to think a day wasted if I did not play ten sets.

I have always enjoyed sport of any kind. I swam and boated, biked and walked, rode and skated. In turn I played tennis, croquet, football, squash and hockey—and this summer of 1906, when my brother Arthur had begun to play polo with his regiment, I even borrowed his sticks and tried polo myself on my ponies, Buster and Mush.

Arthur's polo illustrates my point when I say that my mother doted on her only son. He had one polo pony but wanted a second one as a spare. Father thought it was sheer indulgence to buy him a second pony but mother managed to persuade him to let Arthur have his way. It was the same over a car. Arthur just had to have one when a car was all the new thing, so mother wangled that out of father as well, even though she herself hated motors.

I was nearing the end of childhood. With mounting excitement through October and November and December of 1906, I looked forward to my own 'coming out', set for the beginning of January. I shared a maid with Auriol and I began to acquire some long dresses. On December 16th I wrote: ' . . . I am fizzing with excitement about the week after next. Fitted several times lately for my ball frock.' It was not quite such a splendid coming-out as Auriol's—I think mother had spent all her effort on Auriol and had lost interest by the time it came to my turn. I know the servants used to call me 'Poor little Miss Olave' when Auriol went off to Town with mother and I was left behind in the country. But I was no Cinderella; I was quite happy to be left behind. Indeed, I was still able to say at the end of 1906: 'Thus ends a very exquisite year which nobody can have spent more happily than I have who am really the luckiest being in existence.' I am pleased to see that I appreciated my many blessings!

We had a big house-party for my coming-out. My brother was unfortunately in Cairo with his Regiment or there would have been even more young men around!

Of course, the big thing about 'coming out' was the overnight transformation from child to woman. There was no 'teenage' in those days. One went into long skirts and one put up one's hair and from then on one was able to accept invitations.

There was a luncheon-party the day before the dance. I remember sitting at the table in the lovely panelled dining-room, feeling strange and unsafe and unfamiliar, my head spiked with hairpins like a pincushion. I suppose I must have been turning my head with exaggerated care every time I had to speak to a neighbour for suddenly down the table my father demanded:

'What's the matter with you, Olave? Have you got a stiff neck?'

I expect I went puce in the face but I *dared* not move my head in case my hair fell down.

We had sixty-five guests for the dance which was held in the Great Hall. It was an impressive setting. The hall was lofty, with a magnificent hammer-beam roof supported by corbels carved like angels. The walls were lined with linenfold panelling and above this there were tall mullioned windows. At one end there was a minstrels' gallery where we had the band. We had gathered masses of evergreens from the woods to garland the hall and it looked so festive.

It was Friday, January 4th, 1907, and I was almost eighteen.

I opened the dancing with Arthur H. as my partner. He was another Etonian friend of Arthur's and was quite keen on me at the time, and I was more than a little in love with him. I remember the lovely cotillion I danced, and staying up till 4.15 a.m. 'This,' I wrote—little guessing the wonderful experiences I was to enjoy in ensuing years—'is the moment in all my life most worth living for.'

Bradfield seemed very heaven.

Mother was less flattering. In *her* version of the occasion, she wrote: ' . . . the stout little person flutters like a joyous butterfly amongst her friends in supreme happiness.'

Father was taking Auriol to Cairo as soon as our house-party was over, so this winter I was again mother's sole companion for the two-month sojourn in the flat in London. I hated leaving Bradfield even for a few days, particularly as our lease would be up in May and my parents had still not decided where they would go for their next move. All the same, I found much in London that was thrilling. My love of

music was being intensified by all the gorgeous concerts I attended —
Ysaye, Pachmann ('He is quite mad and laughs and gesticulates all the
time. He is called the May Queen of the piano, he is so ethereal'). In
addition, I was introduced to Grand Opera. I was entranced by
Die Walküre, Gotterdämmerung, Tristran and *Fidelio* at Covent Garden.
I had resumed regular lessons on the fiddle and was becoming a
moderately accomplished player.

As always there was the delight of the theatre: Variety at the Hippodrome, Granville Barker playing in Bernard Shaw at the Court;
Beerbohm Tree doing a season of Shakespeare at His Majesty's; and, of
course, Gerald du Maurier at the Comedy ('As divine as ever . . . I am
dotty over him').

The question of where we were to live after May was becoming
pressing. Mother and I went to see Mells Manor, near Frome in
Somerset but that was dismissed as being 'too poky'. When Father and
Auriol returned from Cairo, they inspected Glynde House in Sussex
but that did not suit either. Eventually, they decided on another
historic house — Hardwick — near Bury St. Edmunds.

First of all, though, we had to pack up Bradfield — and I had to have
my first brush with the law!

It was all due to the pleasurable occupation of laying pennies on the
railway line and then lying low and waiting to see how much they were
flattened when a train went over them. We used to put a pin on each
penny and it flattened into a little sword. It was a stupid thing to do,
for I suppose we could even have derailed a train. Certainly it was
immature behaviour for an eighteen-year-old but then, for all the
sophisticated pleasures I enjoyed on my trips to London, I was incredibly
naïve. My companion in this escapade was Esther ('Babe') Mac-
Gregor who lived in neighbouring Verbeer Manor. Unfortunately,
we were spotted by the driver of a passing train who reported us. We
were caught and eventually summoned by the G.W.R. to appear
before the Chief Inspector at Tiverton Junction. He was extremely
kind and let us off with a caution. In fact, he laughed about it, which
was very understanding of him. I hate to think what the consequences
might have been for us today!

That, with the death of poor Doogy, was the last incident of note
before we left Bradfield for good — though I wrote in my diary that I

'left behind a big portion of my heart in the little dell with the body of Doogy, a few yards north of keeper's cottage.'

I described Bradfield variously as 'Heaven' and 'Paradise' and so it was to me. It is sad to think that the home where I enjoyed so much freedom is now a school for maladjusted boys. Not that I begrudge the boys the beautiful surroundings. They are, by an accident of birth, missing out on so much that life has to offer that they deserve a chance at least of a lovely home. But it seems so depressing that all the lovely panelling has to be boarded up to protect it, that the gracious dining-room with its beautiful ceiling worked in a design of pomegranates and grapes, has to be furnished with plastic-topped tables. However, at least Bradfield is being occupied rather than pulled down and who, nowadays, could afford to maintain such a vast place as a private house?

Hardwick, our next home, was built by Robert Drury in the reign of Henry VIII and rebuilt in 1681. It was a long, magnificent building with pepper-pot turrets at each end and a terrace running the whole length of the house. Inside it was dark and rambling and 'all steps' (my mother dismissed it as 'the big, cold house') and it has since been pulled down to make way for a housing estate. The gardens were the most exquisite I had until that time ever seen. There was a lime avenue and a yew walk; a long rose-covered pergola. Each vista was closed by a classical statue. There was a formal garden in the Italian style with an elaborate fountain in the middle rising above a pyramid of four basins in which Auriol and I made immediate plans to bathe!

With my usual energy, I threw myself into new pursuits and made new friends, but something was lacking. I wrote, 'I'm not as happy here as at Bradfield. For the first time in my life almost I am bored. Horrid child I am to be so when I have everything I can wish for. Except perhaps a hunter.' And even that wish was fulfilled for within a month I had been bought a bay cob called Pedro.

The summer passed in a fierce round of tennis parties. Father had the riding school on the estate turned into an indoor tennis court and as it was a wet summer, a lot of the tennis was played on the covered court ('the only thing we shall regret when we leave here, I think'). I had plenty of partners among the young officers of the Suffolk Regiment stationed at Bury. Typical entries in my diary for summer,

1907, are 'Played 81 games of doubles', 'desperate fights in singles'. It seemed as if I must hurl myself passionately into every activity to smother a dissatisfaction with my life that was beginning to nag at me. Intermittently, I would practise furiously on the piano and violin, wondering if my future lay in music. I started to take singing lessons as well and was promised that I had a voice worth training.

When autumn came and the opening of the hunting season, I found an outlet for my restlessness in the sheer joy of riding:

> October 19th, 1907. Met at 9 and found a cub and ran for a bit and killed . . . Pedro behaved splendidly. He had never seen a hound before and he jumped things nobly but came down once over a very big ditch but I got clear and hauled him up and Robert Bower gave me a leg up, and so on again full of fire.

Actually, Pedro was more hurt on that occasion that I had guessed and for the rest of the season was unable to hunt. Instead, I was lent a hunter—a dangerous, naughty horse called Crispin. He had a nasty trick of rearing but he could certainly go. 'November 16th, 1907—Crispin splendid. Jumped two gates. My first 5 bars!' I hunted regularly three times a week all that winter. Maybe it was as well to have something to do for a lot of the time I was at Hardwick quite alone except for the servants. Mother, father and Auriol were more often in Town or up in Scotland.

> Meet at Chedburgh. Hacked there in awful rain.
> Hunting at Newmarket—18 mile hack back home. Crispin came down twice. Loads of other people did too.
> Nice day on the whole and we jumped quite a lot of very big things.
> Hacked to meet of the Staghounds . . . Found a deer . . . and ran right back to Ickworth Park. 45 minutes nonstop run over very big country, ripping it was, and our horses were splendid. Several snowstorms.

However, by the middle of January, 18 degrees of frost brought an end to hunting for the time being. There was still the thrill of my

B.-P. at the time of their marriage.

(Above) Bradfield, Devonshire – one of Olave's many childhood homes. (Below) a family group at Grey Rigg in 1916. Back row: B.-P. with Peter; Harold Soames; Arthur Soames with Sanchia. Front row: Olave; Hope Soames; Katherine Soames; Auriol and Bob Davidson with Christian and Clare.

first real experience of the social world. Such functions as I had attended before had been small private dances in the homes of friends, and always with my parents in attendance. Now I was 'chaperoned' by an older woman friend and went to the Suffolk Hunt Ball at the Atheneum in Bury, to the County Ball and so on. I meticulously recorded the names of all my partners and the numbers of the dances — and as I danced every dance from 9.30 p.m. to 3.30 a.m., there were plenty of names! I was thrilled with the glamour of the men in hunting pink, of the professional dance band. I note that I 'went absolutely mad' in the Lancers with Robert Bower ('quite the best dancer there') who was Master of the Newmarket and Thurloe Hounds.

Mother, however, declared herself 'Suffolkated' at Hardwick — and the search began for yet another home. I noted gloomily, 'Heaven only knows where we shall land when we next take flight — Birmingham or Upper Tooting!'

CHAPTER FIVE

The Restless Romantic

Years: 1908–1910

It was one thing for my parents to tour the countryside by train and carriage in search of their Earthly Paradise; it was a much simpler proposition with a motor-car. They might never even have discovered the house in Dorset which became their first and last settled home had they not, on January 27th, 1908, acquired the Crossley. It was a bright yellow limousine with a landaulette hood and we were all entranced by it: 'The car is heavenly and so quiet and the chauffeur Williamson drives so awfully well. I adored every second of it.'

Williamson, incidentally, was dismissed shortly afterwards for repeatedly taking out the car on his own without permission! He was replaced by Edward Puddle. 'I think we will call you Edward,' said my father, and so we did. He was never called Puddle again.

It is amusing to read what one could do with a car in those traffic-free days:

> Muz and I shopped in Regent Street and the car was to wait for us.
> A(uriol) and I whirled up to Hampstead Heath and Barnet and Finchley. Lovely, and went so fast and so safe too. It is a joy, that car!

Imagine 'whirling' up the Finchley Road today or driving for pleasure through the suburban wastes of Barnet!

I little realised what significance the place would have for me in later years when I made the following entry: '1908. February 2nd. Dad Auriol and I went in the motor through Richmond Park to Hampton Court. First time I've ever seen it. Quite lovely and the formal gardens are so nice.'

I suppose with the urgent necessity of finding a home, father found it impossible to go abroad that winter for we stayed in the London flat from January to the end of March. I was now nineteen and, on this occasion, loved every minute of my stay in London.

It was a visit packed with entertainment. Quite apart from the delights of motoring which opened up new and hitherto undreamed of opportunities for sight-seeing, we again did the round of museums and picture galleries. During the daytime, also, I was working hard at both the piano and violin, and with my singing lessons: 'Played the fiddle with Mrs. P yesterday. She plays the piano well but bangs away *fff* all the time regardless of me!'

Every evening we visited either a concert or a theatre, or, very occasionally, 'the new cinemetagraph thing'. I was present at Claude Debussy's first appearance in England when he conducted four of his own compositions at one of the Henry Wood symphony concerts at the Queen's Hall. I saw Nikisch conduct. I was once again entranced by Elgar's *Dream* ('too lovely to clap even'); drooled over du Maurier as *The Admirable Crichton* ('too adorable') and was completely bowled over by Shakespearean tragedy.

I am very busy reading *Hamlet*. What a lovely play it is. I think 'the rest is silence' in the last speech is perfectly exquisite . . . Forbes Ro.ertson . . . at the Court Theatre . . . died so beautifully and I wept buckets full of tears.

We 3 to *Othello* at the Kennington Theatre. Forbes Robertson was perfect . . . Never did anybody get into such a passion as F.R. in the 3rd and 4th scenes. He simply shook all over literally and his brown skin made his eyes and teeth shine whiter and he looked and behaved like a wild beast. When he stabbed himself at the end he went and kissed his dead wife and then fell limply and without a sound down 3 steps and lay like a log. So dramatic and awful. I streamed, and loved it, every word.

Perhaps I found the Shakespeare moving because I was in love yet again and found an echo of my own emotions in the grand passions on the stage. This time it was Oliver V. whom we nicknamed 'The Child'.

'Olave – down little flutterer, down,' I chide myself when a telegram arrives saying that The Child has returned to England from a visit abroad. In the next breath I am laughing at myself—'I am an ass!' However, a few days later I am analysing my feelings: '1908. May 9th—A letter yesterday from Oliver but altho' I love him I am not 'in love with' him—a vast difference . . .'

Arthur was home on leave from Cairo ('much better looking— but just as selfish as ever', I noted). Mother was thrilled to have her 'little redhead' at home again. Bridge was becoming a popular card-game and my father played keenly with my brother and sister. 'I can't and won't learn', I wrote fiercely at the time—nor have I ever learned since, not having an inclination for any card-game more complicated than Racing Demon.

There is also an amusing entry in my diary for 1908:

> April 12th—Great fuss going about election at Manchester. Winston Churchill was eventually ejected (as liberal candidate) and the Stock Exchange sent this ribbald (*sic*) telewag 'What's the good of a W.C. without a seat!!'

By the early summer, we had given up both Hardwick and the London flat and had moved to Dorset. This time my father was sufficiently certain of his choice of house to purchase the place—not without some teasing from friends who wagered he would be on the move within two years.

The property, which stood on Crichel Mount, was on the edge of the village of Lilliput—the name which Dean Swift, who lived for a time in the village, borrowed and immortalised in *Gulliver's Travels*. The house was called 'Grey Rigg'. It was a very ordinary modern house of the period, neither large nor small, in complete contrast to the other magnificent country 'palaces' that we had formerly lived in. The house has since been re-named 'Crichel Place' and the grounds have all been sold off and built on, but in 1908 we had a magnificent uninterrupted view south-west over Poole Harbour to Brownsea Island. There, had I but realised it, B.-P. had, less than a year before, held his first experimental camp for boys, from which the great game of Scouting evolved. The island was called Branksea when we first went there.

Hardy (the butler) and Lizzie (one of the maids who had been in our service for years) and I were given the task of transferring the livestock from Suffolk to Dorset. Our wagon travelled via London where it was shunted about from one siding to another. I remember at one point being stranded in a tunnel somewhere near Ludgate Hill but I was more concerned that the horses should not feel lonely than that I myself might come to harm.

Grey Rigg, as my mother correctly stated, was 'the desired compromise between town and country without being aggressively suburban'. Bournemouth was only a short drive away but there was the New Forest behind, moorland for walking and a good shoot for my father. Mother, Auriol and I paid formal calls around the neighbourhood, travelling either in the victoria or in the yellow car, and soon we had as busy a social life as at any of our other homes. As usual, I flung myself wholeheartedly into a whole new range of activities. Swimming and sailing, inevitably, became our main recreations and I also learned life-saving. Arthur had had a serious accident playing polo in Egypt and had to come back to England for an operation, so he was at home recuperating for a good deal of the summer. He was now Signalling Officer to his Battalion and he took pride in teaching me the Morse Code. I worked hard at my music, helped Father make the garden, played tennis, attended concerts at the Winter Gardens – and fell in love again. '1909. January 21. Oh dear! D. . n my heart. It's off again and gone to Gerald P.'

I was not well. I was having recurrent pains in my head which the doctor dismissed as nerves so I was made to lie down for two hours every afternoon. In the summer, my father took me on a cruise to Norway in the *S. Y. Vectis*.

'1909. July 29th. Saw first glacier. Anchored alongside Kaiser's yacht at Odda.' The middle of August saw me back at Grey Rigg and actually *winning* a tennis tournament. 'Great fun. I adored all of it. Singles are so nice – one has only oneself to rely on and to blame.'

If my nerves were troubling me, it was possibly because I was restless and dissatisfied with my meaningless existence. On the one hand, I craved love:

I am ready to love any man, I'm afraid, with my hot heart!

I love Gerald – but only because there's no other!

Ulric proposed but I refused. I am supremely happy it has happened and equally so that it is over.

I had an awful suicidal fit of the blues. Lovely morning and I sat in the sun on the sea shore . . . and made my hanky a wet pulp with salt tears—chiefly about Ulric . . . how I wish I could love him enough to be engaged.

These are typical entries in my diary during 1909. I had an enormous capacity for love yet no outlet for it save my dogs and horses. Where was the man who would kindle a response in me, whom I would recognise with certainty as the one with whom I could readily share the rest of my life? Coupled with this aching emptiness of heart was a sense of inadequacy:

Robert Herrick's:—
    'She by a river sat and sitting there
    She wept and made it deeper by a tear'
is like me. Fussing about doing nothing all my life is making about as much difference to the world at large—as Julia's tear to the depth of the river!

Once again a woman was to have a profound influence for good on my life, as I like to think that many fine women since have, through Guiding, opened the eyes of other young people to the needs of others. Lilliput was a turning point in my life. Through Beckie Manser, my eyes were opened and I saw my pleasure-filled existence as empty, futile and unsatisfying. Through her I began to feel aware of an inner need to be of service—an awareness which, when I met my husband, flared into response to and recognition of similar qualities in him.

I had, while I was at Hardwick (and without my mother knowing) written to a London hospital to enquire about taking up nursing. Unfortunately, I had no qualifications to offer. I was told to get myself trained at a local hospital and then to apply again. That would not have been possible from home; mother would never have tolerated it. It would have had to be a complete break or not at all, so I let the matter slide. Now, in Parkstone, an opportunity arose to take a first tentative step towards concern for others rather than myself.

The Invalid Children's Aid Association, or I.C.A.A., had a seaside holiday convalescent home in Parkstone for children from London. Mrs. Beckie Manser, who was a neighbour of ours at Lilliput, was responsible for obtaining voluntary helpers for this home. She had the idea of organising young women of her acquaintance into a rota to look after the children in the afternoons so that the nurses could have some time off. There was Janet Forde, I remember – such a bun, she was. I used to play Brahms trios with her on the piano and her brother on the viola. There were Joan Bevan and Doris Rossiter and Sybil Pontifex and myself. There were others, too, whose names I can no longer remember. Our job was to keep the youngsters amused and teach them a little if we could. Of course, we were quite untrained but we would encourage them to draw or to work at their copy-books Sometimes we took them on the beach. Occasionally I was even able to have a few of them to tea at Grey Rigg. They adored it there – particularly playing with the dogs – but mother did not like it at all. She considered my work with the children a complete waste of time and stopped my going whenever she could.

But I continued to go and to give what little unskilled help I was capable of giving. These children – some of them crippled – awoke in me feelings of compassion which hitherto had been lavished only on ailing animals. It was really my first contact with sick people, with suffering of any kind. I hate illness and loathe the endless discussion of ailments which passes for conversation in some circles, but I am tremendously moved by suffering – particularly in children.

The summer continued quietly with sailing and tennis, shopping, musical evenings, concerts, work at the I.C.A.A. Home. The other I.C.A.A. helpers and Auriol and I used to bathe from 'The Lido Club House' – our name for a little bathing hut belonging to a Miss Burton. She let us each have a key to the Club House and we thoroughly enjoyed being able to swim on a quiet stretch of beach. There was hardly a house at Sandbanks in those days. There is no other entry in my diary for this year of particular interest except: 'October 14 – Uncle Arthur . . . has just bought Sheffield Park in Sussex.' Later, Uncle Arthur (my father's eldest brother) was to will the property to my brother who later sold it. Today the gardens belong to the National Trust and the public can enjoy the magnificent arboretum, the lakes, azalea groves and bluebell woods planned by my Uncle Arthur. He kept a staff of seventeen gardeners to maintain the place.

However, on November, 1st 1909, we held a dance at Grey Rigg and from that date onwards for the next two years, the events of the Soames family read like a romantic novel.

Auriol fell madly in love.

Up till that time, she had always had everything her own way. She was undoubtedly a great beauty and Mother had made sure that she had had every opportunity to meet suitable young men and enjoy a gay social round. Certainly she had not been without admirers. Now she lost her heart completely to a Frenchman who, for the present, made no response to her obvious infatuation. I noted waspishly in my diary: 'November 7th, 1909—It will do Auriol's heart of stone a lot of good. She has been so accustomed to being grovelled to— and she must grovel herself now.'

In addition, father also was in danger of becoming entangled in an emotional affair so the family beat a strategic retreat from the scene of these double embarrassments. Father let Grey Rigg for the winter and moved us all—family, dogs and servants—to Rutland Lodge in Knightsbridge.

The Fates, had I but known it, were already intertwining the thread of my life with that of my husband-to-be. I was given a new dog —a Clumber spaniel known as Doogy II. Each morning, with Doogy at my heels, I crossed Knightsbridge into Hyde Park to exercise him. The significance of these walks was to be revealed two years later.

In the meantime, however, in default of anything better to do, I plunged once more into the gay life of Edwardian upper-class London.

November 11th—Richter conducts at Queen's Hall. Jan Paderewski soloist.

November 12th—With Arthur to Motor Show at Olympia. 'Dollar Princess' at Daly's.

November 13th—His Majesty's Theatre—I saw 'Trilby' which I have wanted to see for years. Tree absolutely splendidly beastly as Svengali and Viola Tree sweet and sad as Trilby and Henry Ainley 'Little Billee' to the life. I adored it and howled!

I learned to skate at the Prince's Club; I went to see a new play by Maeterlinck, *The Blue Bird*. I revelled in H. B. Irving doing *Dr. Jekyll and Mr. Hyde* ('wonderful and awful'). I found *The Importance of Being Earnest* boring but—an indication, perhaps, of my budding social awareness—declared John Galsworthy's new play *Justice* 'splendid—the finest play I've ever seen.'

The new social awareness, however, saw nothing wrong with a day spent skating in the morning, out with a friend for lunch and a matinée, tea at Stewarts, dinner with friends, a second theatre in the evening, and afterwards to supper at the Savoy! 'I enjoyed it—so gay', was my comment—and that was a typical day.

I was nearing my twenty-first birthday—not that 'coming of age' signified any particular freedom for a girl in the circles among which we moved. A daughter only escaped from the authority of her parents when she married—and I had not yet found anyone whose company seemed preferable to that of my family. I did, however, take a tentative step in the direction of emancipation by joining a Ladies' Orchestra run by a Miss Audrey Chapman. I had to be auditioned by the conductor, René Ortmann, and was absurdly frightened. It was the first time I had ever had to audition—and to play before strangers at that! Evidently my execution was of the required standard and for a short time that winter I was able to make friends outside the family circle, and to meet people whose enthusiasm for music matched my own.

It was not to last long. This was the second winter my father had spent in England and he was not well. 'Dad very sorry for himself so Dr. came—chiefly *malade imaginaire*,' I wrote unsympathetically. My criticism may have been true, but nervous illness, even if self-induced, is nonetheless illness. My father was a very nervy, introspective man, subject to serious moods of depression. It was decided that he and I should go to Cannes for a month and soon I was able to report 'Dad . . . getting better and himself again.'

Auriol had recovered her poise away from Grey Rigg and, with mother, was thoroughly enjoying the gaiety of the London scene. Once again she had gathered around her a crowd of admirers, one at least of whom was persistent in his wooing of her: '. . . old Ford came. He stayed to dinner and asked Auriol again for about the 100th time to marry him—but he is 50! she is only 24!' How shocked I was at the thought of a twenty-six years' difference between husband and wife. Anyway, with my father recovered in health and Auriol restored in spirits, it seemed an appropriate time to return to Dorset.

A day or two before our departure from London, we went to the Palace Theatre to see 'the lovely Russian dancers' who were 'quite the rage just now'. Anna Pavlova was dancing 'The Dying Swan'. Looking round the brilliant, crowded theatre in the interval or strolling in the foyer among the elegant and fashionable audience, life seemed very secure. I had a father and mother whom I adored and who were loving and generous to me; I had a beautiful home; I enjoyed comparative wealth and luxury. The system on which these privileges rested seemed sure and enduring. England was at peace under a beloved King. I was vaguely aware that there was an unruly political party called Liberals and an even more unruly political party known as Radicals, but only a few exceptional and (to me at the time) rather cranky women bothered about politics. Yet within a week I was writing at Lilliput:

1910. May 6th—Heard latest bulletin of the King who is seriously ill with bronchitis.

Sat. May 7th—King Edward VII died at quarter to 12 last night— universal sorrow and bewilderment. So quick—the Queen hurried home from Venice in time.

It was all so different from when Queen Victoria had died. I was not yet twelve then, scarcely aware of what went on outside my sheltered home. Now in 1910 the sense of shock reached even to our part of Dorset and I made comment in my diary on the mourning clothes everyone wore:

May 20th. Friday—King's Funeral. Whole holiday for everybody everywhere! The procession with 8 Kings thro' London was made into a great World's Pageant. We gardened. This is very like a splendid story called 'Ben Tobit' by Andrevsky? of how even when great things happen individuals go on with their small insignificant affairs just the same.

The new reign was to bring violent social upheavals, a cataclysmic war and the complete destruction of the sort of leisurely way of life my parents had enjoyed for so many years. Perhaps a first hint of what was to come can be found in a note I made on June 30th, 1910: 'Polling day for East Dorset By-Election. The beastly Radical Guest got in.' But that was only a By-Election. In the meantime, I was delighted to be back at Grig (as I called Grey Rigg): 'Clean, silent rain all last night and cold this morning. After(noon) Auriol and I go for a wild ride by the sea—and Doogy . . . tears along to keep up.'

That was one of the few times that year that I was really happy with Auriol. She was very unsettled. At rising twenty-five, she was feeling that she ought to be married and settled down, but she did not want to accept 'old Ford' (Henry Ford, the painter). On returning to Grig she had found herself even more desperately in love with Maxime (the Frenchman) who, although he now returned her affection, was unable to marry her. He already had a wife who, tragically, had been in a mental institution for years. Looking back, I can see that it was a heart-breaking situation that, despite all her many suitors, Auriol should have set her heart on the one ineligible man of her acquaintance. At the time, however, I felt impatiently that she had been the subject of too much admiration in London. It had turned her head and, indeed, I confessed to my diary: 'Auriol and I are drifting further and further apart—in fact, we have nothing in common.' It was an intolerable situation and cast its cloud over the whole summer, for one unhappy person in a household affects all the rest:

Dad was rather horrid to Mother and she lay low all day (I wrote in September). She does take things to heart so—and was quite knocked up. He probably didn't mean it—but fixed her with gimlet eyes and she is not strong, poor darling.

Arthur, likewise, was having a complicated love-life and I seemed to be the only member of the family who was completely calm.

October 16th, 1910—It is extraordinary how everybody nearly—beneath a calm and apparently happy exterior—has a skeleton in their cupboards—except for me—who am completely happy—I ought never to be anything else with the glorious home I have and affection and love which I really believe lots of people have for me — do I deserve it — if not, at least I appreciate it.

The storm broke towards the end of the year. Arthur was attending a weekend house-party at which Maxime was also present. What the exact circumstances were I cannot remember after all these years. Perhaps Maxime did not even know that Arthur was Auriol's brother. But imagine Arthur's embarrassment and fury to hear Maxime boasting to the assembled guests of his conquest of Auriol! Of course, Arthur felt obliged to tell Auriol that Maxime was only playing with her. She was desperately hurt and once again sought refuge and oblivion in 'dances and things' (I wrote) in London.

Early in the New Year of 1911, father took her to India and Ceylon for a three months' tour. Time and distance would heal even a broken heart.

CHAPTER SIX

A Wedding in the Family

Year: 1911

1911 opened on rather a forlorn note in my diary: 'To the Fordingbridge dance—nice, but why go!!' I was disenchanted with life, and my half-day a week with the Invalid Children's Aid Association was not enough to satisfy me.

Mother offered her usual selfish panacea and swept me off to the Curzon Hotel in London for a month while Grey Rigg was altered and added to and redecorated. This time the theatres and shopping, the skating and the singing lessons seemed unsatisfactory. I was glad to return to Dorset in the middle of February. A month later, my feeling of restlessness was temporarily assuaged by a new development:

> March 18th—Auriol writes from Ceylon that she is engaged to be married to a man of 40—Bob Davidson. Has a place in Scotland and large estates in Ceylon. Dad likes him and has given his consent and he comes here to ask Mother at Easter. Hurrah! How lovely for her and us!... He gave her a lovely ring and a string of pearls worth £400! I couldn't bear to have anything on me as valuable as that!

One would have thought that Mother would have been delighted that her 'flower' was to be married at last and to such a wealthy man. But, alas, when Easter came and Auriol's fiancé came to stay with us, I had to record:

> April 6th—Mother is awful over it—in bed all day saying he is not good enough!
> April 9th, Sunday—Mother in bed in hysterics most of the day . . . up in time to say goodbye and be nice to R.D. So all is well—

but she has small relapses into awful unreasonableness now and
then—about me too for having a letter from Ralegh and writing
to him. Why shouldn't I?

The 'small relapses' went on all through the summer:

> Mother had a very bad relapse about the wedding and is miserable.
> She wouldn't stop it if she could—but she would love to have a
> son-in-law to be proud of instead of this good-hearted 'nature's
> gentleman'.

This was hardly fair, for brother-in-law Bob was a splendid fellow.
Perhaps mother had hoped for a titled match for Auriol. Certainly in
her eyes a Scottish planter did not have the social graces she would have
wished for, but he was kind and gentle and sincere—and truly in love
with Auriol. He was extremely wealthy, also, and mother's doubts
were in some measure mitigated when he took a lease of the magnificent
Elizabethan mansion near Yeovil, Montacute House, for the first
year of their married life. Her favourite daugher would not be banished
either to the wilds of Kirkcudbrightshire or to Ceylon—which was
some small consolation to our sorrowing mother!

The wedding was fixed for October. Now my mother had every
excuse for frequent visits to London to buy 'things' for Auriol's home
and to help in the choice of her trousseau. She entered into the planning
of the wedding with passionate dedication. 'Dad and I so happy here
alone', I wrote gratefully in my diary in early June.

I escaped for a few days from the endless wedding chatter and went to
Stratford-on-Avon with Friede, my old German governess. F. R.
Benson and his company were doing a season there and it was interest-
ing to compare his productions with the Irving/Tree productions
I had seen the year before at His Majesty's Theatre in London. We
saw the great Matheson Lang as Macbeth and heard Ellen Terry
talking about 'Shakespeare's Heroines'. We made excursions to
Warwick, Kenilworth and Shottery and 'did Stratford à l'Américaine,
Guidebook in hand'.

'What a jolly time we've had. I've never known that aviator,
F. Time, Esq., go so well.' Considering that the year was 1911 and

that aviation was in its infancy, I was very 'modern' using the word 'aviator'. I was, however, passionately interested in flying. The previous year, there had been a display of flying machines at Southbourne as part of a special 'week' in Bournemouth:

1910. July 11th, Monday. — On big hired motor boat round to Southbourne and watched aeroplanes — biplanes and monoplanes — flying round and up and along and about at terrific speed. Perfectly lovely and wonderful — first time I have ever seen or thought with ecstasy of flying and flying machines . . . Want to do it badly ourselves.

Of course, all that the planes were doing that day was circuits and hedge-hopping across the fields. The next day the planes flew higher — particularly Charlie Rolls:

Tuesday, July 12th — Went to watch it at the Aerodrome. Saw lots of lovely flights and exquisite to see them starting. Graham White flew beautifully — then Andemanns came down in his monoplane — neither damaged — and then at 1.15 C. S. Rolls fell down smash in front of us in his biplane and was killed on the spot. Quite awful and ghastly tho' one saw nothing but the wrecked house of cards.

The Hon. Charles Stewart Rolls was the third son of Lord Llangattock. He was the brilliant pioneer of automobile engineering whose partnership with F. H. Royce produced the famous Rolls-Royce car. He established several world records for automobile speeds but was equally enthusiastic about ballooning and flying. He was not quite thirty-three when he was killed; it was such a tragedy. Of course, no one knew until it was given out that the crash had been a fatal one. After that, everyone went home and there was no more flying display that day. Despite the tragedy, I was back at the airfield the following morning to watch the planes again. Today, when the sound of aircraft has become part of the background noise of our daily lives, it seems strange to consider that, even in my remembrance, there was a time when people rushed out of doors and pointed to the sky when an aircraft went over. 'Look!' they would cry. 'A *flying* machine!'

June 22nd, 1911 was the Coronation Day of King George V and Queen Mary. I was invited to stay in London for a few days with Alex Bingel, a girl I had met and become friendly with in Mentone some ten years earlier. The Bingels had a lovely house in Grosvenor Street but for the day of the Coronation they had hired a room on the processional route.

Got up at 5 and after getting squeezed in the terrific crowd in Trafalgar Square got to our room and saw the Coronation Procession grandly — going to and returning from Westminster. A most lovely affair — and so interesting — wouldn't have missed it for worlds. Brother Arthur was signalling officer and very important! but I didn't see him.

I met my cousin Noel Soames during these few days in London. He had been in love with me for some time — ever since I had stayed with his parents in Wrexham the year before. I suppose the excited atmosphere of London at Coronation time had something to do with it for we had a whirlwind romance, heightened by secret meetings in Hyde Park. We became engaged, also secretly — and the engagement lasted a whole week! Poor dear — he was killed in Palestine during the First War.

Back at Lilliput, the summer followed its usual pattern of tennis and boating and teaching 'my waifs', but the pace of affairs quickened as the date of the wedding approached.

October 18th — Drove with Mother to inspect St. Peter's. It is a lovely church for a wedding and this will be a superb affair. I hope I shan't cry! it is such an emotional business.

October 21st — Clothes — clothes such lovely ones Auriol has got.

October 23rd — Preparations start in real earnest. Arrange all the lovely presents in the music room.

October 24th—Servants tea and present party. Marquee put up. Presents pouring in 'thick and fast they came at last'.

Thursday, October 26th, was the day when all mother's planning would come to fruition. The service in St. Peter's, Parkstone was fully choral. Auriol wore a beautiful long cream satin dress and a splendid matching train of cream satin embroidered in silver and pearls in a lattice design of leaves and roses. I myself wore it two years later when I was presented at Court. There was a three-year-old page and six bridesmaids. I was one, feeling strangely awkward in eau-de-nil chiffon and a Juliet cap of pearls. All the family were present, hordes of friends and relations like rabbits.

Afterwards, Auriol and her Robert went off to Scotland, to Cumloden, the Davidson estate near Newton Stewart. I, feeling more than a trifle forlorn, went off to visit relatives in Wrexham and afterwards to stay with the Gubbins in Hereford. Edythe Gubbins was a sister of my beloved Ba Heysham who had encouraged my violin playing. Colonel Gubbins, Edythe's husband, commanded the Depot of the Shropshire Light Infantry in Shrewsbury. Both these dear friends were anxious now to see me as safely wedded as Auriol and, in an effort at matchmaking, introduced me to various young officers at the Depot. One of these young men, John S., did indeed behave as the Gubbins hoped! He took me out on several occasions and at last proposed marriage.

'I can't give you an answer yet,' I replied. 'I am not sure of my feelings. Look—I'm going to Jamaica with my father after Christmas. I shall be away two months. I will give you my answer when I return.'

I still was not sure what I was looking for, hoping for, waiting for.

I opened my diary on January 1st, 1912 by writing: 'Well, I do hope, Olave, you will have a better year this time than last.'

I was soon to know.

On Wednesday, January 3rd, 1912, my father and I set sail from Southampton on the *R.M.S. Arcadian*. I wrote home to my mother from the first port of call: 'There is only one interesting person on board and that is the Boy Scout man.'

CHAPTER SEVEN

Strange Courtship

Year: 1912

Sie Bower was a member of the family with whom we had been friendly in Suffolk. Her brother Robert was the Master of the New-market and Thurloe Hounds who was 'quite the best dancer there' at my first public ball at the Atheneum in Bury St. Edmunds in January 1908. Sie used to visit us frequently at Grey Rigg. She had something of a reputation as a fortune-teller and used to read our hands. On each occasion, I solemnly recorded her prognostications in my diary and it is interesting to see how often she was right.

1908. August 20th — Sie Bower left. She told my hand yesterday. My character I knew without being told but she says I shall be in a motor smash in about 2 years. Marry (a soldier p'raps) in about 3. Go out to India in about 6 and have 3 babies. *We will see if she knows.*

Two years later she read my hand again:

1910. September 25th — Sie tells us all our fortunes. Mine is not a nice one . . . I am still to have a bad accident which she told me of 2 years ago. I shall go on being a mollusc as I have always been for two more years and then wake up and be a person.

Sie was staying with my mother when my first letter arrived from the *Arcadian*. 'Olave will mention in her letter the man she is going to marry,' she said.

I did not, fortunately, suffer the motor smash but everything else she foretold came true — my marrying 'the Boy Scout man' who was a soldier, my going to India, the number of my children—but most of all her prediction about 'waking up and being a person'. I had been withdrawing more and more into myself this last year. I remember arriving at a friend's house for tennis and seeing a number of cars and carriages outside. I was filled with panic. 'It's going to be a big party— I can't face it,' I said to myself—and went home.

In such a state of diffidence, I probably should not have minded if the *Arcadian* trip had fallen through. It very nearly did. The Baker sisters (one of whom had been a bridesmaid at Auriol's wedding) had booked for the cruise and urged us to join them. When my father applied for tickets, however, the passenger list was already closed. We only obtained berths at the last moment when two people had to cancel their booking.

We drove from Grey Rigg to Southampton to join the ship. It was bitterly cold. Passengers were stamping about on the quayside waiting for a tender to take them out to the *Arcadian* which, on account of a dock strike, was anchored out in deep water. A raw fog added to the gloom of the winter morning.

A little group of the still novel Boy Scouts were drawn up to await the arrival of the boat train from London. With their bare knees and rolled up shirt-sleeves, they should have been blue with cold in such conditions but they were bubbling over with excitement. As the train drew in, they sprang smartly to attention.

'There's B.-P.,' someone said and I watched, amused and interested, as the hero of Mafeking inspected the Scout Guard of Honour. Two days later I was introduced to him:

1912. January 5th—. . . supremely happy sitting lazily loafing on deck all day. Make friends with Daisy Goodwin—daughter of Albert Goodwin the painter. Also Lieut.-General Sir Robert Baden-Powell 'The Boy Scout' who is so nice. He talks so nicely about Mafeking and all his interesting experiences and is so modest and sweet . . . Ripping day.

There had been no difficulty over that first conversation. The General seemed to recognise me.

'You live in London,' he said.

'No,' I replied. 'In Dorset.'

He looked puzzled. He had obviously been so certain that he knew me.

'But you have a spaniel,' he insisted. 'A brown and white spaniel.'

It was my turn to be surprised.

'Yes,' I said.

'And you have been in London? Near Knightsbridge Barracks?'

'Indeed, yes—two years ago.'

That satisfied him. He told me how he used to try to read people's character from their manner of walking—he had included a passage on this subject in *Scouting for Boys*. At the very time, during the winter of 1909–1910, when our family were at Rutland Gate, he was at his mother's house at 32, Prince's Gate. I would walk daily with Doogy II in Hyde Park and he, hurrying one morning from his home to the Barracks, had noticed what he chose to call my 'quick, determined gait' indicative of 'honesty of purpose and common sense as well as a spirit of adventure!'

It was an amazing coincidence that we should meet in this way. It was an even more amazing coincidence that we should have the same birthday—22nd February.

That evening we were both at the Captain's Table for dinner. My father and B.-P. soon discovered a mutual interest in painting and talked eagerly together of water-colour techniques. They were almost of an age—B.-P. was only three years younger than my father—yet already to me he was not just another parent-contemporary. How can I describe the instant recognition the one by the other of the perfect, the only complement in love? It was indeed a 'marriage of true minds', a meeting with the compleat partner such as is granted to only a privileged few. Ours was a rare love, a rare happiness. I thank God daily for the wonderful way in which His Divine Hand led us both to come together.

I still cannot imagine what it was about me that attracted him. He was famous, talented, experienced. I was such an ordinary person, not at all clever, with no experience of life whatsoever. Yet within five days I was writing:

Have B.-P. to myself all day—till 11 p.m.—much intelligent

conversation on religion etc.—sitting aft watching the phosphorous
balls of light whilst other people dance . . .

Do sports—and win potato race—in intervals between sitting
with B.-P. on the top deck—Yes, I'm up against it!

. . . Up before dawn again just to see him and kiss him.

It was necessary to be circumspect. Shipboard romances are notorious
and it would not have done for a distinguished General of fifty-five
and the founder of Scouting which in five years had exploded into a
world-wide Movement, to be caught flirting with a girl of twenty-
three. That is how other people might have viewed our relationship.
I do not think anyone ever realised how deep and passionate was our
love for each other—not even after we were married.

Many, many years before, when he was serving in West Africa,
B.-P. used to chaff his officers about their excitement when letters
arrived from their wives in England.

'Just you wait,' one of them warned him. 'You'll get it badly
one of these days.' Now that day had come. We were helplessly,
deliciously, ecstatically in love with one another—yet no one must
know.

Hence the stolen kisses before dawn. Hence the secret little notes
that were 'posted' in a cleat of one of the lifeboats. Hence the elaborate
subterfuge of his going forward on the ship after dinner and my going
aft, and meeting secretly at a pre-arranged point on the boat-deck. I
had to endure the attentions of a Major D. who was returning to a
colonial appointment in Bogota. He looked like a sheep and was quite
keen on me. I had to dance with him politely but noted in my diary:
' . . . the beloved Scout is always there. He gives me a photo album
and sketches . . . I *adore* him.'

The long, hot, lazy days passed all too quickly. We cruised along
the coast of Venezuela, past the string of small islands that fringe the
coast: Santa Margarita, Curaçao. Flying fishes kept pace with the ship
as it moved through the dark-blue glassy sea. We called at Porto
Colombia and Colon. Everywhere there were excited Boy Scouts to
meet him. We went to watch the Panama Canal being constructed. I
did comment in my diary on the building work at the Gathun Lock
but for the most part I viewed all the new sights through a haze of

love. Even my first sight of the Pacific at Panama rates no more than a passing reference.

Our time together was rapidly coming to an end. B.-P. had come on the cruise for a rest before embarking on an arduous tour of the States. He was continuing on the *Arcadian* as far as New York, then returning to England from the west coast of the States via Japan, New Zealand, Australia and South Africa. He would be away until August. Father and I were to disembark from the *Arcadian* to spend two or three weeks in Jamaica, returning to England in the *Tagus* in the second week of February.

Fortunately for us, the weather for the long trip from Colon to Kingston, Jamaica was stormy. We could count on being alone on deck.

January 23rd. Tuesday — Sail at 2 — out to sea and she pitches like anything but oh! I'm so happy all day with him — He sketches away and I talk and we laugh together — even when we try to be serious the imp of mirth sets in. We feel and think alike about everything ... Perfect bliss.

He gave me a Scout 'Thanks Badge' in the form of a swastika with the Scout fleur-de-lys superimposed. The right-handed broken cross or swastika (so-called from the Sanskrit word for 'well-being') was an ancient sign of good fortune that had appeared in many civilisations even as far back as the Bronze Age. Later, when the Nazis adopted the left-handed broken cross as their symbol and it became synonymous with evil and oppression, the Scout Movement abandoned the use of the swastika as a Thanks Badge, but in 1912 it was still a symbol of good. I was touched that he should give me this token of thanks and I wore it on a fine gold chain around my neck — but underneath my dress!

Even if he could have produced a ring in mid-ocean, we felt it was not right at that moment to become engaged. We did speak — half jokingly, half in earnest — of asking Captain Custance of the *Arcadian* to marry us, for we were wildly in love and dreading the separation that lay ahead. But we both knew in our hearts that it was not the right thing to do. There were too many people who might be hurt by a hasty marriage. So we had to be content with an 'understanding'—that some day, somehow, despite the difference in our ages, despite his comparative poverty and my wealth, despite his loyalty to his mother and what I knew would be the opposition of my parents, we would come together.

On January 26th, the *Arcadian* was to sail from Kingston for New York, taking my beloved Robin with her. The night before, my father and I moved our luggage from the ship up to the Myrtle Bank Hotel where we were to stay. After dinner, I strolled down towards the harbour. By 'chance', B.-P. strolled up from the harbour. We sat down together on a little bridge—a 'dangletoes', he called it. I cried and cried. I just could not bear the thought of being parted from him for so long. Next morning, I hurried down to the harbour to see him before the ship sailed. Unbeknown to me, he had hurried up to Myrtle Bank with the same purpose. We missed each other by minutes so that when he did eventually find me at the ship, there was no time left to talk and, anyway, there were people around. So all we could do was shake hands and say 'Good-bye'.

I had no one with whom I could share my feelings. My father, with his usual aloofness, had noticed nothing and, in any case, Robin and I had agreed to keep our 'understanding' a secret until he had finished his world tour and could consider ways and means of making our marriage possible. Meantime, he filled my thoughts by day and my dreams by night. I went through the motions of taking an interest in Jamaica but my mind was with Robin in the *Arcadian*. I found the 'funny little social circle' of Jamaica constricting—meeting the same limited group of people at every house we visited—but to drive home at night after a tennis party 'along the dark bumpy road lit by fireflies' would bring thoughts of my darling crowding into my mind. 'Ah Robin—you are always there.'

Within ten days, a bundle of letters had arrived from him, posted from New York. He must have sat down in his cabin the moment he went on board.

R.M.S.P. Arcadian
26 Jan.

It is much worse than I had expected, to be on board and no b.e.

to be found. It is exactly the feeling I had when my two mates had been killed in Matabeleland—one kept looking round expecting to see them as usual at the camp fire—whereas, they were dead. I rouse up from my work—(for I am working all I know) look around and the stitches suddenly tighten as I remember there is no little friend on board . . .

Like all his letters on this tour, it was signed not with my name for him, Robin, but with a little sketch of a robin. Oh, those enchanting little drawings!

'No letters from you yet . . . ' and the robin's mouth is turned down at the corners, its tail droops.

'A bundle of your letters awaited me . . . '—a perky robin with its tail up.

'Please send some more . . . '—a hungry robin with its beak open.

'I must show you my scrapbooks of this trip . . . '—an eager robin with a big book under each wing.

In this first letter from the *Arcadian*, as in many of his later ones, Robin addresses me as 'b.e.'. This, very unromantically, stands for 'bulgy-eyes' for he said he loved the way the surrounds of my eyes bulged when I laughed. The reference to 'stitches' alludes to one of those private codes that all lovers have—in this case that his heart was 'stitched tightly' to mine so that when he felt a great upsurge of love in his heart, it made the stitches pull tighter.

On February 9th, my father and I boarded the *Tagus* for our return voyage to England. Imagine my surprise and delight to be greeted by gifts and—more important—a bundle of letters written aboard the *Arcadian* as Robin steamed northwards from Jamaica to New York. On arriving there, he had sought out the *Tagus* (having ascertained that that was our return vessel) and had bribed the steward to ensure that the letters were delivered—and privately—to me.

. . . The more I think of it, the more marvellous it seems—I mean the coincidences which happened with us—our birthday for instance; and the band playing Faust music, and then our time (at Myrtle Bank); my having seen you walking with your dog; and then all the little points which we have in common.

Just wonderful.

Please don't marry Major D. right away, will you? . . .

He tried to comfort what he knew would be my distress at our long separation:

Do you remember my story about my poor little dog 'Taffie' who died because I was away for a week—He would not eat, and moped, and died. Well—I've come to sympathise more than ever with him during the past few days—I have not wanted any food and I am much lighter (and, I've no doubt, much healthier) in consequence . . .

I do wish I had not to write you scrappy notes but could tell you direct what I want to say. I expect you will be starting very soon . . . to go Eastward to meet me. Yes, you may imagine that we are going away from each other. Not a bit of it. I'm on my way to come and see you, going Westward, via America and Australia, and you are going Eastward—so we are bound to meet in time! . . .

He wrote playful, tender letters, addressing me as 'little mouse' because, as he said, a mouse is 'a little beast that keeps gnawing'.

It's 5.15 a.m. of our last day at sea. I've just been on deck and had to return below because there is a gale blowing with rain and splendid lightning—and it is all from behind us so it is shoving us along with quite a warm wind. It is impossible to believe that tomorrow we shall be in ice and snow at New York. It feels just as warm as the Tropics . . .

I am trying to make up for laziness on the voyage by extra work at the end of it—but you keep putting your oar in and interrupting me; one moment it is that radius of your eyebrow where it says . . . (and here followed a sketch of my eyebrow!) . . . ; the next you want to show me again your swagger pink satin shoes . . . but you mustn't do it. Run away and play. I'm fearfully busy and have not time to sit down and write to little girls—so I just send this letter to say so.

All the same I hope you will not think evil of me if I become a rather bad correspondent after this as I shall be overdone with work these next 6 weeks . . .

I think one of the most distracting things that you give me to keep me off my work is the last I saw of you and b.e.; but they were not 'little bulgeys' then, they were B.E., big Brown Eyes suddenly melting as we shook hands with, 'Well—Goodbye', in a most casual way . . .

As the *Arcadian* steamed further north and the weather became cooler, the cold light of reason enters his letters:

> Last Day on board.
> 30 Jan.
>
> . . . you agreed with me that it was hopeless to talk or think sensibly while on board this ship—and I have not been able to do so yet . . .
>
> But although so woolly and blind, yet I see the 'difficulties' looming very large: especially on my part and that is as regards money—even if my age were forgiven.
>
> People cannot live on less than 1200 to 1500 and that is pretty low—but I don't see where it is to come from in my case.
>
> Do you see any hope? Post a line at Colon.
>
> How I wish we could talk instead of writing. As you say, pen and paper is a rotten medium (though I must say you get over the difficulty marvellously well for your letters are just *you* talking).
>
> I am awfully sorry that the voyage is over—It brought me the happiest time I ever had—not only the 7th heaven which I might have hoped for, but I got the 8th! . . .

I did 'post a line' at Colon (for the *Tagus* made the same calls in reverse as the *Arcadian*). Once again I viewed the Panama Canal, Porto Colombia, Cartagena through a rosy glow of happiness. At no time in my life has my diary recorded so vividly the *colour* of the various places I have seen on my travels. We visited the Pearl Island of Santa Margarita, called at Port of Spain: 'Out at sea. Hot and happy—and I drift and dream in the sun and Robin is in them all—such jolly dreams of where we shall live and what we shall do—together.'

I had a telegram from him on our birthday, February 22nd, but then had to possess my soul in patience until I reached England before I could receive any further word from him. '1912. March 3. Sunday — Cold . . . wet . . . so I think of and write to Robin. It is just awful to think I shan't see him till August . . .'

We arrived back in England on March 6th but I had to wait until April 1st for Robin's first letters from America to reach me.

> The Waldorf Astoria.
> New York.
> 9 Feb.

b.e.

You keep turning up in such funny places. Why do you do it?

In the middle of watching a steel ingot being cast at Carnegie's works in Pittsburgh — there you were enjoying the wonderful glare, bang, rattle and roar just as much as I was.

When I was in the middle of a speech at a luncheon yesterday who should I find sitting beside me, wedged in between me and a Jewish judge, but b.e.!

When I was reviewing Boy Scouts, when I was stamping about the platform waiting for the night express with the thermometer at 15° below zero, when I was taking tea in a dear little house over-looking the great frozen lake at Detroit, when I was — oh well — I'd just like to know when or where b.e. didn't turn up . . .

We always had a wonderful affinity for each other. At the very time that he was writing that letter, I was confiding to my diary:

He is never out of mind — unconsciously I feel him always with me and it is heavenly — and yet just too awful to have to wait so long for his return. If I feel like this now what will it be like in August! My eyes see only your eyes Robin — my ears only hear your voice.

Our 'understanding' was supposed to be a secret but if my diary for these months is anything to go by, everyone who met me must have realised I was in love. Day after day, I poured out my heart in ecstasy and as each batch of letters arrived, I was inspired to even further transports. April 20th is a typical entry:

He *is* perfect—he is all that is sweet and kind and nice and noble and clever and artistic and sporting and simple and unaffected—I call it quite marvellous to be so unspoilt after all the adulation and gush he must have had. Ten most delicious letters from him at last.

In one of those letters he wrote:

Nearing San Francisco, 5th March. Oh! Why aren't you here at this moment! Running through the Sierra Nevada . . . The line keeps twisting and turning among the mountain spurs and precipices, through splendid fir forests, all in deep, clotted fresh snow . . .

Oh! In the few minutes that I have been writing we have run out of the snow into quite a different world . . .

Oh! Fruit trees all in blossom!! For goodness' sake come and look! Isn't it good? There's a house—just the spot—such a view—and a dog scampering about the lawn, a trout-looking stream below and a quaint little dovecote made like a little house on its pole . . .

Nine days later a further batch of letters arrived. I was thrilled to receive them 'but they aren't nearly as nice as the last', I noted with concern. What had gone wrong? Was our 'great love' all in my imagination? I could not believe I was mistaken. We had only known each other for three weeks before we had to separate but they had been such wonderful weeks. Surely he was not having second thoughts already. I waited in agonising uncertainty until his next letter arrived.

I read it with mounting dismay.

I cannot quote the letter for in my distress I tore it up, but I can still remember as if it were yesterday what it said. His mother had written (he informed me) to tell him that his brother, Frank (who up to that time had been Mrs. Powell's principal supporter) had fallen ill and was unable to make so generous an allowance as hitherto. Would Robin please increase his allowance to his mother and to his sister Agnes. 'I am old and I am poor; I have nothing to give you,' he wrote to me in despair. 'By the time I have paid my mother's allowance, I shall scarcely be able to keep a dog. If only my dream could have come true!' He went on to offer me my freedom. It would not be fair to expect me to live in penury.

The poor darling—it was typical of him to think of my happiness first. I dashed off a reply by the first post. Of course he was not to worry, I assured him. I had enough for both of us. We would manage somehow. Our dream *must* come true.

Then I had to wait—a long, long wait while my letter chased him round the world and his reply came slowly back by sea.

May 4th. Would I could go to sleep till August the 20th.

May 7th—He has his work and lots to distract him . . . and here am I sitting waiting . . .

May 12th—Thundery—a do nothing sort of day . . . I.C.A.A. seems tedious.

May 18th—13 weeks today Robin lands. It seems further off than ever now—and he is literally so. Read his *Aids to Scouting* and *Matabele Campaign* and can't believe—don't in fact—that the Robin *I* know is that wonderful man who knows and has done so much. He is now becoming very dream-like but oh! *so* lovable.

June 4th— . . . he is really coming me-wards now.

June 13th—Drive into Bournemouth and send off my photo to fetch Robin home from Durban. It is the oddest of feelings—this being in love with a memory of a man!

June 15th—It is so funny not knowing if we are going to marry each other or not—for me it is 'Robin or no man'.

There is much more in the same vein and much in deep despair; then at last on July 21st: 'Oh Joy again! All is well and what a glorious world it is and how happy I am! A dear stitchy letter and at last he has written to Dad.'

My secret—if it still was a secret—was out at last. I could discuss Robin freely with my family and friends. The relief was exquisite.

Now that he was beyond the 'half-way' mark of his world tour, his letters arrived with increasing frequency—humorous letters, tender letters, descriptive letters, lover's letters.

What a glorious mail! (he wrote from Melbourne) I'm just like a camel when he's having a drink out of his water bag. Don't you know how his inside hangs out of his mouth and he gurgles and drinks the water down his long neck—well, poetical though the simile may be, that's what I feel like—stitches bulging with pleasure!

Ten days later he wrote from Government House, Adelaide:

(the tour) . . . is all an enjoyable adventure, but through it all I keep looking on to something that you could not guess in a month of Sundays. It is so silly and so petty and childish that I know you'll despise me for it—whisper—
I want go to Peter Pan and the Tate Gallery with someone.

> Govt. House
> Adelaide.
> 24 June.

Oh --- .. ---..!

Why do I say that? Well because, as I was driving out in the motor yesterday with Lady Bosanquet, my hostess, she suddenly said 'There's Olive'—I jumped out of my half asleep attitude and yelled 'WHERE?' Then she pointed to a silly olive tree. And when I had gradually got back my equilibrium (i.e. my previous semi-comatose condition) I kept humming to myself 'Sweet olive oil—sweet Olave—sweet oil' and now I'm boiled if it hasn't coiled itself to simple 'OIL'—Fancy being called Oil!

During the long voyage from Australia to South Africa, he must have written to me several times each day—sometimes thinking on paper, sometimes reminiscing, sometimes breaking into nonsense verses:

> On board the S.S. *Themistocles*
> 9th July 1912.

. . . my neighbour at table . . . partly broke off as she looked at me—I was staring hard to my front, far far away from what she was saying—I was looking across the saloon at two of the round ports which were, as a pair, close together with a beading above them which made them look like eyes with a brow—and a clever brow at that—over them! ...

... Oh another coincidence! You don't mean to say that YOU ever played by the Round Pond? That was MY playground. Oh I can show you where Red Indians lived and hunted. The Texas plains are within sight of it, where I've drawn an unerring bead on the wary bison (London sheep). The grizzly who lived under the chestnut trees towards the Albert Memorial—but why go on? if you never played there you never met them: if you did play there well of course you know all about it. Are you by any chance Wendy? ...

When are you coming to Town, Miss Soames,
When are you coming to Town?

When am I likely to get your complicity
In giving my mother the happy felicity
Of welcoming *you* to our home-domesticity?
(You'll find matters ordered in sober simplicity).
    When are you coming to Town, O
    When are you coming to Town?

    Come in and look at my quaint curiosities,
Relics of wars and of savage ferocities,
    Beautiful caskets and awful monstrosities
(Some of them really are simply atrocities!)
    When are you coming to Town, O
    When are you coming to Town ...

and so on for verse after verse.

On August 14th I received a letter which told me that the photograph I had sent to Africa 'to fetch Robin home' had indeed arrived.

Durban Club. Natal.
19th July 1912.

Oh! I can't write what I feel at this moment—but I can't go to bed without writing a line to catch this mail.

When we arrived today I scarcely dared hope, and when a bundle of nearly 90 letters was handed and one after another failed to show the familiar writing I was beginning to despair. But then there came in the registered packet! I pretended entire indifference before my 'staff'! But at a convenient moment I clutched it and rushed to my room and tore it open.

It is a *beautiful* photo.

Thank you a thousand times, b.e. Oh, I can't tell you what I thought. I think you would have been glad you sent it if you could have overheard what I said to myself and the questions I asked. Could this really be b.e.? And could she really be sending it to *me*?

But she has sent it and in such form as my dear old Aunt went for when choosing some biscuits to send to me in S. Africa — she ordered a kind 'that would wear well in the pocket'.

I have kept this in my pocket ever since I got it so that I can take a nibble at it every now and then. Oh I must cable and thank you — otherwise you won't know for weeks how pleased and grateful I am.

And the letter is signed with a positively euphoric robin drawing!

Eager though he was now to return home, Robin loved his stay in South Africa. It had meant so much to him throughout his career.

Durban Club. Natal.

20 July 1912

I *have* enjoyed coming back to this old place Durban. I have known it for so many years and the old inhabitants of it know me so well, that it is like getting home after being in so many new and strange places.

And it is beautiful. This morning I got an early morning walk along the shore of the lagoon — under palm trees along the esplanade — with their tops brilliant in the rising sun and stems in violet shadow. The lagoon reflecting the pale blue overhead light and hazing off into grey mist — and Indian natives going to market in gorgeous red draperies with yellow fruit on their heads. Just glorious. Luncheon in an open air café facing the ocean while the surf comes roaring in . . .

(Above) The Scouts' wedding present, 1913.

(Below) With the children, Heather, Peter and Betty, at Pax Hill, 1923.

Heather Peter Betty

Robert Baden-Powell

1923

Dressed for a private audience
with Pope Pius XI, 1933.

At the Girl Guides' World Camp,
Camp, Foxlease, 1924.

How the artist in him showed in his letters!

Johannesburg. 26 July.

... up on the top of Spion Kop amongst the silent graves looking across the immense panorama of sunny veldt and flat-topped ridges fading into violet distance. Peace seemed scarcely the word for the solitude and dumbness of it.

Such a contrast to what those scarred old rocks had seen and heard.

Then yesterday we travelled up to the border of Natal circling round Majuba with its great sphinxlike bulk pretending that nothing harsher than a baboon's cry had ever been heard there—and our train plunged away from it into the tunnel of Leings Nek under the graves of the two big fights on the pass—into the Transvaal, where at every station, in the glaring jolly sun, were Boy Scouts and men of my Police to greet me.

It *was* good—and you think I enjoyed it—especially as we journeyed all day without the slightest suspicion of what was about to happen to us.

Well it's a thing I can't describe. But the train ran into Johannesburg station and I stepped out to find a dense mass of people all over the station and on the roofs and trees. Mayor —Defence officers covered with uniform and medals. Police by hundreds. 300 Boy Scouts. 54 Mafeking garrison. Deputation of 200 ex-Constabulary men—Bands—ladies—cheers—

For nearly an hour I was going round shaking hands, lumpy in the throat as could be (mind you I had left Ladysmith at 4 a.m.). Then there was a sudden heave—and just the sensation of aero-planing. I was being carried above the heads of the crowd—such a row you never heard.

I had had it once before after the war and I remembered how a kind man held my pockets shut to prevent valuables falling out— that's all that occurred to my numbed brain so I clutched my pocket tight myself so that my valuable little possession should not be lost...

I received this letter on August 17th. Only a week to wait now:

6

'My heart beats time to these passing seconds—passing quickly at last . . .' Surely he would come straight to me at Lilliput when he landed at Southampton on August 24th.

But he didn't!

CHAPTER EIGHT

A Partnership Begins

Year: 1912

He didn't come. Instead, he went to London to his mother and immediately afterwards to Norway, taking his nephew Donald for a fishing holiday. He felt he had to honour a promise to take the boy on this trip — a promise made before he left England the previous January and before he met me. I wrote angrily in my diary on August 26th: 'Jolly way for a lover?!? — to treat his loved one?!? Of course he is squashed with work and must take his nephew to camp as he promised to — but — oh dear!' My family knew that I had been counting the days to Robin's return. Now they witnessed my distress that he had gone away again. It made my father very angry indeed. He wrote to Robin.

I never did hear exactly what he put in the letter — but it worked.

My poor sweet received the letter in Norway in the middle of September. Immediately, he abandoned his holiday and telegraphed that he was coming to Grey Rigg. I learned later that he had been in a state of near despair when he learned that all berths were taken on the steamer from Christiania, but he managed to persuade the Captain to give him the First Officer's cabin. He arrived in London on September 14th and immediately wired to say that he was coming to Parkstone by train. I drove to the station in the brougham to meet him but he was not there; he had missed the train. A further telegram arrived. I met the next train from London. This time he was on it.

We reached Grey Rigg in time for dinner but, poor darling, in his frantic haste to reach me, he had forgotten his razor! It was amusing, really — the great B.-P. himself, the man who had given the watchword 'Be Prepared' to countless men and boys, being so flustered with love that he forgot his razor! Hardy, our butler, lent Robin his own razor, with the result that he cut himself shaving and had to appear at dinner with sticking-plaster on his chin!

I cannot remember anything about that dinner. I only know that afterwards, mother and I adjourned to the drawing-room leaving the two men together. Shortly afterwards, Father brought Robin in to us and said 'Well, Olave, I suppose it's all right' — and we were left alone.

The next day as the train carried him back to London, he wrote:

I cannot *yet* realise it!

My life was spread out green and placid like a quiet calm lake when bang comes a dynamite bomb out of an aeroplane, splosh, bang, spurt, and upsets the whole caboodle. And you're the bomb!

I can't be the same being who walked the deck of that ship in the North Sea during Thursday night, with a grip clutching his throat with a mighty fear — to find himself on Friday night in a dazed condition in the South of England — and on Saturday the happiest man in the whole of England — and on Sunday the happiest man in all the world! (and likely to remain so). Can it be me? . . .

Once the engagement was announced, the fuss began: 'September 20th, Friday — It was a day — and now every paper is full of us — and I see myself everywhere and reporters and Kodaks pester us — it is a joke.'

Mother, of course, had hysterics — just as she did when Auriol became engaged. Robin was too old; he had not enough money; he was not good enough, etc., etc. I think really that she was a bit jealous that I, the ugly duckling, 'poor little Miss Olave', was marrying a man who was a national hero and a world figure. However, she did come round and, in fact, provided my wedding-ring. When she married my father, she bought the wedding-ring because he was so absent-minded and would probably have forgotten all about getting one! Whether she thought Robin might be equally forgetful, I don't know but she gave him a ring for me.

Robin had written from Grey Rigg to prepare his mother for the shock of the announcement of our engagement. It was a letter typical of his Puckish sense of humour:

Dearest Mother,

I have been wondering what to give you as a birthday present, but I think I've got one now that will please you (as I hope and believe) – and that is a daughter-in-law for you!

Olave Soames whom I met on board the *Arcadian* travelling with her father promises to make a very good one. I hope you will like her half as much as I do. She has only one fault (and both George and Frank told me that in getting a wife you must overlook a fault or two if she is on the whole what you want). Her fault is that she is young, but she has an old head on her shoulders and is clever and wise and very bright and cheery . . .

So I came here . . . last night to dine and sleep, and to have a talk with her father . . . I must tell you all about it when I get back on Monday – and get your consent and good wishes.

He followed up the letter in person and wrote to tell me of the interview:

32 Prince's Gate, S.W.
17th Sept.

Bless you!

Why can't we cut out Tuesday 17th just as we did Mon. 26 March on my way across from America to Japan, 180° meridian. I don't quite see how I'm going to exist 32 whole hours before I see you.

Oh Olave I can see you laughing now had you heard my poor dear old mother's little detective question about you. When I had said all (and I was as full and long-winded as if I had been talking about *myself* to little girls on the *Arcadian*) – she thought for a time and then suddenly asked very gently 'Is she – rather small?'

I was cruel enough to squirgle and to hum and haw till the dear old lady had begun to picture a slightly hunch-backed deformity before I told her the dear girl was as tall as I was. And I showed her the 'biscuit' and she was very pleased but said (as I did) it doesn't really show what you are like – and I practised the very slightest deception – will you forgive me dear? – I said 'Yes but photographers generally know which way to take a person to show their best points.' And I've not even told her that I think Olave's is

a most beautiful face and full of character. So she is at present
delighted with the dominant idea that however plain you may be,
though that point is skilfully treated by the photographer, you are
very cheery and bright, a real playmate, and yet that under it all
you can be invaluable to me as adviser and helper in my work—
I warned her that she could not see it at first glance probably, but
it's there. Of course, that appeals to her more than the absence of the
hump—Oh you dear thing why aren't you here so that I can *tell* it
all to you instead of writing it all in the midst of an appalling pile
of work that awaits me.

Now I must shut up—I'm going to take my early morning walk
via the spot where I first saw 'The Girl and the Dog.'

Oh tomorrow do be quick and come!

I went up to London on the 'tomorrow' to meet the 'dear old lady',
my formidable future mother-in-law. My first impression of Henrietta
Grace was that she was very sophisticated, cold and aloof—indeed, a
real Victorian 'grande dame'. At first she was reserved—no doubt concerned that I was so young—but within a year she had melted completely and had fully adopted me as a very welcome daughter. I
also met Robin's sister Agnes on this occasion. She resented me but
had to tolerate me. I am afraid there was never any love lost between
us. She was a terrible snob and would have liked her brother to make a
much better match. She was always fluffing round her mother when I
was there, listening, snooping—like Tabaqui in *The Jungle Book*!
Robin's mother would unbutton if ever we were alone, which happened
occasionally, but would shut up whenever Agnes came in.

I can visualise the old lady now, sitting very upright in her armchair,
'receiving'. She would come downstairs and be established in her
place by McPhail, her maid. Then, although she was eighty-eight
when I first knew her, she would hold court at tea. It was the fashion
to announce that one would be 'At Home' on certain days of the week.
Anyone could call for tea and in Henrietta Grace's home one was
always sure to meet famous and eminent people.

While I was in town, I went with Robin to Greenwich to inspect
the ketch-yacht, *The Mirror*, given by the *Daily Mirror* to the newly-
formed Sea Scouts. It was Saturday, September 21st and it was my

first appearance in public with B.-P. We were cheered and cheered. It was all exciting and somewhat overwhelming.

Even a week later, the newspapers were still full of gossip about our engagement which had created such a sensation – fifty-five-year-old General to marry unknown girl of twenty-three! There were letters and telegrams galore. I wrote over two hundred letters of acknowledgment in that first week alone.

Inevitably, there was speculation as to whether marriage would bring an end to Robin's Scouting activities. One small Scout wrote:

I am dreadfully disappointed in you. I have often thought to myself 'how glad I am that the Chief Scout is not married, because if he was he could never do all these ripping things for boys.' And now you are going to do it. It is the last thing I should have expected of you. Of course, you won't be able to keep in with the Scouts the same as before, because your wife will want you, and everything will fall through. I think it is awfully selfish of you.

On the whole, however, the Movement accepted with pleasure the idea of a married Chief, once it realised that I was a friend and not an enemy.

. . . I couldn't help smiling (Robin wrote after a Scout Rally in Birmingham the day after our visit to the Sea Scouts in Greenwich) when I found that there was just a tiny bit of anxiety underlying their thoughts as to whether marriage was going to take me away from the Movement – but when I told them how you had already begun to help in it That day there was such a general gasp of relief and then a general wave of pleasure at the possibilities open under your help . . .

. . . *You are going to make a huge difference in the Movement.*

You probably don't realise yet how enormously it has depended on the *personal* touch. No amount of regulations or written stuff could enthuse the men and the lads to a fiftieth of the extent that the personal brotherhood does – and you and your smile will do a tremendous lot.

I never thought of it till I saw it already at work yesterday.

Scouting is now such an accepted part of the everyday scene that one tends to forget its impact sixty-odd years ago. The 'experimental' camp on Brownsea Island had taken place in 1907 with only twenty-four boys. *Scouting for Boys* had been published in weekly parts at the beginning of 1908, not with the idea of founding a new Youth Movement but merely to offer some fresh ideas to existing leaders of young people. It was boys themselves, really, who started Scouting as a *Movement*, not my husband. They read his book and were thrilled by it. They formed themselves into groups and called themselves 'Patrols' as he had described. They put on hats and scarves and shorts like the boy in the drawing on the cover of the book. They began to call themselves 'Boy Scouts', and yet more boys wrote to Robin asking how they could 'join'. It all happened so fast and with such enormous enthusiasm that he just had to organise things and that was how the Scout Association was formed. It fired the imagination of boys everywhere to such an extent that within two years it had spread right round the world.

Little wonder, then, that the boys should be concerned whether there was a threat in this strange young woman their beloved Chief was to marry. I am so grateful that they accepted me, for I could not have fought them all for my Robin.

He wrote from Cheshire on September 24th:

. . . It was a wonderful demonstration not only by the boys but by the people. We motored for *miles* through them – thousands and thousands – and it was for you, darling, I believe they were out. One great black miner shouted 'Luck to your missus' – and great cheers followed it.

On September 30th, the Surrogate came to arrange about the special licence for our wedding which we had decided should take place before the end of the year. I remember that Robin 'proposed' formally to me outside the door of the room just as we went in to sign all the documents. He slipped a ring on my finger – a simple little affair that an American Scout had given to him. Not for me the 'lovely ring and a string of pearls worth £400' that I had recorded when Auriol was engaged; Robin's simple band of metal with its embossed fleur-de-lys had no financial value but it was as precious as rubies in my sight.

We went down to Hampshire to a big Scout Rally and stayed with Sir Harry Crichton, the County Scout Commissioner. He was having a big house party for the occasion at his home, Netley Castle. After dinner, Sir Harry invited Robin and me to see his library and music room. However, no sooner had we followed him in than he left us alone, shutting the door behind him. Save for one precious day alone on Brownsea Island immediately after our engagement, we had had very little privacy since it had been announced. Now Robin seized this opportunity to clasp me in his arms.

I tried to push him away. 'Stop it,' I said. 'Suppose anyone came in! Whatever would they think!'

'What does it matter,' dismissed Robin, kissing me ardently. 'We're engaged.'

I still was not happy about it. 'We mustn't,' I said. 'People will think we have just come into the library to spoon.'

So I went across to the piano and started to play, just to indicate that we were *not* spooning. Whereat the door opened and Sir Harry's scandalised face appeared round it.

'Really, you two!' he exclaimed in a disappointed voice. 'I didn't leave you alone to do *that*!'

There were not many opportunities to be alone. There were relatives to visit so that I could be 'approved': 'To Aylesbury to be inspected by his stern Aunt Con' (Lady Smyth). 'Inspected by Lady Flower' (another aunt-in-law). There were Scout functions at which I had to be introduced – I made my first public performance alone and my maiden speech on October 12th when I presented a Shield to the Parkstone Scouts. Somehow, the shyness that had burdened me of recent years seemed to fall away under Robin's influence. There were other things to see to, besides Scout affairs. There was linen to buy for the flat we had taken in London at 35, Rutland Court. There was my Marriage Settlement to be arranged.

All the time there was the frustration of having just a few precious moments together and then we would be parted again – 'Oh dear heart, I am longing for Wednesday. What a fearful time it is to wait . . .' Inevitably, there was newspaper speculation about the wedding. It

began with a simple statement: 'A large muster of Scouts will act as a
guard of honour to the bride and bridegroom and hail them as they
leave the church . . .' Then the imagination of the journalists added
further elaboration:

> The first week in December has been fixed for the wedding of
> General Sir Robert Baden-Powell and Miss Olave Soames. The
> ceremony will be performed in the parish church at Lilliput, in
> Dorsetshire, where a large congregation, including many Army
> and Navy men, will assemble . . .

Some papers took a speculative line:

> . . . the point to be settled is what part the boys who owe him
> allegiance will take in the coming important event of his marriage.
> That it will be a festival day goes without saying, but that some
> more than ordinarily exciting parade and demonstration of Scout
> loyalty will be arranged is generally expected.

Other papers let their imagination run riot:

> A guard of honour of Boy Scouts will surround the bride's
> house and link up with the church, so that she may walk through a
> regular army of embryo soldiers. Afterwards a great ceremonial of
> Boy Scouts will be held at Lilliput, the bride and bridegroom
> inspecting the escort and accepting a wedding gift from them . . .

It was too much. Neither of us felt we could face such publicity on
what was, for us, such a specially important day. So we decided to
marry swiftly, quietly and secretly.

On Wednesday, October 30th, 1912, at 12.45 in the afternoon —
just a year, almost to the day, after Auriol's wedding and a good
six weeks before the date canvassed in the newspapers — Lieutenant-
General Sir Robert Stephenson Smyth Baden-Powell, K.C.B. made me
his bride. It was the same church as for Auriol's wedding: St. Peter's in
Parkstone; the same vicar, Rev. the Hon. R. E. Adderley. But whereas
Auriol wore white satin and was attended by six bridesmaids and a

page, I wore a simple blue costume and was attended only by 'Azzie' — Robin's sister, Agnes. Where Auriol's service was fully choral, ours was brief and simple, with no music at all. Where Auriol had hundreds of guests, we had only my father and mother, Robin's brother, Major Baden-Powell, as best man; General Kekewich, C.B., the Defender of Kimberley and an old friend of both Robin and of my own parents; my brother-in-law Bob Davidson (for Auriol was still not well after the birth of her first child) and my dear friend who had foretold it all, Sie Bower.

The church bells did ring in honour of the wedding but not until after we were already on the train for London.

I wrote in my diary that day: 'Is it really true, my darling Robin truly my very own—after these months of waiting and wondering. He is mine—and I am his for ever.'

CHAPTER NINE

A New Life

Years: 1912–1914

We only had a week away after the wedding—at Mullion Cove in Cornwall—for there were so many Scout functions and rallies already booked ahead for Robin to attend: Nottingham, Macclesfield, Sussex, East Yorkshire. I accompanied him to them all and was proud and thrilled by the wonderful reception accorded him wherever he went. It was the sort of reception given nowadays to footballers and pop idols!

I had known that Robin was an important man but not until I married him did I realise *how* important he was, how famous, how much a national hero. Moreover, I was immediately transplanted on to a social plane of which I had no previous experience. As I have already mentioned, my parents were wealthy upper-middle-class. After my marriage I found myself mixing with the aristocracy. It was another world altogether, particularly in the class-conscious era before the First World War.

In those days, the Court page of *The Times* used to carry accounts of weekend house parties and it will illustrate my point if I quote two of them:

December 1st, 1912. Lord and Lady Zetland have a large party staying with them at Aske Hall, Richmond in Yorkshire, and their guests include Lord Scarbrough, Lord and Lady Lamington, Lord Bolton, Lord and Lady Glamis, Major and Lady Evelyn Collins, and Sir Robert and Lady Baden-Powell, who were married only a few weeks ago.

December 10th, 1912. Lord and Lady Brownlow entertained a

weekend party at Ashridge, Berkhamsted, which included the Duke of Norfolk, and General Baden-Powell and his wife.

The grandeur of these house-parties, however, meant little to me.

Strangely enough, this change in my circumstances seemed to alienate my mother. I know she resented my leaving home and I think she was, in addition, slightly jealous that I was enjoying the sort of life she would have desired for herself. Moreover, I think she felt annoyed that I had made a 'better' match than Auriol. Our relationship deteriorated markedly after my marriage. For the moment, however, I was content just to be with Robin.

I wrote in my diary on November 28th: '. . . My parents have been good to me but nothing that I could ever have imagined was ever so marvellous as this joy and love of my Darling.'

Our first home was a flat at 35, Rutland Court, only a few yards from Rutland Lodge where I was living in 1910 when Robin saw me walking Doogy in Hyde Park. It was close, but not too close, to Robin's mother; made travelling relatively easy to the Mercers' Hall (of which ancient Livery Company Robin was the Warden) and was, of course, convenient for Scout Headquarters, by now installed in their present address at 25, Buckingham Palace Road. It was convenient, too, for me to attend sittings with Mr. Léon Sprinck, a Russian artist in pastel, who was doing my portrait as a wedding gift from my godmother, Aunt Ger. This picture how hangs at Foxlease, the Guide Training Centre in the New Forest. My first portrait, by Lionel Baird, had been painted in 1904 when I was a child at Luscombe. There have been two others since: one by David Jagger (a companion to his magnificent painting of my husband which hangs in Baden-Powell House). The Jagger portrait was painted in 1930 and depicts me in British Guide uniform with my personal Standard. The other portrait, by Mrs. Wheatley, shows me in the World Guide uniform (blue/grey as opposed to the navy blue of the British uniform). This painting hangs in the Commonwealth Guide Headquarters in London.

I was ecstatically happy—except for one thing: it soon became apparent that Robin was not well. He had always driven himself hard, imposing a strict regimen of rising at 5.0 a.m. or even earlier in order to fit in all the things he wanted and had to do. Even before

he left the Army to devote himself entirely to Scouting, he had been
famous for his versatility as artist, writer, actor and soldier. His output
of books and paintings was stupendous. Once before, in Africa, he had
collapsed through over-work. Now, with the constant demands of the
rapidly expanding Scout movement and after a punishing world tour,
the poor man was exhausted.

Tuesday. 10th December—R. to Dr. and seedy. Tea party here.
To open Walworth Scout Exhibition. Bouquet, cheers and speeches
—all nice. But Robin is ill—oh—horridly bad—Temperature 102—
with an old sort of fever.
December 13—Robin bad still. It is lovely nursing him...
Wicked posts and a pessimistic doctor.

He pulled himself together for our Reception at the Mercers' Hall
on December 17th. We had been aware that many people had been
disappointed by our secret marriage so we decided to invite all our
friends to a late wedding reception. Scouts provided a Guard of
Honour and entertained the guests with carols. All our wedding
presents were on display—except one, that from the Movement.
Every Scout in the country had contributed one penny, bringing in a
total sum that was sufficient to buy a 20 h.p. Standard landaulette car.
We could hardly bring that into the Mercers' Hall. In any case, it was
not quite ready; it was being specially sprayed in Scout colours—
very dark green with a fine yellow line running round, and the
Scout badge discreetly painted on the panel. There was a silver figure of
a Scout on the bonnet. This magnificent gift was 'officially' presented to
us on behalf of the Association by the Duke of Connaught on
May 17th, 1913—the thirteenth anniversary of the Relief of Mafeking.

It was a wonderful wedding reception—but Robin had to take to his
bed the following day.

I was not the only person to be anxious about his health. At the
reception I had been approached by Lady St. Davids, mother of
Roland Phillips who was one of Robin's most ardent followers in
Scouting.

'What are you going to do at Christmas time with that *dear* man?'
she asked me, and then went on to offer us the use of her house near

Haverfordwest in Pembrokeshire. Roch Castle was a formidable-looking but comfortably modernised fortress set in a commanding position above the village, with a big view over the surrounding countryside. The weather was vile but it did not matter—it was our first Christmas together, and Robin could rest and paint. But when we returned to London the doctor declared him still unfit—he must have a *complete* rest and change. So Robin decided to give me a glimpse of a part of the continent with which he was so closely connected from his 'former' life. He booked our passages to Algiers for January 14th.

There was one thing we had to do, though, before we left England, something we had promised ourselves ever since that letter Robin had written to me from Adelaide in June 1912—we went to see *Peter Pan* together.

We left Southampton on the *Prinz Eitel Friedrich* and had a stormy crossing of the Bay of Biscay. The weather did not matter. Here we were, just a year after our first meeting, on another ship and married.

After a week of exploring the countryside around Algiers, Robin had a surprise for me: we were to have a week's camping expedition in the mountains that edged the Sahara. This would be an entirely new experience for me!

We left Biskra on foot accompanied by two mules and two Arab guides armed to the teeth against attacks by robbers. Rahmoun led the mule carrying the two tents and the camp furniture; Ibrahim's mule carried the rest of the baggage. We had to take water with us as the only streams we should encounter were salt and brackish. It was all delicious fun and such a novelty for me. Sometimes we abandoned the tents and slept out under the stars. I have kept a note of some of our 'menus': breakfast—tea and hard-boiled eggs; lunch—cold chicken and biscuits spread with Nestlé's milk; dinner—cold chicken and chocolate and oranges. The diet was varied with fish caught by Robin, if we were lucky enough to encounter a stream. Of course, in those days there were not the 'convenience' foods and gadgets available to campers today so we had to improvise. Robin poked gentle fun at my efforts when addressing a Scout rally at Parkstone on our return:

You see a lady here in a beautiful black hat and a white coat (the local paper reports him as saying). I saw her not so long ago scrubbing out a saucepan. We were living the simple life in the desert. We only had one pan and it had to be used for frying our fish and also for boiling our coffee. After the lady had fried the fish she had to get some grass roots and sand and scrub the pot out before we could make the coffee. The lady was quite able to do it and she did it well. She also did the washing. But I must stand up for the Scouts and the mere man—she had to fall back on me to do the ironing!

(I never did master ironing—I once tried to iron a shirt but it went brown and stuck to the iron!)

After our camping trip we went on to Carthage and Tunis, then sailed for Malta where Robin had been Assistant Military Secretary from 1890 to 1893 under the then Governor, Sir Henry Smyth. Now we stayed at the Palace with Governor Sir Leslie Rundle. He was Chief Scout of Malta and invited all the Scouts of the island to tea in the Palace Armoury while we were there. We returned to England by way of Sicily and Italy, arriving back at Tilbury on March 1st. We had been away almost two months and Robin was immeasurably better in health.

We had been looking for a house before we left England. We both loved the country and now a garden was going to be necessary for I was expecting our first baby. We were on the top of a bus going from the Cavalry Club to Hamptons when I told Robin of my hopes. It had to be a boy, and, of course, it would have to be called 'Peter'.

We took a lease on Ewhurst Place in Sussex and moved in on April 13th, 1913. It was a modest red brick house outside Robertsbridge, with seven principal bedrooms and staff quarters. The grounds were lovely, with wide lawns sloping down to the River Rother and a splendid view of Bodiam Castle. I loved to watch the Downs behind the castle; they changed colour continually according to the time of day, mauve one minute, blue the next.

Robin was immediately caught up in his Scout work again and I felt very frustrated that I could not go everywhere with him. Despite the coming baby, however, I had to take lessons in curtseying for I was to be 'presented' at Court on May 7th.

It is one of the few occasions in my life when I can remember what I wore; clothes have never mattered much to me. Most of the time I

B.-P. at Pax Hill with his dogs, Shawgm and Twm.

(Above) Olave with her family, 1951. Back Row: Peter; John King; Gervase Clay; Robert and Michael B.-P.; Michael King. Front row: Carine B.-P.; Heather; Olave; Betty; Nigel Clay; Wendy B.-P.; Timothy King; Robin Clay (Gillian and Crispin Clay not present); (below) visiting crippled Guides at Heritage Croft School, Chailey, Sussex.

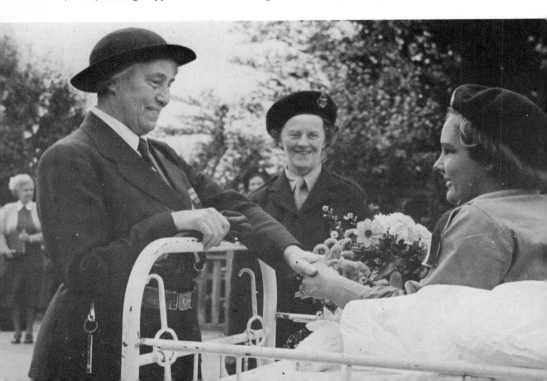

just don't *see* clothes, and fine apparel makes me feel awkward. However, for this memorable event—even though it was so impersonal and all over in a moment—I had a gown of white satin embroidered with leaves in silver. Over this I wore Auriol's silver-embroidered wedding-train and I carried a bouquet of white roses.

1913 was a blissful year, the first of many equally so. My dear friend Sie Bower came to stay with us and saw her prophecy come true: I *had* married my soldier, the first of my three children was on the way and I had 'woken up and become a person'.

It seems incredible now, when money seems to decline in value from week to week, that we could afford such a large establishment. My father had settled some capital on me as a dowry when I married. The income from this, added to Robin's pension, plus anything he might earn from his writings, made us comfortably well off. Being Chief Scout carries no salary! We were able, I note from my diary, to start our household at Ewhurst with two maids, Annie and Lizzie. Annie Court had been a housemaid with us both at Luscombe and at Bradfield. When she saw the announcement of my engagement in the paper, she wrote to my mother asking if 'Miss Olave' would need a maid. Mother replied that I should only be keeping a very small staff as I should not be at all wealthy but Annie came nonetheless. At Ewhurst Place she worked hard as 'everything'. One of my I.C.A.A. boys from Parkstone, now a Scout, joined us as 'Boots'. We had a gardener, and a cook who was as hopeless as I was but was later replaced by a treasure. We had to have a cook for, as I have already mentioned, I was hopelessly inexperienced. She used to come in with a slate and say 'We are having mutton today' and that was all I had to do—to agree! In May, Annie introduced her brother, Ernest Court, to be chauffeur and to look after the horse. Later, Annie's sister came as parlourmaid. With the addition in June of a butler and a 'Tweeny' we were, for the present, adequately cared for!

It was inevitable that all the staff should become embroiled in Scouting. On June 21st, the 1st Ewhurst Scout Troop was inaugurated. The opening meeting was on our lawn, using for assembly the Union Jack that flew over Mafeking during the siege. Court and the gardener became the Troop's Assistant Scoutmasters and I became the proud possessor of a warrant as Scoutmaster!

7

That summer saw the first of many 'Royal' occasions together when we were invited to a State Ball on June 26th in honour of the visit of the President of the French Republic. There were so many 'firsts' in 1913. July gave me my first really important Scout 'occasion', the Imperial Scout Exhibition at Bingley Hall, Birmingham. The pattern had already been established of holding a big Scout function every two years. There had been the Crystal Palace Rally in 1909, the Windsor Rally in 1911. Now the Association were trying out an event in the Midlands. Six thousand Scouts were under canvas for a week and many thousands more, with members of the public, came in daily. Prince Alexander of Teck opened the Exhibition on July 2nd and I was detailed to escort the Prince and Princess round the various displays. I was impressed beyond measure by the wide scope of the exhibits, indicating how much Scout training catered for 'the whole man'. Equally staggering was the terrific interest evinced by the general public. Nothing like Scout training had been offered to young people before.

It was practically my last public appearance that summer except for the Eton v. Harrow match on July 11th, concerning which I noted: 'Jolly . . . Harrow badly beaten but apparently nobody looks at the cricket.'

We had always been a family for coincidences. Our baby son, Peter, ran true to form by arriving on our first wedding anniversary. Robin was thrilled. It appears to have been quite a public event for there were reporters on the doorstep at one o'clock in the morning awaiting the birth! We had over two hundred telegrams of congratulation and the Duke of Connaught graciously wired from Canada offering to be Peter's godfather.

Auriol had a second daughter in the summer of 1913 and Arthur married Hope Parrish in December. I made my peace with Mother, and Robin became Master of the Mercers' Company. One way and another, it was quite a year.

We little guessed, at the beginning of 1914, how the year would end. January started with the usual round of friends down to Ewhurst for the shooting; trips to London for the Mercers or for Scout business; endless proud showing off of Peter to friends and relatives; interviews and photographs for various periodicals; conferences and rallies in which I was playing an increasing part. The shy girl who fled from a tennis party a few years before because there might be people there she did not know, was now regularly addressing public meetings. I was gaining in self-confidence, too:

7th May, 1914—I go with Baden (B.-P.'s brother) to excellent Boys Brigade demonstration at Albert Hall. Prince Alexander of Teck (new Governor Gen. of Canada) in chair. Made rotten speech. Why aren't they all Scouts? Drill will not make self-supporting men of 'em though a very good machine. I cheekily told their Chief Sir W. Smith so!

I had become completely dedicated to my beloved husband's cause and wanted nothing else from life but to be with him. Even baby Peter was frequently left with his nurse as I accompanied Robin all over the country on his tours.

Oh, what a husband and what a man I have married (I wrote ardently in May 1914). The perfect man if ever there was one— perfect mind and heart filled only with noble ideals and kindness and goodness. A tongue that never lies or slanders and an eye that sees the best in all things and all men.

The movement was expanding rapidly, spreading like a flood tide throughout this country and, indeed, the world.

'Saturday, 13 June—Queen Alexandra reviews *10,000* Scouts on the Horse Guards Parade. A grand sight. She was so pleased, pleasant and nice and sent for me to talk to.' There were rallies in Nottingham and Worksop, in Leeds and Chesterfield, in Norwich and Liverpool, in Oxford and Sheffield. Boys, boys, boys. Hundreds of thousands of lively, enthusiastic youngsters, dedicated, eager to be of service.

Was it just chance that set my husband in their midst to lead and inspire them? For if ever there was a time when the youth of this country needed to be alert and prepared, it was the summer of 1914.

CHAPTER TEN

The War Years

Years: 1914–1917

Robin and I had planned a camping and fishing holiday in Norway for the summer of 1914, and in the early autumn we were to sail to Cape Town for a tour of South Africa. However, as soon as events pointed to war, we cancelled both trips. Robin circulated his Commissioners asking for the mobilisation of all Scouts, ready to be of service in whatever capacity required. Even before the actual declaration of war, Scouts were guarding bridges and telegraph lines against possible sabotage. As soon as hostilities began, they acted as hospital orderlies, messengers in Government Departments and assisted the Police. Perhaps one of their most arduous and responsible jobs was a day and night patrol of the coast from the northern tip of Scotland right round to Cornwall. They did this all through the war. 'Men of the Second Line', my husband called them—boys doing a man-size job even in the worst possible weather. No wonder the Movement grew stronger rather than weaker as the war progressed.

Of course, during the first few days, the country was full of wild tales of German spies at large in the community, of acts of sabotage at home and fearful casualties abroad. I solemnly recorded in my diary that Russian troops had been seen going through Scotland to Belgium. So rife was this rumour that when staying in Perthshire that week, I hurried down to the station to watch for them on the trains. Two days later I noted: 'Russian rumour denied by General Ewart who commands Scotland and ought to know.'

Robin was eager to be back with his regiment but Lord Kitchener told him that Scouting was the very best service he could give to his country. He did become Adjutant-General for the New Army and, as Hon. Colonel of the 13th Hussars, he had certain responsibilities with his old regiment. Mostly, however, in that first year of the war, he spent his time touring Scout units, encouraging, recruiting, inspiring.

So many young men of our acquaintance were soon to be killed in the fighting. Our own gardener and chauffeur left us to join up. At the beginning of October, my brother Arthur returned from France 'wounded in the head and very unnerved. The scenes he has seen are *awful* and they have had a fearful time.'

I could not do much myself as yet towards the war effort for I found I was expecting a second baby. However, I bought a 'type-writing machine' and helped Robin with his Scout work.

Robin's mother had lived to hold one of our children in her arms but she did not live to see the second. She died on October 13th, 1914 at the age of ninety — incredibly alert right to the end. As if that were not enough sorrow for Robin, every day brought news of more and yet more young men we knew being killed in France; and on November 5th that dear jolly man (General Kekewich), whom we used as children to call 'The Happy Egg' on account of his baldness, shot himself out of despair at being no longer of service to his country. He had earned a high reputation during the Boer War, he had attended our wedding and was one of Peter's godparents. It was terribly sad.

So many of Robin's contemporaries were dying. It made me acutely conscious of the difference in our ages, made every minute together that much more precious. Field-Marshal Lord Roberts had died, who had given the order for the column that got through to Robin in Mafeking. We went to his funeral at St. Paul's Cathedral on November 19th:

Very impressive and beautiful. A terrible day — bitterly cold and wet for his last journey. He died in such a happy way, though, amongst his Indian troops within the sound of guns. Robin would like to end like that.

Despite the dreadful slaughter in Flanders, there was still a certain gaiety in the attitude of young men to the war. Eric Walker, the Secretary of the Scout Association, had joined the Royal Flying Corps. With the same panache that characterised the Battle of Britain pilots in the last war, he 'parked' his aircraft by Ewhurst Church on his way over to France one morning in February of 1915 and popped up to the house to have breakfast with us!

Robin had been longing to get back into uniform. His opportunity came in late March when he went over to France to visit his regiment at the Front. 'Thank Heaven, not to fight,' I wrote gratefully in my diary.

There were two new additions to our household that summer. 'Jimmie', a small car, was purchased in May; and Heather, our second child, was born on June 1st. Robin taught me to drive and within a few weeks I felt completely confident. Thereafter, I was much more mobile and usually chauffeured Robin to his various engagements. He did not like driving and very rarely took the wheel.

In 1915, the war was still not having much effect on the lives of those of us who were at home. There were shortages, of course, and the newspapers were full of news from France; but even so, dear Heather's christening was still an event, given half a page of coverage in the daily paper! July 13th was the only fine day of that week, I remember. Three hundred Scouts lined the road from Ewhurst Church to our home and entertained the guests at the garden party we gave in the afternoon. For a few hours, we all forgot the war.

Normally we could not forget it. We could hear the big guns booming somewhere across the channel. Court came home on leave, wounded. Friede, my dear old German governess, came to stay but now she was classed as an 'enemy alien' and had to report regularly to the Police. News came that Eric Walker had been shot down and was a prisoner-of-war in Mainz. Robin went over to France again in July and then we went on a five-week tour that took us to Ireland. 'Extraordinary feeling of revolt and hatred of the English', I observed.

During his last visit to France, Robin had been greatly impressed by the work of the Y.M.C.A. in providing recreational facilities for the troops. Their huts offered refreshments, news, concerts and a dry, reasonably warm refuge in which to write letters home. Robin could see that the number of huts was woefully inadequate to meet the needs. Once back home, he prevailed upon the Mercers' Company to put up the money to provide a hut at Val-de-Lièvres, Calais. It was to be staffed by men and women connected with Scouting and he arranged that I should be one of the first 'staff'.

I was absolutely delighted to have this opportunity of doing something *real* at last towards the war effort—but what to do with the babies? My mother disapproved strongly of the idea of my going. It seemed mad and unnecessary to her—another black mark against Scouting—but I managed to coax her round a bit and she agreed in the end to look after the babies for the three months or so I should be away.

After innumerable inoculations, meetings and instructions, I set sail on Thursday, October 7th, 1915—for France. Y.M.C.A. Recruit No. 269 had been called up for duty. There were eight of us on the staff—five men and three women. Our billet was a horrible little box of a cottage but it was close to the Mercers' hut. The weather was appalling so it was as well we had not very far to wade through the mud. Conditions were primitive. There was an out-door earth closet; and our infrequent baths were taken in a tin tub and the bathwater afterwards emptied into the street outside! Inevitably, I took in a number of stray animals as pets—a kitten, an Airedale dog and a rabbit which for no apparent reason earned the name of Boots.

We called our hut 'The Mercers' Arms'. Stella Ashton and I were the 'barmaids', dispensing chat and sympathy along with the cocoa and cigarettes. Maybe the chat was the most acceptable service. One Tommy said to me 'You don't know what it has been to us chaps to have you ladies here!'

The work was hard. Sometimes I wondered whether I could stick it out, particularly on the anniversary of our wedding and Peter's second birthday. But I knew it was a worthwhile job and it was marvellous to see what happiness it brought to the tired and dirty Tommies. Moreover, it was important to me personally. For the first time in my life, I was doing a *real* job of work *on my own*. It was good training and I was under discipline—both of which were to fit me for the life I have lived these many years 'when self-discipline has been the quality most often needed. Meantime, however, I had no inkling of the public life that lay ahead of me; rather was I drawing on past skills: playing my fiddle at a Christmas concert for the troops, and singing. 'I know a lovely garden' was one of the sentimental ballads I put across, I remember. It left one feeling lumpy about the throat and scarcely able to sing because one knew the men would be thinking of home.

Meantime, Robin had been whipping up enough support at home

to start up another Y.M.C.A. hut at Etaples, this time sponsored by the Scouts. He particularly wanted Stella and me to open this one so after Christmas we moved there from Calais. It was even harder work here, for there was only one man to help us. The first day we were short of water, short of food, short of change.

6th January, 1916—My wig! This is something like 'some hustle'. We have just one hour free in the day but all the rest is going for all one is worth. We eat when we can, what we can, where we can!

Etaples was a dirty, loathesome, smelly little town which seemed even worse because we were so frustrated by lack of help. Extra hands had been promised from England but there were delays over permits so we had to struggle on short-handed through the beastly winter weather. Then, at the end of January, I was badly hit by 'flu. I staggered into the hut part-time for two days although I had a soaring temperature but then was ordered home.

When we went to Grey Rigg to see the babies, Peter did not know me at all after so many months away and was very shy with both of us. This, I was to discover, was one of the penalties of the life I was to lead in the future—the long periods of enforced separation from my children.

Let me be frank and admit that I have never been a doting mother. I loved my children but my darling Robin was the person who mattered most in my life. I always put him first and the children a long way second in my affection. Indeed, as they grew up, they would probably say they came third with me for by then I was so completely involved in Guiding. I am aware that I can be criticised on this account but let me say in extenuation that Guiding was at first partly an extension of my great love for Robin; then it developed far, far beyond my expectations or even my imagining and to lead it properly demanded no small personal sacrifice. I realise now that I missed a great deal through being away from my children so much, though not so much as might be expected. Most children in our walk of life at that period were, in any case, left largely in the care of their nurse and nursery-maid. If the main burden of bringing up my children was lifted from my shoulders, it was only a repeat of what my own mother had done with Auriol,

Arthur and myself. For example, I see in my diary for July 17th, 1921, I made an entry: 'Peter had lunch downstairs with R. and me in a grown up way for the first time.' He was then almost eight. It seemed to me at that time quite natural that he should still be taking his meals in the nursery with Nannie; today, such an arrangement would be unthinkable. My children assure me, however, that they never felt neglected. Indeed, they have told me how excited they used to be whenever we were coming home. I think I am very much closer to them today than ever I was during their early years. Robin, of course, was absolutely wonderful with them and they adored him. For example, I see that I wrote in my diary in 1917: 'Babies heavenly and the nursery feels rather full now with three! I think Robin is a better mother than I am and gloats over them.'

Peter, to our desperate anxiety, was a very frail baby. He had rickets and spent a lot of time on his back. He also suffered from constantly recurring attacks of gastro-enteritis. Nowadays, with modern medical skills, these ailments would no doubt have been promptly cured, but in the state of knowledge in 1914 to 1918, he was constantly under the doctor's care and all this illness made him late developing. He did not walk until he was three. We were advised that he should have bracing sea air and he spent nearly a year at Bexhill, much of the time in a nursing home, until after our third child was born in April of 1917. She was to have been 'David' but arrived as Betty instead.

We had been somewhat dismayed on our return from France in 1916 to learn that the owner of Ewhurst Place had been killed in action. Our tenancy was for the moment secure but the house was going to be put up for sale. We could not possibly raise the capital to buy it and, even if we could have done, it was not as conveniently placed as we should have liked.

To travel down from London, one had to take a train from Charing Cross to Robertsbridge, then change to the branch line, the 'Rother Railway', from Robertsbridge to Ashford. It was a funny little line. One bought one's ticket on the train. The conductor would move precariously along the *outside* of the coaches, even while the train was in motion. One would be sitting in one's seat when suddenly the carriage door would open, letting in a blast of wind and rain, and there was the conductor. After collecting all our fares, he would climb out through the door again and proceed to the next compartment!

We looked at a number of properties during the next few months and eventually settled on Little Mynthurst Farm near Horley, a dear quaint fifteenth-century place, though a trifle awkward inside with lots of low beams and communicating rooms. We took it on a short lease and moved there in September of 1917—with three children, the staff, three dogs, two doves, pigeons, rabbits, ducks, chickens and goldfish!

CHAPTER ELEVEN

The Girl Guides

Years: 1916–1918

I suppose that to most people, my name is synonymous with Girl Guiding. It must seem all the more surprising, therefore, that I should come thus far through the story of my life with scarcely a mention of that Movement.

Scouting, like Topsy, had 'just growed'. Following the publication of *Scouting for Boys* in 1908, thousands of youngsters had demanded an organisation to guide them in its practices and precepts. The result was the Boy Scouts Association.

The perusal of *Scouting for Boys*, however, was not confined exclusively to boys. Their sisters read the book with equal avidity. It opened up new and appealing vistas to these young female Edwardians, visions of a life where women could face the world on equal terms with men, where they would be trained and equipped to cope with whatever emergencies might arise. The idea chimed in perfect tune with the growing demand for women's suffrage. As this account of my own girlhood must have demonstrated, there was nothing at all for girls to do in the Edwardian era except wait to be married. They had no freedom of action, no training for life, little education compared with boys. Needlework, painting and music were almost the only activities considered suitable for young ladies. Now, after centuries as second-class citizens, women were beginning to dream of freedom and equality with men. *Scouting for Boys* turned that dream into reality for at least a few girls in 1908 – although I myself was utterly oblivious of this trend at the time, being wholly absorbed in my pets, my tennis, my hunting and my romances!

Soon there were little groups of unofficial 'Girl Scouts' sporting such unsuitable patrol names as 'Wildcats' or 'Nighthawks'. In an effort to emulate the Scouts, they marched around, festooned with water-bottles and whistles, their haversacks bulging with bandages, hoping to find some injured person on whom they could practise their newly-acquired skills.

When the Scouts held their first big Rally at the Crystal Palace in 1909, the 'Girl Scouts' turned up and demanded to be inspected by my husband. He had to do something about them. He could not allow them to be Scouts. That would have scandalised the parents and dis-gusted the boys! So he decided to organise them into a sister move-ment which he called 'Girl Guides' and he asked his sister Agnes to run it.

She was a very gifted woman and extremely clever but thoroughly Victorian in outlook. She organised a Committee from among her elderly friends and asked Mrs. Lumley-Holland to be Chairman. These ladies did their best but they were not really in touch with the younger generation; their ideas were based on the old-fashioned women's organisations. Agnes wrote a handbook adapted from *Scouting for Boys*, which came out under the title of *How Girls Can Help the Empire*. I am afraid that Robin and I called it 'The Little Blue Muddly'. Actually, she did the job very well having regard to the strict conventions of the times. Before 1914, the dead hand of Queen Victoria still rested heavily on anything to do with the female. Whilst encouraging young girls to take a first tentative step towards indepen-dence, Agnes had at the same time to allay the fears of their parents that Guides might in any way become 'unwomanly'. The result was a not very exciting programme. The Guide Committee worked from one room in Scout Headquarters and were, in fact, concerned largely with the issue of badges and the publication of *The Girl Guide Gazette*. Things did not, therefore, go too well with this young organisation, though the outbreak of war gave more direction and purpose to its activities.

As the war progressed and women played a greater role in the national effort, it was inevitable that the Girl Guides should feel a need for a more up-to-date approach. As yet there had been no organisation on a national scale, only sporadic local growth. Robin began to receive letters from all over the country begging him to *do something* about Guiding.

It meant a clean sweep of the Committee and that would include Mrs. Lumley-Holland!

He made an appointment to see her at her house, I remember. He was very nervous. It seems incredible that the man who could face Chief Dinuzulu or King Prempeh, who had earned the name among the Matabele of 'The Wolf That Never Sleeps', who could withstand a seven-month siege in Mafeking by the Boers, should be apprehensive of one elderly lady; but such was the case. Not for nothing, however, had he earned a reputation for guile in his campaigns. When he was ushered into her drawing-room and asked to wait, he selected a chair with its back to the light. Thus, when Mrs. Lumley-Holland entered the room, she would be facing the window and he might be able to read from her face something of what was going on in her mind. It was not her face that betrayed her, however — it was the egret in her bonnet. It was all a-quiver! Robin realised that she was even more nervous than he was. After that, he felt confident to control the interview which ended, as he had hoped, with Mrs. Lumley-Holland's resignation.

Robin now set about reorganising the Movement. He succeeded in obtaining a Charter of Incorporation and set up a new Committee of younger women, with himself as Chairman. Agnes became President and held that office until H.R.H. The Princess Mary took over in 1920. Agnes then became Vice-President, which position she held until her death in 1945.

The new Committee began to organise Guiding along Scout lines, using the scheme of de-centralisation that Robin had found worked so well in all his other activities, whether in Scouting or in the Army. There was to be a Commissioner appointed for each county who would be responsible for organising Guiding in an area where she was known and where she herself knew which women to call upon for assistance.

I had already, as early as September of 1914, offered my services to the Girl Guides but had been turned down by Agnes and her Committee. I think they considered me too young. I had swallowed my disappointment at being rejected and had done what I could to help by typing Robin's letters for him. After the reorganisation, however, I felt emboldened to offer my services again. I was in the Guide office one day with him and with the Guide Secretary, Miss Macdonald. I asked tentatively 'Who are you having in Sussex? Could I be of any help?' Little did I realise what would ensue from that casual offer!

Miss Macdonald put me in touch with Miss Maude and Mrs. Jennings who were organising Guiding in Crowborough and Brighton respectively. They asked me to see what I could do in my own part of Sussex. So, warrantless, with scant knowledge as yet of Guiding but with great enthusiasm, I plunged in. I started Guide Committees all over my District with such success that I was asked to take on the Division of Rye. It was thrilling. Guiding began to catch on with the same enthusiasm that had accompanied Scouting a few years before. Girls saw in it opportunities to be of positive service to their country. Soon individual women were starting companies and organising local supporters' committees. In March 1916, I was granted a warrant as County Commissioner for the whole of Sussex. I flung all the energy of my twenty-seven years into the work. There was never any shortage of girls; the problem, as always in voluntary work, was leaders. Out of twenty letters I wrote, perhaps only one would meet with any response. I had to persuade, cajole, and sometimes even beg for help, support, money, premises to meet the ever-hungry demands of the growing Movement.

April 7th, 1916 – Write letters by the yard about Girl Guides in Sussex and I must get things going without any delay.

May 7th, 1916 – I go to Woking to stay with Lady Betty Balfour and talk over amalgamation of her daughters' 'Girl Scouts' with Girl Guide Association.

May 12th, 1916 – To Sheffield Park for Girl Guide meeting of D.C.s etc. of this county appointed by me. Duchess of Norfolk, Lady Leconfield, Lady Monk-Bretton, Mrs. Jennings, Miss Maude, etc.

I suppose if I had not had the good offices of an excellent and trusted Nannie for the babies, I could not have done so much. I see from my diary that, in addition to travelling constantly about the county to find and enthuse suitable young women to be Guide leaders, I was in addition touring the *country* with my husband and supporting him in his Scouting. In July alone I went with him to Bath and Bristol, to

Oxford, to the Isle of Wight, on a tour of Hampshire, and deputised for him for a week's tour in the North of England when he was unwell.

Later, when our children were at boarding school, we were at pains to arrange our tours as far as possible to avoid school holidays or, if that were not possible, to take the children with us if it could be arranged. In these early days, however, with all the urgency of building up the two organisations that were making such a positive contribution to the national effort, we felt obliged to put our personal lives aside as so many other members of the community were doing. Even so, there was a great deal of fun to be had as well.

May 31st, 1916. – Scout and Guide Office staffs entertained – came down by coach for lunch. Scout Band. 70 for lunch. Scout rally and display on lawn. Tea for 400 Scouts 70 Guides.

Later, as the two Movements grew, the numbers at Scout and Guide Headquarters increased to such an extent that two days had to be set aside for entertaining them. They were such happy parties and it is a pleasure for me today to meet elderly people who were once on the staff and who remember those summer outings.

Miss Alice Behrens, a woman of outstanding character and a Guide leader up north, helped Robin with the new organisation. She used to stay with us whenever she came south. I remember one weekend in the summer of 1916; Robin was going fishing – a favourite recreation. Alice and I walked down with him to the river. We sat on the bank in the warmth of the late afternoon and talked, in between casts, of the subject that was dear to us all.

'Alice,' said Robin, reeling in his line for another cast. 'It's time you got your Commissioners together to talk. You ought to be planning how you can make Guiding grow into a national movement of greater value, as my Scouts have grown. Why don't you have a conference? Choose a good centre somewhere in the middle of the country and call them together.'

That was how the Matlock Conference of October 1916 came about. There were twenty-six Commissioners at that first gathering. Today there would be more like twenty-six hundred. I attended as County Commissioner for Sussex and spoke on the subject of 'Organisation'.

To my intense surprise, I returned home as Chief Commissioner, having been elected to that office at the Conference. Later, in February 1918, I was made Chief Guide.

It was an enormous challenge and one that I was proud and happy to accept. It seems quite incredible that in so short a space of time between my marriage in 1912 and the Matlock Conference of 1916 I should have travelled so far. The shy, diffident girl had developed into a confident woman. I can only thank my husband for this transformation. Not that he influenced me in any conscious fashion; he never said 'Do this' or 'Do that'; he expected me to make up my own mind about things, to write my own letters and speeches, to run my own show. But he had this marvellous ability to awaken in me qualities and talents I had no idea I possessed. He built up my confidence; he gave me encouragement; he inspired enthusiasm.

It was as if all the pent-up longing for a purpose in life had at last found an outlet. The abortive attempt to enrol as a nurse; the intermittent help given at the I.C.A.A. Home in Parkstone; even the three months' service with the Y.M.C.A. in France—all these were as nothing compared with the sense of 'belonging' I felt when I started Guiding. Again, so much of what I had dismissed as a wasted girlhood now, in a roundabout way, showed itself to have been a preparation for the life that lay ahead.

All the many friends I had made—and kept—from Devon to Sussex, from Cumberland to Berkshire during the family peregrinations, were to help me now as I travelled from one end of the country to another finding Commissioners, organising, coaxing, enthusing, 'spreading the word'. Even if the friends were not themselves prepared to put on uniform, they could often introduce me to someone who would.

All the walking and riding and tennis that had filled my earlier years contributed to the robust constitution that has enabled me to cope with a punishing programme for nearly sixty years.

The love of the out-of-doors, fostered by the cycle rides and picnics on Exmoor, the days out shooting with my father, the primrose and blackberry forays—all these enabled me to appreciate that part of Guiding which seeks to inculcate in youngsters a joy in nature and in open-air pursuits.

Even the peripatetic existence I had as a child enabled me to adapt readily to the constant changes of scene forced upon me by public life. Indeed, until about a year ago, I do not think I had spent more than five successive nights in one bed since my marriage!

It was wonderful to be working 'in harness' with my husband, striving towards a common goal, imbued with the same ideals. We had the same sense of values, the same sense of humour, our ideas were in accord on everything. Working together, we could achieve much more than the sum of what either of us could have achieved separately. We were leading brother and sister Movements, we could travel together and contribute to each other's work. There could scarcely have been a happier arrangement.

There had to be a snag somewhere!

As usual, it came from my mother. She was so very Victorian in her outlook. She condemned suffragettes and any form of 'Women's Lib.' whatsoever—even the comparatively modest freedom Robin offered to girls through Guiding. She just did not understand him or his motives—or the change he had made in me. It was bad enough my marrying and leaving home; it was worse to put on a Scout uniform and go to France—but at least that was only for three months. But to take up Guiding . . . !

I wrote sadly in my diary:

She has become estranged and, knowing nothing about Guides, is quite violently 'anti-Guide' which is so awkward and difficult and even absurd! . . . I can't understand her strangeness and apparent turning against me.

CHAPTER TWELVE

The Coming of Peace

Years: 1917–1919

The war was going badly. There were air-raids over London. Robin was caught in one in early June 1917 while waiting for a train at Liverpool Street Station. Several people were killed. This was a very different kind of warfare from the professional campaigns he had experienced in India and Africa, though perhaps Mafeking compared, with its involvement of civilians in the danger. The horrendous side of flying, however, did nothing to spoil my own passionate interest in aircraft.

I wrote only a week after the June raid: 'I wonder when we shall all be flying as a matter of course like we motor now.'

I could have done with the use of a private plane in those early years of Guiding for I was constantly travelling. 'There is always too much to do', I wrote despairingly in my diary in December of that year. It was true then and it has been true for over fifty years since!

Robin, too, was driving himself hard, but whereas in 1917 I was only twenty-eight, he was now sixty and should have been taking things more quietly. He was always over-tired and suffered dreadfully with constant pains in his head. He used to call his headaches 'fivers', which was a relic from his Army days when Col. Baker-Russell used to say, 'I have a head I wouldn't sell for a fiver.' Try as I would, I could not persuade him to do less. All I could do was endeavour to see that the house ran smoothly – and even the staff seem to have had their ups and downs that year:

22nd October, 1917 – Mabel (new cook – Annie's sister) came and I hope she will do. The 'nursery' department doesn't always fit in smoothly with the 'kitchen' and/or 'house' staff!

9th November, 1917—Rather an upset in the 'ménage'. This nurse will have to go!

Furthermore, I was worrying about money. Everything was costing more. We were constantly travelling and entertaining, both of which ate into our modest income. But with all this, I could still write with feeling on our wedding anniversary: 'Tuesday, October 30th, 1917— Our wedding day—and each year makes us love each other more —though it seems to reach the top all the time, and cannot become "more"!'

Early in 1918, I went to France again. This time, however—and it shows how much respect Guiding had already earned—I, recently appointed Chief Guide, went as 'a woman of standing' to investigate the conduct and conditions of the Women's Auxiliary Army Corps.

The Corps had been organised by Dame Helen Gwynne-Vaughan. They did magnificent work in France and, needless to say, were a *succès fou* with our men out there. Equally needless to say, human nature being what it is, one or two girls had babies and had to be sent home. This led to wild rumours of 'immorality among the W.A.A.C.s'. There were letters and questions in the papers, much misunderstanding and exaggeration. The Government decided to send out a small party of 'women of standing' who would look impartially into the allegations and report on their findings.

Violet Markham was one of our party. She was some fifteen or so years older than I was, a small, bright-eyed woman who had already made her mark. She was a prominent Liberal, a granddaughter of Joseph Paxton, the designer of the Crystal Palace. Her father was a wealthy mine-owner in Chesterfield and she had in her youth espoused the miners' cause, working tirelessly to improve the working and living conditions of the miners and their families. When she moved to London, she championed with equal vigour the cause of women in domestic service and sought to improve their lot and to raise their status. It was as Chairman of the Central Committee on Women's Training and Employment that she was included in our party.

I remember one amusing incident connected with her. She was always known as 'Miss Markham'. Only her most intimate circle of

friends knew that she had been married for nearly three years to Lieut.-
Col. James Carruthers. He was serving in France at the time of our
tour and was able to join his wife for a short leave. Naturally, they
shared a bedroom, and the following morning the W.A.A.C. who
went in to call Violet reported in shocked tones that '*Miss* Markham
was in bed *with a man!*'

Strangely enough, Violet was called in during the last war to
investigate similar highly-coloured rumours of immorality in the
Women's Services. That was when she coined the phrase 'Virtue has
no gossip value' — a comment I have often had in mind when considering the attitude of public and press to Scouting and Guiding.

I cannot really see how any 'Commission of Enquiry' was going to
detect signs of immorality, short of extracting confessions from the
culprits! However, we toured various W.A.A.C. camps in Boulogne,
Etaples, Abbeville, Dieppe, Le Havre, Rouen and Calais. We inspected
quarters, talked to the girls and were able on our return to give a
reassuring account of the splendid work they were doing and to
declare our satisfaction with their hostel accommodation. We also
spent a lot of time being lunched and dined by colonels and generals
who were anxious to reassure us of the respectful attitude of their
men to the W.A.A.C.s! It was an interesting experience — but I think
I preferred my service as a barmaid at the Mercers' Arms.

My relationship with my mother was deteriorating so rapidly during
these months and she was writing such odd and unkind letters that I
determined to 'have it out' with her. We met on 'neutral ground' at an
hotel in Bournemouth and spent a whole morning in bed arguing! At
last I managed to make her understand the importance of the work I
was doing with the Guides and we became reconciled. It was a relief to
me once again to enjoy a happy, loving relationship with her.

By the summer of 1918, hope of an ending to the war was in the air.
The lease on Little Mynthurst would soon be up and we did not wish
to renew it. We dearly wanted a house of our own, with a view and
some land — a permanent place where we could settle down with our
three babies and put down roots. Father made us an unexpected gift of
£1,000 which helped us to make up our minds to begin looking for
another house. If the war was coming to an end, we could perhaps
begin to plan ahead a little.

In the middle of October, Robin was sent abroad to France and then to Spain for an indeterminate period on some confidential work for the Foreign Office. I hated his being away but could not accompany him. I filled in the weeks attending various Scout and Guide rallies along the south coast and finished up at Grey Rigg for a few days with my parents, where the children joined me.

November 10th, 1918 — Letters and play with babies and wild rumours about that peace declared. Went to bed and asleep and suddenly woken by dear Robin kissing my eyes — got back at last. Brought news that the Kaiser has bolted.

Two days later, we gathered up from estate agents a handful of 'Permits to View' in the Bentley area, put our bicycles on the train for Farnham and set out in search of a house. We looked at several during the morning — all unsuitable — and were tempted to call it a day. However, we had sandwiches with us so we propped our bicycles against a gate and sat down by the roadside to have our lunch. That was when we noticed the 'FOR SALE' sign on the gate. 'Blackacre Farm', the house was called — a forbidding name. We had no letter of introduction as this particular house was not on our list, but we thought we might as well have a look at it. After eating our sandwiches, we pushed our bikes up the half-mile drive with mounting excitement. This surely was the place we were seeking — high up on a hill, facing south with a wide view over the Surrey/Hampshire hills. The owner was away and the maid was reluctant to allow us in. Eventually, we prevailed upon her to let us look over the house and we knew immediately that this must be our home. The price, when we learned it, was high — higher than we could afford. The owner would not let and we were in despair. Surely we were not to have a vision of Paradise only to be denied entry! Once again, father generously came to the rescue with the balance of the purchase money and Blackacre became ours. But it had to have a better name, something that would symbolise the place it held in our affections. We christened it 'Pax Hill' — the hill of peace — for we had discovered it during that first week of peace after the Armistice; and a 'hill of peace' it was to prove over the next twenty years, the haven to which we returned so gratefully after our tours, the house that was always full of people and laughter, the home where we saw our children grow to maturity.

Gradually life in England resumed a peaceful, if different course. The men returned from France often so different from the boys who went out there. Social barriers were breaking down. Ernest Court, our chauffeur, came back to us commissioned after a distinguished career in the Royal Flying Corps. Eric Walker was another who came back from prisoner-of-war camp in Germany, but for many there was no coming back. Numbers of Robin's pre-war Scouts would not return to lead the Movement they had joined so enthusiastically. Roland Phillips, Lady St. David's son and the finest of Scouts, was just one of the many splendid young men who gave their lives. His memory is perpetuated in Roland House, the building at Stepney Green which he gave to the Scouts of East London as their Headquarters.

In December we watched from the windows of the Cavalry Club in Piccadilly the Victory procession led by Haig and Plumer and Birdwood.

That first Christmas of the peace was so happy. The babies were old enough to share the enchantment of it all. We were excited at the prospect of moving to Pax Hill at the end of January. Nothing prepared me for the urgent telephone call from Bournemouth on Boxing Day telling me that my father had been drowned. I left everything and rushed down to be with mother at this agonising time. Barely four months after this tragedy, my sister Auriol also died, as a result of the epidemic of Spanish 'flu that swept through the country.

Robin and I had accepted an invitation to tour Canada and the United States early in the spring of 1919. My leaving her at this time of double bereavement revived Mother's hostility to Guiding. I was distraught. I felt a deep duty towards my mother but on the other hand, all arrangements had been made for the tour and to have cancelled it at the last moment would have caused disappointment to the thousands of youngsters who were expecting us. I decided to go ahead with the tour but my decision hurt mother exceedingly.

It was not a good start to the Peace.

CHAPTER THIRTEEN

Pax Hill

Years: 1919–1920

Among the passengers on the *Arcadian* on that propitious voyage of 1912 had been a Mrs. Juliette Lowe, a wealthy American lady with homes on both sides of the Atlantic. She had met Robin in London and had been so impressed with his ideas that she had carried them back to the States and had started Guiding there. The name, however, did not suit Americans. 'Guide' implied a half-breed Indian who looked after people going on hunting trips in the mountains. The name had no romantic connotations in the States. Mrs. Lowe's young ladies, therefore, chose to call themselves 'Girl Scouts', as had the first unofficial Guides in England. Robin did not approve. 'Scout' to him meant '*Boy* Scout'. The more he protested, the more the American ladies dug their heels in. There is something about the determination of women! 'Girl Scouts' they were and 'Girl Scouts' they remain to this day—one of the few defeats my husband suffered in a long career! Now, in 1919, seven years and a world war after its inception, Mrs. Lowe was anxious for Robin to see how 'her' Movement was shaping and for him to give her the benefit of his advice.

We were to have sailed on St. George's Day, April 23rd, but there was a strike of dockers. We kicked our heels in Liverpool for a week and eventually got away on the *S.S. Baltic* on the 29th. We landed at Halifax, Nova Scotia, in a snowstorm and stayed three days with the Governor there, making brief visits to Scouts in the surrounding district. Then came a whirlwind tour in the States: Boston, New York, Washington, Baltimore, Philadelphia. Everywhere we were besieged by reporters and photographers, fêted with luncheons and dinners.

People are *so* kind and hospitable here and *so* well off!!

Dine with Hammonds. A big opulent affair rather like Buckingham Palace!

I had become used to enthusiastic crowds in England but nothing
prepared me for the reception we had in the States—gatherings of
3,000 at a time, luncheons and dinners with 1,200 guests, a Victory
rally in Carnegie Hall and so on. Today, Scouts and Guides are so
much an accepted part of the social scene that it is easy to forget that
only fifty years ago they were new and exciting. We gave all we could
in the States in the way of advice and encouragement. While the
spirit of these Girl Scouts was heart-warming, they were not very well
organised and we felt they had much to learn.

Our hostess in Boston was Mrs. J. J. Storrow. She was prickly at
first for she felt that American Girl Scouts 'didn't need to be told from
England what to do'. When she met Robin, the hostility fell away.
'Sir Robert', spoken with an American accent, sounds like 'Sir Rabbit'
so you can imagine that within a short time he had been nicknamed
'Brer Rabbit' by her.

After two weeks, we returned to Canada to stay with the Duke and
Duchess of Devonshire at Government House, Ottawa. From there, in
between the usual round of sight-seeing of hydro-electric plants, paper
mills and grain elevators, we both worked hard to promote Scouting
and Guiding. Here, too, we began to work out the pattern we were to
use on later tours. Sometimes we attended functions together; more
often we would divide forces, for there was much for me, in particular,
to do. There was in these early years a pathetic lack of organisation
among Guide leaders. Robin would address a Rotary luncheon, I a
women's meeting. He would seek support from the local Chamber
of Commerce, I would visit schools, and so on. Always there were
Scouts and Guides to meet us on the station platforms, mayors to greet
us, civic receptions, conferences, rallies, parades—and speeches,
speeches and yet more speeches to make. We visited Montreal, Toronto
and Quebec, everywhere welcomed with wild enthusiasm by the
thousands of young people who were flocking to join the world
brotherhood and sisterhood of Scouts and Guides. It was thrilling but,
oh, so exhausting. By the time we boarded the *S.S. Grampian* for our

voyage home, we were only too grateful to keep to our cabins and sleep. We recouped our strength on the ten-day voyage back to England and by the middle of June we were home again at beloved Pax.

Already the house was bursting at the seams. Mother was looking after Auriol's three little daughters for the time being but Robin and I had undertaken to have them as soon as we had sufficient accommodation, as their father was going back to his business in Ceylon. Mother, who was now a very wealthy widow, helped us financially to add two wings to Pax, one for the servants, the other for visitors and for our three additional 'children'. We also added a large music room in which Robin arranged his presentation swords and caskets, his medals and the many souvenirs he had of Scout tours in all parts of the world. Five-year-old Peter laid the first brick of the extension on July 16th, 1919 and just a week later that distinguished and eccentric architect and designer of Portmeirion, Clough Williams Ellis, lunched with us to see what progress was being made. He had designed the servants' wing. It was not one of his more inspired efforts for the bedrooms all faced north into an avenue of plane trees while the corridors faced the view to the south!

We were to have eighteen blissful months at Pax Hill before our next big overseas tour.

Gradually, after all the changes of the war years, the staff settled down to the happy band who stayed with us for many years. We engaged a young Guide, Grace Fisher, as under house-parlourmaid. Nurse Hilda Austen joined us to look after the six children and soon she and 'Bear' Court (as the children used to call him) were engaged to be married. That involved more building for we erected a cottage for them in a corner of the paddock. Inevitably, the cottage was christened 'The Bear's Den'.

Sometimes I wonder how I fitted everything in!

Mother had moved to London so at least it was more convenient to visit her there on my frequent trips to Guide Headquarters. Her style of living still maintained the leisured state of pre-War days: 'September 30th, 1919—Drive with Mother in a stately landau with 2 prancing chestnuts! So unlike me!'

'There is always too much to do.' I think that will be found engraved on my heart when I die. If I had not had a blessedly fit body, I just could not have managed. Quite apart from tours and rallies in different parts of the country, there was the work at Guide Head-quarters which increased as the strength of the Movement increased. I would dash up to London two or three times a week, fitting in com-mittee meetings and maybe half a dozen interviews with potential leaders. The Movement was gathering momentum abroad as well and leaders had to be selected and trained to foster development in these other countries. Careful thought had to be given to the adjustments that had to be made in the programme to adapt Guiding to the needs of other cultures.

I could have filled all my days, and nights as well, with Guiding affairs but always tried to get home to Pax for the evening. Every minute in that beloved house was precious, each day filled with the multitude of small details that go into the bringing up of a family of six and the running of a home. My diary is full of such mundane but, to me, important entries as:

All to church and children stayed for the sermon for the first time.

Babies all played our form of 'Beg o' my neighbour' with howls of mirth. Heather was the cleverest at it.

Betty was able to reach up to open my bedroom door in the morning for herself for the first time.

However busy we were, Robin and I always contrived to be at home with the children for Sunday tea in the nursery. It usually ended in riotous romps and games. Robin was marvellously sweet with the children. No matter how much they bully-ragged him, he would laugh. He was never too important to play the fool with them.

He adored children and it was a nightmare to him at Christmas that some child in Bentley might be forgotten and go to bed on Christmas night without a toy. After tea on Christmas afternoon, he and Major Wade used to go round all the cottages in the village where there were children. They would have with them a sack of surplus toys from Pax Hill. Outside each cottage, they would place a parcel. They would then knock on the door but leave before anyone arrived to open it.

If the children were learning new skills, so was I. It would have been no good my attempting to lead Guides if I could not myself join in their activities so I would slip into Bentley for an occasional half hour to see Mrs. Eggar, the local Commissioner, to 'learn my knots' and other Guiding technicalities.

H.R.H. Princess Mary became Guide President in 1920. From the very beginning she took a close personal interest in all our work. Nor was she a 'nominal' Président. She insisted on making the Guide Promise and sent for me to Buckingham Palace to enrol her on December 16th, 1920.

The Royal Family have always given great support to both the Scout and Guide Movements. The Duke of Connaught was first President of the Scouts, succeeded later by the Duke of Gloucester. The late Duke of Windsor was Chief Scout for Wales and also launched the Prince of Wales Fund to develop Scouting. The Queen Mother was a Guide Commissioner in Scotland before her marriage and continues her interest still as Patron of the Girl Guides Association. I see that we had an evening reception at Guide Headquarters in March of 1928 'to meet the dear little Duchess of York . . . H.R.H. is most entrancing and sweet and delightful to all.' I am proud that H.M. the Queen and Princess Margaret were both keen Guides, the latter taking over as President of our Association on the death of the Princess Royal. Princess Anne was a Brownie, Prince Andrew is a Scout and now Princess Margaret's own little daughter, Lady Sarah Armstrong-Jones, has enrolled as a Brownie, which makes three generations of our Royal Family being members of the two Movements. It is a wonderful compliment to my husband's vision and imagination that his pro-gramme can appeal equally to the occupant of a palace or of a mud hut in Africa.

One added attraction of Pax Hill was that it was only a few miles from Aldershot where Robin's regiment, the 13th Hussars, had their headquarters. As their Hon. Colonel, he used to enjoy entertaining the officers at Pax Hill, or would motor over to Aldershot to dine in the Mess, or take the children over to watch a gymkhana. In view of the Duke of Gloucester's later accession to the Presidency of the Scout Association, I am interested to note the following entry for September 18th, 1920:

Robin to shoot with Col. Booker at Chawton. They all came back to tea here after the shoot — Col. and Mrs. Booker, Major Bertie Hoare, poor Col. Twist whose nice pretty little wife died lately, Col. Marchant who was Robin's A.D.C. years ago and H.R.H. Prince Henry who is attached to the 13th for a time. Nice boy.

Tea was our 'sociable' meal of the day, the one at which we entertained the most.

June 7th, 1921 — About 40 members of Women's Institute to tea. Had it on the lawn and they strolled about and played feeble games very happily.

August, 1921 — Visitors in house. Visitors for tea. Two lots of campers camping on drive. 70 others (Dutch and English) camping in field near river. Have them all for tea on lawn.

We frequently had odd tents pitched on the wide shady verge of the half-mile drive up to the house, for Robin was also President of the Camping Club of Great Britain. Members would turn up unexpectedly, sometimes in dreadful weather conditions, and we would feel obliged to take them in.

September 2nd, 1920 — . . . Home by afternoon train. Find two families of amateur campers in pouring rain waiting to camp on the drive. Put them into the hut for the night.

We had many, many visitors. There were almost always one or two people staying the night, usually on Scout or Guide business. I found it easier to cope with several visitors at a time because they entertained each other. Robin also enjoyed having friends over at the weekend for fishing, his favourite out-door pursuit.

Guests were not allowed to upset his routine, however. Of course, with his many public duties, he was often away or had to spend the night in London, but whenever he was at Pax, he slept on the verandah, whatever the weather. He did not seem to feel the cold out-of-doors. He could sleep with only a light blanket over him and his feet sticking out at the bottom of the bed, yet during the evening indoors, he would sit close to the fire wearing a Jaeger suit *and* a dressing-gown over it.

Every morning, even up to the age of eighty, he would be up at early dawn and do a series of physical exercises. He made himself tea, ate some fruit and was sitting at his desk by 5.0 or 5.30 a.m. In the quiet hours before the household stirred, he would work at his monthly article for *The Scouter*, his weekly article for *The Scout*, at books, at urgent letters, plans and so on. He claimed that he put an extra month into each year making use of these early morning hours.

At half-past seven or a quarter to eight, he would come upstairs to bath and dress. I would be up by that time and we would call the dogs and go for a two-mile walk before breakfast—always the same walk, to the outskirts of Froyle village. We timed it to a nicety to be back for breakfast at 8.45.

Robin liked baked apple and cream and porridge for breakfast. He was not an 'egg and bacon' man; he rarely ate meat. In fact, he was most abstemious over food, though he did enjoy a glass of port after dinner. Breakfast was an unhurried meal. The post usually arrived in the middle of it and Robin's secretary, Eileen, would come strolling up across the lawn to join us. (Eileen Nugent had been Robin's secretary since 1914. In 1920 she married Major A. G. Wade, Secretary to the Scout Association, and they made their home in Bentley.) We would go through our always enormous mail together and Robin would toss letters over to Eileen, telling her how to reply to them. Then he would disappear into the study and I would settle at my desk in the drawing-room to deal with my own letters. I have developed a fair turn of speed on the typewriter and if my style of 'setting out' in regard to margins, punctuation and use of capital letters is hardly up to secretarial college standards, at least it is quicker than writing by hand—and it is personal to me!

By 11.30, Robin would have finished dictating to Eileen and would come striding into the room, rubbing his hands in the dry 'washing' way that had become a habit with him.

'Come on, Mum,' he would say. 'Drop it.' And out we would go with the dogs for another two- or- three-mile walk until lunch-time.

As he grew older, I endeavoured to make him lie down and doze for half an hour after lunch but then there would be another walk, a longer one this time. We never did less than seven miles in a day when we were at home, which probably accounts for our excellent health.

We would have tea by the fire, often with visitors, more rarely (if we were lucky) by ourselves. Then there would be time to prune the roses or fix the pergola in the garden. Or in winter Robin would settle down with the newspapers, or with some minutes or reports he had to read, until it was time for a light supper and early bed. Even if we were entertaining, he would make some excuse that he had 'one or two things to see to' and would slip away to bed by 9.30. But every night he would come into my bed for 'armchairs' — just lying in each other's arms, revelling in being together. He was so sweet, so loving. Yet all the time, he had this brilliant, driving energy, hatching out wonderful ideas that had to be translated into words. Writing, writing, always writing. He really was an incredibly talented man. In addition to the thirty-two books he wrote and his countless newspaper and magazine articles, he was also a talented sculptor and an artist of no mean ability, using his brush with equal facility in either hand. Some of his finest paintings are the animal studies he made in Kenya when he was in his eighties.

All this talent — yet I took him so much for granted! It is a measure of our love for each other and also of his touching humility, that never at any time was I in awe of him. Despite the difference in our ages, despite his eminent position in public life, we were completely in accord with one another. We never had a thought apart. He was the pivot of my life. I adored him.

Throughout this account of my life, I speak of my husband as 'Robin' or 'Darling'. To him, after we were married, I was no longer 'B.E.'. He called me 'Mum' in front of the children and 'Dindo' in private. This was our own contraction of 'Darling'.

We were not great ones for giving dinner parties on account of Robin's preference for early nights. We tended rather to do our formal entertaining by means of garden parties. Our grounds of eight acres were very lovely, with smooth lawns and rose-beds and softly cooing white doves. We could accommodate up to a hundred and fifty people at a time quite easily, even if we were driven indoors by weather to the music room. I would have an ice-cream man there with his cart and guests could have as many ices as they wanted. Usually the local

Scouts provided some form of entertainment or the Bentley Country
Dancers, dressed in orange and white, would put on a display. Gradually the jaunty music would set our feet tapping and soon we would
all join in—hostess and guests and servants all together, swinging
round in 'Old Mole', 'Newcastle' or 'Hunsdon House'.

At the beginning of December 1920 we received an important
invitation for an overseas tour from no less a person than the Viceroy
of India, Lord Chelmsford.

India had been one of the very first overseas countries to adopt
Scouting. At first it was run by European leaders for Indian Scouts.
Its simple creed of friendship to all and belief in God appealed equally
to Hindus with their 'perfect way' and Mahommedans with their ideal
of brotherhood. The general principles of the Movement are applicable
to all races. Fifty years ago, nationalism was beginning to be a force to
reckon with in India and there was some feeling that no warrants had
been issued to Indian nationals. Congress started its own, all-Indian
Scouts. Then other parts of that vast sub-continent decided they
wanted *their* own Scouts so that by 1920 there were the Agra Scouts,
the Seva-Samiti Scouts, Mrs. Annie Besant's Scouts of South India, and
so on. It was quite contrary to the spirit of Scouting to have so many
rival organisations, nor were they affiliated to the Association in
London. The World Association policy is 'One country—one
Movement'.

There was a big all-India Scout conference in Calcutta in 1920 after
which the Viceroy invited Robin to India with the purpose of recon-
ciling all these rival groups into one federated body. As Guiding was
also developing fast among some of the more enlightened Indian
women, I was invited as well. Guiding could do much to help bring
Indian women into the twentieth century.

It was not the sort of invitation one disregarded—and even if Robin
had not felt the visit to be of vital importance to the future of Scouting,
he would have rejoiced at this opportunity to show me the India he
had so loved when he served there as a young subaltern from 1876 to
1884.

We had only a month to make our preparations—and that involved
the purchase of a complete wardrobe suitable for the tropics. Special
thin uniforms had to be made for the day-time, evening dresses for the

many State functions we knew the visit would entail. I loathe buying clothes at the best of times so that such a rush as this was a nightmare.

To crown everything, on Christmas Day Heather began to feel ill. The doctor diagnosed scarlet fever!

There are Guides and Brownies everywhere throughout the world,
whether it be St. David's, Pembrokeshire (above) or Korea (below).

Olave in South Africa, 1942,

CHAPTER FOURTEEN

India

Year: 1921

We sailed for India on the *S.S. Narkunda* out of Liverpool on January 7th, 1921. The doctor had changed his mind about Heather's complaint; it was not scarlet fever after all. 'Pretty nasty leaving home *and* those babies too for so long.'

It was a fascinating three-week voyage – though it had its irritations, of course: 'January 8th, 1921 – ... The Austen Chamberlains sit at our table with the Captain – and he *will* talk politics!'

In some ways, it was almost like a royal progression. Gibraltar was all decorated with 'Welcome to the Chief Scout' in lights; at Marseilles, the Eclaireurs, or French Scouts, were out in force to greet us and give us lunch; there were waving, cheering Scouts at Port Said. Even the passengers of the *Narkunda* stumped up over £300 for the appeal made by the Prince of Wales in aid of Scout funds.

We arrived in Bombay on January 28th and stayed in a guest bungalow in the grounds of Government House – known affectionately as No. 1, India, being the nearest point in India to England. M. Georges Clemenceau, the French statesman, was also staying with the Governor at that time and, sitting next to him at dinner, I was relieved of the embarrassment of my poor French because the lady on his other side spoke the language fluently.

We immediately plunged into a round of visits and lectures. One of my own first engagements was to address a large meeting of women on the subject of Guiding. There were Hindus and Parsees, Anglo-Indians and Europeans. At that time, Indian women did not, on the whole, mix much with European women. It is a tribute to Guiding that, once the Indian women took it up, the barriers between the races began to come down.

After four days in Bombay, we travelled overnight to Delhi. We had been given a sleeping car on the train but had little sleep. At every halt—and there were many—there were enthusiastic Scouts and Guides to greet us and garland us with flowers. We hung out of the train to talk to them and clasp their hands—and I hope they did not observe that Robin and I were both wearing uniform jackets and hats over our pyjamas and nightie respectively!

In Delhi we stayed at Vice-Regal Lodge. This was not the impressive Lutyens structure which was built later in New Delhi but an earlier building. Guests were accommodated in tents in the grounds— though 'tent' is a word that evokes a deceptive picture. Each pavilion was a sumptuous room, thickly carpeted, richly furnished and hung around with curtains. We were assigned a bearer, Mahrwatti, who attended us for the rest of the tour. He looked after our luggage, laid out our clothes and was generally invaluable. He was always smiling and courteous, immensely capable, anticipating our needs and guarding our possessions.

It is a great privilege to have experienced something of the grandeur of the British Raj in India. I have visited the sub-continent six times in all but no later visit has had quite the impact of the first.

We lunched with the Viceroy and his wife and discussed the plans for our tour. It was all very grand and royal. The Viceroy was Chief Scout for India and Lady Chelmsford was Chief Guide so they were well acquainted with the problems that lay ahead of us.

Lord Chelmsford was anxious that Scouting should be used as an adjunct to education in India. There were nearly ten million boys of Scout age but many of them were lacking in any opportunity to learn about health or hygiene, quite apart from the moral principles and strengthening of character Scouting could offer. There were already over a third of a million Scouts in India but this was only a fraction of the potential number. Even so, the difference of approach of these boys from non-Scouts was too outstanding to be dismissed as accident. For example, they helped to regulate the vast crowds at the *melas* or religious festivals; they had laboured with admirable courage on the rescue work following the Quetta earthquake. This, in a country where death and disaster are so often accepted as inevitable, denoted a marked improvement of attitude. Guiding, too, could help break down the traditional conventions that kept Indian women in the background.

Encouraged by Lord Chelmsford's support, we set out on our tour.

The Viceroy had kindly directed that for the next month we should have the use of a special saloon car attached to the trains – sometimes goods trains – we used. It was really a comfortable travelling flat with bedroom and drawing-room accommodation. Although we stayed with various provincial Governors when we were spending more than one night in a city, the saloon car was a useful 'base' where we could relax in between engagements or sleep comfortably as we covered the vast distances between one State and another.

Robin was thrilled to see and feel India again. He had such happy memories of his service life there. Of course, on that first visit he had been on military duty; now he came with the message of peace and brotherhood. There were changes in him and changes in India, but still the challenge of the country remained – the vast distances, the poverty, the caste system.

We visited Agra. We motored out from Jubbulpore to see the Marble Rocks where Rudyard Kipling set the 'Bee Rocks' in his *Jungle Book*. We saw a *mela* at Allahabad where two million pilgrims came to bathe in the Jumna and Ganges rivers. We went to Lucknow where Robin showed me the bungalow home he occupied in 1876. Benares, Ranchi, Madras. We would travel for hours on end in the train, past big bumpy mountains, tall scraggy palm trees, fields of pepper and cotton, delicious bullock carts and flocks of goats, absurd biblical wells and ploughs, and always the colourful, picturesque people. I fell in love with it all, even the heat.

Everywhere we went, at all hours of the day and night – even at 3.30 in the morning – there were Scouts and Guides begging us to leave the train for a few minuts to talk to them, to be photographed with them. I was amazed that we were received so kindly. Although I appreciated that it was necessary to keep up the dignity of the British administration in India, I could not help contrasting the opulence of Viceregal Lodge and the various Government houses we stayed in with the appalling poverty of so much of India. I began to feel disturbed at the conditions many of them suffered. Again, I was shocked at the contrasts between wealthy, high-caste Indians and those of low caste. We met one Indian ruler with a £1,000 diamond in his turban and his horses' hooves painted with gold leaf. In Madras I attended a purdah tea-party of seven hundred women and was sickened by the sheer opulence of their jewels, even decorating their painted feet.

In Madras, Robin came face to face with the extraordinary Mrs. Besant. She was over seventy when we met her—a tiny woman, white-haired, but with a formidable personality. She always wore Indian dress. It must be exceptional for an Englishwoman to wield a considerable influence in the politics of another nation but this is what Annie Besant did in India.

She had abandoned her vicar husband (and her Christian faith along with him) as far back as 1873. Since that time she had come under the influence of the notorious Charles Bradlaugh and had published *The Gospel of Atheism*. Then, with equal enthusiasm, she had become a Fabian, had organised the Matchmakers' Strike of 1888 and had formed the Union of Matchmakers. Her restless energy took her to America and finally to India in 1893. There she became fascinated by Eastern mysticism and decided that India was her spiritual home. She was convinced that she had been incarnated there in several previous existences and I believe she embraced the Hindu religion.

Here at last in India was a country to which she could devote her restless energy. She flung herself with enthusiasm into the cause of Congress, tenaciously advocating Home Rule for India, even though this brought her into frequent conflict with the British administration. At the same time she did a great deal for the cause of education in India, founding the Hindu College in Madras. However, when Gandhi started the Civil Disobedience campaign in early 1919, she was quick to see the dangers inherent in violence. She, who only two years before had been imprisoned for non-co-operation, refusing loyalty to the Crown, now realised how necessary it was for the British to remain in India if any sort of progress towards independence was to be made without a revolution. The tragic bloodshed of 1947 when Independence was finally achieved only goes to show how far-seeing she was. In Scouting she saw an opportunity for forwarding her educational aims and to this end she formed the Scouts of South India, an independent but enthusiastic body of some 25,000 Scouts not affiliated to the official B.-P. Scouts.

This then, this diminutive tigress, this thorn in the flesh of the British administration, this stormy petrel of Indian politics, was the woman Robin had to win over. As elsewhere throughout this tour, as on so many occasions before and after, his charm and good sense won the day and Mrs. Besant agreed to bring her Scouts of South India into the federation. We celebrated the occasion with an eight-course dinner cooked and served by one of her Scout troops. The meal was served Indian fashion, with the guests sitting on mats on the ground. Afterwards, Robin named Mrs. Besant Hon. Commissioner for India and invested her as a *proper* Scout. During the ceremony he had one of those unaccountable lapses of memory that come to us all on occasion — he forgot the Scout Promise and Mrs. Besant had to prompt him! It was something of a triumph for Scouting, in view of the old lady's previous antagonism to the Crown, that she now promised 'to do her Duty to the King'. She lived to a great age and died somewhere in the nineteen-thirties. She certainly was one of the most arresting characters I have met.

The long tour continued to Calcutta where we stayed with the Governor, Lord Ronaldshay. The Viceroy and Lady Chelmsford were also at Government House so there was yet another dizzy round of luncheons and dinner parties. 'They *do* entertain a lot in these places!' I complained in my diary.

We had a brief holiday in the Himalayas. Their beauty and magnificence was such that Robin was up at all hours trying to capture in paint his impressions of them. His sketchbooks were filled with pictures of towering snow-peaks, rosy in the morning light; of plunging gorges; of picturesque Tibetan characters seen in the mountain villages. All these are preserved in the giant scrapbooks that I have kept ever since we were married — a wonderful souvenir of the rich and varied experiences we have had in all parts of the world.

We left India satisfied with a job well done. The rival factions had been united, both Guiding and Scouting had received a stimulus and the whole organisation there had been set on the right lines. What *was* needed, however, was an Organising Commissioner sent out from England to *keep* it on the right lines. But where could the Scout Association raise the money to pay such a man?

We went on from India to Burma and sailed up the Irrawaddy to

Rangoon. We were leaning idly over the ship's rail watching the river bank slip by when we noticed a small boat with the name painted on its side: 'Alison'.

'Alison!' I exclaimed. 'Alison Cargill—it must be. Her father is Chairman of the Burma Oil Company.' (Alison had helped me to organise Guiding in Scotland in 1917.)

It seemed like a sign. When we eventually returned from our tour, I wrote to Sir John Cargill explaining our problem. He generously gave us enough money to send out the Commissioner we felt India needed. It was a wonderful gesture with wonderful results—and all thanks to a little boat called 'Alison'.

Scouting and Guiding in Burma have, alas, been suppressed since the revolutionary régime took over in 1962; but in 1921 both Movements were as enthusiastic as in India. But Burma was hot and clammy and we were grateful to move on to the cooler climate of Ceylon. We stayed at Temple Trees in Colombo. I was to recall that visit some forty years later when I stayed there as a guest of Mrs. Bandaranyke, the Premier of Ceylon—but on the more recent occasion, there were machine-guns on either side of the front door!

Our return journey included visits to Egypt and Palestine where we were entertained by Lord Allenby, Sir Herbert Samuel and Mr. (later Sir) Ronald Storrs—all men whose careers have been identified with the turbulent politics of the Middle East. It is an indication of how far the situation there has deteriorated that in 1921 I could record attending a rally in Alexandria of Greek, Armenian, British, French, *Jewish* and *Egyptian* Scouts.

We left our ship at Marseilles and returned home by way of Paris. After all the state and splendour of our visit to India, we had to fight and scramble our way on to the train for Calais! But we were on our way home. We had been away three and a half months, we had travelled twenty-two thousand miles by boat and train, by rickshaw and pony.

'Babies and Mother at station and we all nearly *burst* with joy. And Pax looks *too* lovely and home-y. Oh *what* a home coming!' It could so easily have been a disastrous home-coming. If at times in this account of my life I sound wary when mentioning the press, it is because both Robin and I have suffered on more than one occasion from misrepresentation of our words—though it would only be fair to say that on the whole the press have treated us generously and honestly. On this occasion, we held a press conference to give an account of what had been achieved in India.

'Do Indian Scouts use the same Law and Promise?' asked one reporter. Robin, ever a man to be careful in his words, answered honestly.

'They have to translate it into their own language,' he explained. 'Sometimes it is difficult to find an exact equivalent. For example, the Indians have no specific word for "honour" in our sense—only "standing" or "prestige".'

The newspaper report the next day carried the statement 'Chief Scout says that Indians have no honour'! You can imagine the embarrassment this caused and what explanations had to be made.

CHAPTER FIFTEEN

Double Harness

Years: 1921 — 1927

This account of my life would become tedious were I to itemise all our activities between the two wars. I can only mention the highlights. They were wonderfully happy years, full of laughter and fun as the children grew up; full of stimulus and challenge as we travelled the world; full of hard but rewarding work as we saw our two Movements grow in strength and quality.

Of course, inevitably, there were irritations and disappointments. Though I was able to maintain enduring friendships outside my family, I did not enjoy the same easy understanding with my mother or my brother. 'I just *can't* get on with him', I wrote despairingly in August of 1921.

June 2nd, 1922 — A troublesome 'scene' with Mother over my going away in Guide uniform and it *is* difficult and trying.

October 19th, 1922 — Had a most trying letter from Mother again yesterday abusing me about Guides. I *still* don't know what she dislikes in it and I don't think she knows herself and it is merely an obsession for no rhyme or reason.

Similarly, I was also wrestling with the question of religion. As I have mentioned earlier, I had had a traditional 'C. of E.' upbringing which had sufficed during my girlhood. Now, with my growing maturity and experience, and particularly meeting people of so many diverse religions, I was questioning what seemed to me the empty formality of the services I attended.

August 21st, 1921 — I *can't* go to church. It puts my hackles up.

January 8th, 1922 – R. and I to church. Much too 'high' for me, and only adds to my conviction of how terribly off track the parsons are.

I had been hearing a good deal about Christian Science on my voyages to and from India and explored that in some depth but did not find there the answer to my needs. I believe sincerely in the existence of God and in His Power in our lives – the way my own life has been wonderfully and clearly guided is just one illustration of this – but I have not found myself drawn to any one particular sect or denomination of Christianity more than another. For example, the elaborate ritual and incense of Roman Catholic services hold no meaning for me, although they may for others. They come between me and my idea of God. I believe in God rather than 'Religion'. I believe in God quite easily. I have no doubt that there is a Power, bigger than ourselves and supreme over everything. For want of a better word we call it 'God'.

I also believe whole-heartedly in the 'after-life'. I think it is extraordinary that for all these centuries the Christian Church has disapproved of communication with those who have 'passed on'. Yet, after all, that is exactly what Christ did – coming back and talking with His disciples. His teaching urged people to see the after-life as a continuation of this one.

I believe that we are here in order to leave the world a little better than we found it. God works through us to make the world a better place. I find very appealing the idea in Eastern religions that one can come back again to earth in another existence to remedy any mistakes one has made in this, and so seek perfection.

In times of grief and doubt I have turned to God for strength and comfort, but what *is* the Truth? Maybe I soon shall know.

1921 closed with visits to Buckingham Palace to discuss with Princess Mary what the Guides' wedding present to her should be when she married the Earl of Harewood the following February. We gave her a silver box, a Guide badge in diamonds, and three silver statuettes – little realising that the present would be two-way.

The Girl Guides Association had been offered by a wealthy lady,

Mrs. Archbold Sanderson, a property near Lyndhurst in the New Forest. It was called 'Foxlease' and, with its ample accommodation and sixty-five acres of grounds, it would be ideal as a training centre for Guiders. It was a tempting offer, for we badly needed such a centre. But the conversion of the property from a private residence, and its equipment as a training centre, would cost a deal of money. Moreover, maintenance of the house and grounds would be a constant drain on our resources. Had our young Association the funds to meet such a responsibility?

The answer came from Princess Mary.

All the 'Marys' in the Empire had contributed towards a present for her wedding. Half of this sum, plus the amount raised in entry fees to view her wedding presents, the Princess handed over to the Girl Guides Association. We received about £10,000 – a tremendously generous gift and more than enough in 1922 to make Foxlease a viable proposition. It was typical of Princess Mary's practical and active Presidency of the Movement.

She was interested in every detail of our activities. Whenever I returned from an overseas tour, I had to report to her about it.

4th May, 1927 – Lunch with Princess Mary at Chesterfield House to tell her all about South Africa. Saw her two nice little boys who insisted on being kissed! (The present Earl of Harewood and his brother, the Hon. Gerald Lascelles.)

If ever there were any unseemly gossip in the papers about Guides – as inevitably happens from time to time – I had to enquire into the matter on her behalf and give her the facts. She was no 'nominal' President and, indeed, seemed to enjoy joining in the informality of Guide activities. 'Foxlease' was opened officially by her on July 23rd, 1923 and thereafter she would visit it frequently and would join in like any ordinary camper.

Saturday, 17th July, 1926 – Meet H.R.H. Princess Mary at Brockenhurst station and drive with her to Foxlease. Guiders line drive and cheer her wildly. She has coffee and talks with the Commissioners in the house and then visits each different group and sees some jolly displays. She has tea in camp too out of a mug and then joins in jolly camp fire. She enjoyed it immensely.

June 10th, 1932 — Princess Royal enjoys herself immensely and stays till quite late, seeing camp doings, cooked a 'damper', sing-song, etc. and glorious sunshine made it a perfect day. She loses her shyness too with us.

Peter went away to prep school in January 1922. Although I had not worried unduly about leaving him behind when we went off on trips abroad — probably because he was in his home and surrounded by familiar faces — I minded dreadfully about handing him over to strangers.

He was a shy little boy, very frail, very undemonstrative. 'A *nice* little chap, with no vice anywhere.' I adored him but I don't think I ever understood him. If I had, I might better have realised what an ordeal it was for him to occupy the limelight from his earliest years. He had been enrolled as a Wolf Cub in October 1921 on his eighth birthday. Less than a year later, thousands and thousands of excited Scouts and Cubs gathered at the Alexandra Palace to greet the Prince of Wales with a Posse of Welcome on his return from his World Tour. We arranged that Peter should lead him by the hand into the arena. Not until years later did I learn how terrified he had been. 'The only thing that gave me any comfort,' he was to write in *The Scouter* 'was that the Prince's hand was shaking even more than my own.'

The year closed with another 'Royal' occasion when my beloved Robin received the G.C.V.O. from the King. It was, we felt, a recognition of the value of his work in Scouting — but I think we derived every bit as much pleasure from the birthday present he received from Scout H.Q. staff two months later — 'a wireless broadcasting apparatus'. It was such a novelty and so thrilling to be able to hear a concert actually at the time of its performance without being there. Little did we dream of the marvels of communication that were to develop over the next fifty years!

In March of 1923 Robin and I undertook a three-month tour of Canada and the United States during which I made my own first broadcast. I have made so many since that I am no longer intimidated by the medium but at the time I recorded the new experience as being 'very un-nerving'. Later in the year I spoke over the air from the old 2LO station at Savoy Hill.

2nd August, 1923 – Broadcast about Guides for 8 minutes. Rather fun speaking over the wireless – just read out a thing in a room alone. It's a sort of jam jar on a tripod!! How wonderful it is.

Nowadays, 'Pause for Thought' or whatever current B.B.C. programme needs my voice merely makes an appointment and sends a representative with a tape-recorder down to Hampton Court. I can broadcast comfortably from my own drawing-room and, if a plane goes over and spoils the quality of the recording, or if I make a mistake or have a tickle in my throat, it is a simple matter to do it all over again.

In my diary for 1924 I record the year as 'opening badly'. Betty, Yvonne (Auriol's youngest) and Peter were all down with whooping-cough, 'all trains stopped with a rotten strike of engine drivers . . . Labour Government comes in under Ramsay MacDonald.' I am not sure at this distance of time whether I regarded the last item as part of the general gloom!

It is interesting to look back and see what events were of sufficient importance to me to warrant inclusion in my diary at this time. They range over domestic and public events:

1st March, 1924 – All the children now have breakfast and lunch downstairs with us instead of in the nursery.

April 10th – To Grantham. Call on Hardy, Dad's poor old butler, now partially paralysed and living alone in pokey rooms.

May 28th – To tea (quite awful!) with Duchess of Rutland to meet Queen of Roumania. To State Ball in evening. Delightful.

July 4th – Call and see Lady Harewood (H.R.H. Princess Mary) at her house in Belgrave St. about a guide 'fuss' in West Riding.

July 10th – Garden Party at Pax. Band of 13th Hussars played. Over 100 guests.

August 31st – Scouts from overseas came to tea. We expected

4 Indians and 6 South Africans—and instead of that 27 came!
Great fun though and they did enjoy seeing Robin in his own home.
The music room with all its curios is invaluable for amusing people.

One could hardly say that life lacked variety, and it was that very
variety that gave our busy lives their unfailing interest. There were the
six children with their varying temperaments and skills—all now at the
stage when we could go on camping trips together, or play tennis
together. I was only in my mid-thirties and could easily cope with
several sets in an afternoon. All six children rode—with varying
degrees of skill—and followed the local hounds with enthusiasm. We
had four ponies at this time and would hire a couple extra for the
holidays. We started up our own hockey team in the winter of 1925/26.
Peggy and Joan, the Jackson sisters, enthused us with the idea. They
were both mad keen and played for England. Our team was drawn
from Peter, Heather and myself; Mrs. Douglas Eggar and her sons (who
lived in Bentley); Major Wade (the Scout Association Secretary) and
his wife, Eileen (who was Robin's secretary); 'Penny' (Miss Dorothy
Penicuik Clerk, our governess); Margery, our nursemaid; Mrs.
Roberts the cook; and Court, our chauffeur. We played with great
enthusiasm, even if we were not particularly good.

I was here, there and everywhere on Guide business. Robin did not
now attend as many Scout functions as formerly. He saved his strength
for the big occasions and, particularly, for overseas tours; but he was
often away fishing, or in Town for meetings and dinners, reunions and
levées. I always found his home-coming delicious. He would arrive
back by the last train from, say, a Mercers' dinner, looking quite
splendid in evening dress with all his medals and orders. He would
sit by the fire with his Ovaltine and tell me all about the guests and the
speeches, making it so amusing with his wonderful gift of mimicry.

We paid another visit to the States during April and May of 1926.
On this occasion we were invited to lunch with President Coolidge.
He had a reputation for being dour and uncommunicative. There was
a story, no doubt apocryphal, that a young thing, seated next to him at
a banquet, began gaily: 'Mr. President, I have a bet that I shall get
more than three words out of you during dinner.' The President
replied simply: 'You've lost'—and went on eating.

At least we did better than that—but it was hard going!

We were due to be photographed with him on the lawn of the White House. A number of Scouts were rustled up to set a suitable 'scene'. They were in position, we were in position, the photographers were in position. All that was needed was the President. He walked stiffly out from the house, posed in the place indicated while the photographs were taken, then turned round and stalked back into the house without saying a word to anyone—so perhaps the story of the young lady's 'bet' was true after all.

I daresay many such stories have accumulated over the years about my husband and myself. One at least I can vouch for, having noted it in my diary at the time.

I had taken Peter and Heather and two friends to visit Romsey Abbey. Urged on by the children, I wrote in the Visitors' Book 'O. Baden-Powell and party of 4.' There were a number of visitors to the Abbey that day, moving round singly and in groups. We had to pass the table with the Visitors' Book as we left the Abbey and here we were detained by an excited church official. He indicated a completely strange middle-aged man who was reading out an inscription to *his* family of four and whispered:

'Your little boy will be interested to know that that is General Baden-Powell over there!'

I was used to an 'aura' surrounding my husband. One Danish Scout refused to wash the hand my husband had shaken! When at last it was borne in upon him that hygiene demanded that the ban be lifted, he insisted on bottling as a keepsake the water the hand had been washed in! Now, to my great embarrassment, I found myself being invested with the same sort of aura. In June 1926 I record a report reaching me that a Dorset Ranger Guide had said ecstatically 'You know, I actually touched her coat . . . isn't she wonderful and so ordinary!' I wrote: 'It is blessed that they realise one is human but it *is* a responsibility to feel they care so!'

We must have visited thousands of rallies up and down the country and abroad between the two wars, sometimes together, more often separately, as the two Movements grew and became more demanding. As his years increased, however, Robin liked less and less to travel on his own. In the summer of 1926 he went to Switzerland for the opening of the Scout International Chalet. I felt bound to keep a Guide appointment in England. He wrote:

21 Aug. '26

Darling Dear,

I am so homesick! Never again to a new place without my wife to share the fun. I keep turning to you and talking to you all the time . . .

23 Aug. '26

. . . as we have tea out in the hotel garden and as I invited Dame Katherine (Furze) to tea with me, every delegate of course took her for my wife, especially as she was in Guide uniform! — most compromising! . . .

Our next big overseas tour was our visit to South Africa 1926 to 1927. We were to be away nearly eight months so we let Pax Hill, complete with staff, took the children with us and put them in schools near Cape Town. Thus we were able to see them fairly frequently and were able to spend the long Christmas holiday together in a rented cottage at Gordon's Bay.

Robin was so happy to show me the country where he had spent so much of his soldiering life and I, for my part, was impressed and moved by the reception he received. How the survivors of Mafeking loved him! Unfortunately, he was not well during a great part of this tour. He was now sixty-nine, rising seventy. On more than one occasion I had to deputise for him. I was particularly moved in Durban when a dinner was held for former members of his South African Constabulary. One old chap had travelled three hundred miles to see Robin and was so disappointed to miss him — but at this time Robin was so weak and tired with a fever that he spent most of his time in bed and I kept him going on Benger's Food. He was incredibly plucky and determined. In Johannesburg he rose from his bed to review and talk to 6,000 Scouts who had assembled to greet him because he did not want them to be disappointed. It was so hot that even some of the Scouts collapsed but he kept going somehow until the end of the meeting, and then went straight back to bed again.

This was the biggest tour we had yet undertaken and I found myself working at a formidable pressure. Nobody who has not experienced it can realise the amount of sheer hard work that goes into such a tour.

People say it is 'so easy' to travel, everything planned and arranged, but not a bit of it. I had to write dozens of letters for each bit of a tour, every moment planned to the last detail. First, the letter to say we were coming, and preliminary tentative dates. Then I had to write to other places in the vicinity or on the way, to ask if they would like us to visit them too. Then we had to fit them all together to suit their climates and their other plans and their school holidays or terms. Then where to go and how long to spend in each place, and what to do and who to see. Inevitably difficulties would arise. There would be hurried changes in the travel schedules, trying to fit in with everybody's plans.

Clothes were another big consideration. I had packing lists which ran: 'Best evening dress, 2nd best evening dress, short evening dress, garden-party dress, hat, gloves, evening bag, etc., etc.' That one was for grand, formal occasions. I had another list for Scout and Guide functions which read: 'Camp overalls, uniform shirts, hat, belt, gloves, skirt, jacket, etc., etc.' One had to be prepared for any occasion and any climate.

It is not just the round of rallies and parades, receptions and luncheons, displays and tea-parties and dinners, visiting sick youngsters in hospitals, thousands upon thousands of handshakes. Such a programme in itself is fatiguing – particularly the handshakes! In addition, however, there are countless speeches to prepare.

I have always made it a practice to speak without notes but it has taken years of discipline to perfect the art. In Bulawayo in October of 1926 I see that I wrote: 'Robin and I both gave speeches. I don't like talking in front of him yet.' Every talk or speech needs to be carefully prepared. An unthinking comment or thoughtless phrase can give offence, can be 'distorted' by the press. Every speech needs to be different, too. A rousing message to end a big rally would be in quite a different key from a persuasive explanation of our aims designed to win financial support from the local Chamber of Commerce. The audience at a Rotary Meeting in the States requires a different approach from a group of ladies in purdah in India! We were frequently asked to broadcast and these talks demanded yet another approach for one could not see one's audience or gauge its reaction to what one was saying.

Arriving by rickshaw for a rally in Poona.

Olave wears a sari during her 1961 tour of India.

With Asian (above left) and African (above right) Guides in Kenya; (below) with
King Constantine at the XIth World Scout Jamboree, Marathon, Greece, 1963.

In addition to the social events on our programme, we had to plan our movements ahead and make the necessary bookings on ships and trains and planes. We had to interview leaders and prospective leaders, study and discuss local problems. We had to write letters by the hundred.

Robin was always punctilious about letters and expected me to be the same. Every letter we received was answered, if possible, the same day. Every person we stayed with had to be thanked, as had everyone who contributed to the arrangements for our tours. Wherever we halted and talked, there had to be 'follow-up' letters to strengthen any impact we might have made. My typewriter, 'Beetle', went with me everywhere. Indeed, I had a travelling office, a black bag called 'L.J.' (for Long Journeys) which had its own check list: spare typewriter ribbons, eraser, carbons, etc., etc. It was a very different kind of luggage from the violin and tennis racquet that accompanied me everywhere as a girl.

Robin used to like to draw a personal 'Thank You' card relating to some aspect of each tour—a custom I have preserved since his death though I myself have not the skill to do the actual design. We usually had the card printed somewhere along our journey and during the last —usually hectic—week of the tour, hundreds of these would be addressed and posted. The card he designed for the '26–'27 South African tour showed all five of us waving goodbye from our return vessel, the *Caernarvon Castle*, with an outline of Table Mountain in the background.

This particular tour was an important one for South Africa. Scouting and Guiding were going ahead with great enthusiasm, despite there still being some anti-British feeling. (For example, Mrs. Hertzog, the Prime Minister's wife, would not support the work.) So far, however, membership of the two Movements was allowed to the white population only. The coloured and African people were restricted to two related organisations for boys and girls known respectively as 'Path-finders' and 'Wayfarers'. Once again, as in India in 1921, we had tactfully but firmly to urge the policy of 'One country, one Movement'. I am happy to say that, though the policy of the South African Government today may still be one of apartheid, this does not obtain in Scouting and Guiding. Indeed, at the 1971 World Jamboree in Japan, the South African contingent had one black Scouter among its three

10

leaders, and had black African, Chinese African, Indian African as well as white African Scouts making up the party.

On this tour we were entertained at Government House, Pretoria by the Earl of Athlone and Princess Alice. Robin was still in frail health at the time and I recall with gratitude the charming and friendly welcome we had, and how Princess Alice helped us unpack, and insisted on arranging for a nourishing rice-pudding to be prepared for Robin who was still on a milk diet.

Later, on her return to England, Princess Alice took a very active part in Guiding, becoming a hard-working President of the Imperial Committee. She has always been sweet and demonstrative and at times it is difficult to know which to do first on meeting her – salute, curtsey or be kissed!

This tour was the beginning of my love-affair with Africa. I was fascinated by the endless miles of loneliness in the bare, stony Karoo Desert; by the breathtaking splendour of Victoria Falls; by the fantastic rock-piled landscape at World's View where Cecil Rhodes is buried.

We were constantly amused when people asked us on our return to England how we had enjoyed our 'holiday'! They little realised how exhausting the tour had been. The constant 'giving out' to other people drains one of vitality. One has always to be cheerful, always smiling, always interested.

Just occasionally I would question whether the effort and discipline and sacrifice were worthwhile but such doubts were only fleeting. We both believed whole-heartedly in the value and importance of the work we were doing with young people throughout the world. Any Movement which forges links of understanding between peoples of different race and creed must be of value. Any Movement which inculcates self-discipline and moral standards, which develops character and skills, which seeks to put the needs of others first, cannot fail to do good. It is a tribute to my husband's genius that so many other organisations and educationalists have chosen to use his methods – which were quite unique when he introduced them. Indeed, Scouting and Guiding remain unique among Youth Movements in that they are the only ones that are international in scope and that seek to develop their members physically, mentally *and spiritually*. So if the job, over the years, has been a demanding one, it has been worth while. At the same time it has afforded wonderful opportunities for travel. We had the privilege of seeing places and meeting people on a scale not granted to many and we felt the wonderful exhilaration of seeing good results coming from our personal effort. The sheer enthusiasm with which we were received by young people everywhere was in itself a tonic to the spirit, and if at times we felt in a state of near exhaustion physically, we were both blessed with resilient constitutions.

I, being thirty-two years younger, recovered more quickly than Robin. On boarding ship for a return voyage, the same practice almost invariably obtained. I would retire to bed in my cabin and stay there, flat on my bed, completely exhausted, hardly eating at all, and dozing most of the time. That seemed to put me right quicker than anything and after three days of 'loafing', as I called it, I would be 're-charged' and thereafter able to enter fully into shipboard life. I became a competent deck-tennis player and even at the age of sixty-two was able to win the mixed doubles championship aboard the S.S. *Cavina* on my way home from the West Indies.

Robin, on the other hand, preferred to recoup with bracing early morning walks round the deck, with painting and sketching. He was never idle. Often, during a long voyage, he would take the opportunity of working on one of his books. Then 'Beetle' would come into service and I would type away in our cabin by the hour, transcribing his notes and preparing his manuscripts. The dear man rarely relaxed except with fishing. That, apart from painting and visits to the theatre, was practically his only recreation.

How he used to love to slip away up-country when we were on tour, for a few days' privacy in some fishing-lodge miles away from people; or, at home, to spend a week with Heather fishing for salmon in the Spey or the Wye. At Pax Hill he would come back from a sticky day in Town, change into shorts and an old floppy hat, and stroll down with his rod to the Wey for the evening rise. The River Wey formed one of the boundaries of our parish at Bentley and when Robin formed the Bentley Fly-Fishing Association, he and his fellow-members re-stocked the river with trout and did much to clean up the river and repair the banks along their beat.

What wonderful years they were—working together, playing together. I can never be sufficiently grateful for the life we shared.

CHAPTER SIXTEEN

Recognition

Years: 1927 – 1930

Quite suddenly, it seemed, the children were grown up. In the spring of 1927, we had our own two and Auriol's three girls at home and Peter at prep school. Two years later they were all away at boarding-school. Christian, Clare and Yvonne (Auriol's daughters) went first. That meant that Penny, our governess, had only Heather and Betty left in her care. Peter started at Charterhouse in September of 1927. It was Robin's old school and he was very keen that his son should follow him there – though the school had to lower their very high standard somewhat to include him! In April 1929 Heather became a boarder at St. James's School, Malvern, and a month later Betty departed for Westonbirt, so for the first time since we moved there in January of 1919, the nursery was empty and the garden at Pax Hill undisturbed by the shrill sound of children's games. It seemed oddly quiet but at least Robin and I were free, provided it was term-time, to travel without having to make complicated arrangements for the children. We could tour around the country looking up relatives and old acquaintances: 'Call at Winchester on Tuffield who was Robin's trumpeter when he joined the 13th in India in 1876.'

We were once again free to visit rallies *together*, instead of having to divide forces. At a gathering of Scouts in the Welsh Marches in 1928, we were given a black Labrador retriever puppy. We christened him Shawgm after the counties represented at the rally: *S*hropshire, *H*erefordshire *A*nd *W*orcestershire, *G*loucestershire, *M*onmouthshire. Dear Shawgm! He was my husband's inseparable companion for ten years.

We also had a dear stupid Airedale called Pooh Bar (for *P*eter, *O*lave *O* *H*eather, *B*etty *A*nd *R*obin), a Welsh terrier called Twm, a cocker spaniel called Estyn and a Sealyham called Pat. I have always loved having dogs around me.

Of course, our holidays with the children were now more precious than ever. We went on wonderful camping trips. We had quite a fleet of cars during this period: Jimmax, an 18 h.p. Standard saloon; Jimmajor, a 14 h.p. saloon; Jimmy, my little 9 h.p. two-seater, and Jimminor, a wee green trailer. On the camping trips, Court would drive Jimmax, towing Jimminor with all the equipment. I would drive Jimmajor carrying the family.

Occasionally, Robin would take a vacation with Peter or Heather alone. On these expeditions, he would write every day giving details of their various activities. As always, his letters were vividly written and full of humour. At the beginning of 1929, we had taken Christian, Heather and Betty on a cruise to the Mediterranean, North and West Africa and the Canary Islands, so during the following Easter vacation from school, Robin gave Peter a fishing holiday in Belgium.

The inn was in the village street just opposite a big barn and the village manure heap (he wrote concerning their stay at Villers-sur-Lesse). The houses in the village were clean and neat but each had its manure heap. They seem to be connoisseurs in manure and there was a constant aroma of it everywhere . . .

We walked to the railway station which was the office for granting licences to fish. The station master wanted all sorts of information before granting it – among others wanted my photo of identification – and was very stiff and autocratic till he spotted my Legion of Honour button badge. Then he asked, more politely, my profession. Directly I told him 'General' he was all politeness and smiles. He took down more particulars of age, date and *day* of birth, and *where*, etc. etc. and finally handed me licence to fish in any part of Belgium whatsoever, for which I paid him 15 Francs down (about 1/9d.!).

1929 was a memorable year. There were some 'special' occasions, such as a delightful and intimate dinner-party we attended at St. James's Palace in May as guests of the Prince of Wales ('H.R.H. a very considerate, kind, genial host'). Mostly, however, I remember 1929 for the great 'Coming of Age' Jamboree of the Scout Association at Arrowe Park, near Liverpool. Only one incident marred that gathering for Robin — the peerage that King George bestowed upon him!

That probably sounds an ungrateful thing to say but my husband really was upset about it. He was a man entirely free from personal ambition, wholly content with his work, his hobbies, his family and his larger Scout family — yet fated to receive countless worldly honours and rewards. These he accepted not on his own behalf but as tributes to Scouting. He had already been created a Baronet before our tour of India in 1921, had received the G.C.V.O. in 1922 and the G.C.M.G. in 1927; but a peerage, he considered, was too much. Moreover, he felt that becoming a 'lord' might raise a barrier between himself and the boys he led. He liked always to feel that the boys viewed him as one of themselves, that they would not be shy of approaching him.

When the letter came from the Prime Minister, Mr. Ramsay MacDonald, indicating the King's intention, we talked it over and both agreed that Robin should decline the honour. However, 'Belge' Wilson of the Scout Association urged him to accept. He said the King's gesture honoured the whole Movement; that it would give Scouting a 'boost'. Eileen Wade, his secretary, also urged that it was his duty to accept. The Duke of Connaught added his voice and eventually, I remember, my husband snapped: 'Oh, do as you damn well please!' and stamped off. Someone must have sent off a telegram of acceptance immediately for on August 1st, when the Prince of Wales opened the great Jamboree, he read out a telegram to the assembled Scouts:

It has given me great pleasure to mark this signal event in your history by conferring a peerage on the Chief Scout. Ever since its inception, he has been the mainspring of this great adventure, from its small and almost humble beginnings until today, when you number nearly two million in your ranks. The recognition of his valuable services to the cause will be welcomed by all who realise the importance of training the world's youth both in mind and body . . .

George, R. I.

The whole great arena erupted in cheers and shouts and there was only one glum face in the whole vast assembly—my husband's!

The Prince of Wales was really a bit naughty about the Jamboree. He had expressed a desire to see all over the vast camp and it had been arranged that his 'inspection' should begin at 10.0 a.m. which would give the Scouts time to have their breakfasts and clear up their camp-sites. However, he was invited to play golf that morning so he turned up early at the Jamboree, without warning, and no one was ready for him. Of course, it did not really matter; he saw a camp genuinely at work and not a special show. On the other hand, even boys do not always like to be caught on the hop, in 'scruff order'—particularly, perhaps, when they have been hoping that some specially (to them) important badge may be noticed.

It was a wonderful Jamboree. We ourselves stayed at the Royal Hotel at Hoylake; we knew from the experience of previous Jamborees that Robin would have no peace or privacy at all if he stayed at the Jamboree itself. We even managed one or two walks along the beach alone together. But we visited Arrowe Park every day.

August 5th, 1929—Wander round from camp to camp—all the nations having their groups in bunches, and you step out of India into Finland, or across a rope from Italy to Mexico, and they all have their gate-ways and gadgets well made.

The closing day, August 10th, brought Robin's big 'surprise' present. I had been charged with the duty of finding out secretly what he would like. I asked him casually if there was anything he particularly needed. 'Yes,' he replied. 'A new pair of braces.' I duly passed on this information. As every Scout in the *World* was being asked to contribute one penny to the present, there was quite a con-siderable sum involved. In the end, he was presented with a Rolls-Royce car (christened 'Jam Roll'), a trailer caravan (known as 'Eccles'), his portrait by David Jagger, a cheque for £2,800—*and* a pair of bright green braces!

There were large house parties at Pax after the Jamboree. The library was used as an overflow dining-room. Leaders of overseas contingents filled the guest bedrooms, slept in the summer-house, in the new caravan, in tents on the lawns. We entertained contingent leaders from France, Japan, Hungary, Jamaica, Canada, Egypt, Norway, Ceylon, India, Australia, South Africa, New Zealand, Rhodesia and the United States—princes sitting down with farmers, counts of ancient lineage with carpenters. It was an exhilarating if exhausting summer but eventually the last visitors departed and peace enfolded our beloved Pax again. 'Went blackberrying—such a joy to be quiet. Most soothing recreation—if prickly!'

There were more excitements to come. On October 18th of that year, Robin received the Freedom of the City of London. We enjoyed the rare privilege of driving through cleared streets and lines of cheering people to the Guildhall where Robin was welcomed with a long address and received a magnificent gold casket containing his 'Freedom'. Afterwards, we drove immediately behind the Lord Mayor's coach to the Mansion House where a huge luncheon banquet was given in our honour. I sat between the Lord Mayor (Sir Kynaston Studd) and Lord Reading (the former Viceroy of India). We even had a mounted police escort back to Scout Headquarters afterwards. It was all most exciting and impressive.

Another ceremony—very quaint and of brief duration—took place on October 30th, our seventeenth anniversary and Peter's sixteenth birthday. Robin was 'introduced' to the House of Lords by Lord Hampton and Lord Glentanar (two 'stalwarts' of Scouting). Mother and Christian accompanied me to watch the ceremony and we all had a jolly tea afterwards in the House of Lords tea-room. Many years before, Robin had been invited to stand for Parliament. 'All right,' he had wired back. 'For which side?' He did not trust politicians and, although now a member of the Upper House, he did not allow himself to become embroiled in its business. He only spoke very occasionally, when he felt he had some useful contribution to make to its debates. He once wrote: 'The world seems divided into talkers and doers. There are too many talkers. The doer is the man we need—the man whose vision is not limited by narrow party considerations.'

In between these two slices of pageantry, there was an excitement we could well have done without—Pax Hill was burgled. We all slept through it, including the dogs. We think the burglars were after the gold 'Freedom' casket for it had been on display in the window of the Goldsmiths and Silversmiths Company in London. However, when Robin came to take the casket home after the presentation, he found there was a special container to go with it—a black box with a lid and two doors at the front. The night of the burglary, we had had the 'doors' open to admire the casket without taking it out of its box and, just before we went upstairs to bed, we shut the doors. So there was nothing to see but a plain black box. I suppose the intruders shone their torches round and just took what was immediately obvious. They did not apparently search for anything. However, the house was stripped of most of our treasures: cups, salvers, clocks, all our wedding silver including the gift from Robin's regiment, the inscribed Mafeking silver gun, even the silver christening mug the Duke of Connaught had given to Peter. It was a sad blow, not for the financial value of the goods which were, in any event, insured, but because most of them were irreplaceable. So many were tokens of love and respect and loyalty from all over the world, items which gave pleasure also to our many visitors. We never recovered any of them. We could not replace the items so we bought a second Rolls-Royce with the insurance money. It was really of greater value to us than the silver as we could use it.

Except for this terrible mishap of the burglary, it had been a wonderful year. At seventy-two, Robin was far more fit and fresh than he had been for a long time. It was wonderful to see him so full of happy vigour. Thus it was almost as if we were turning back the clock to 1912 when we set off in January of 1930 for a repeat of the cruise on which we had first met. The *Arcadian* was no longer in service and this time we sailed on the *Alcantara*. It was delicious seeing it all again. We made a sentimental journey to the Myrtle Bank Hotel in Jamaica, and to the 'dangle-toes' bridge where we had parted so sadly eighteen years before. We visited the Panama Canal again, only now it was completed and we had the fun of pulling levers and 'helping' to put ships through the Miraflores Lock. We went on to New York where at a Scout luncheon we met 'the nice crippled Governor of New York —Frank D. Roosevelt. He spoke well.'

In July, I 'presented' my niece Christian at Court. She was seventeen, the age at which girls 'came out' in pre-War 'Society'. Being a débutante in those days had a special ritual. We stayed overnight at the

Rubens Hotel in Buckingham Palace Road. We wore the prescribed ostrich feathers in our hair and the regulation evening dress with train and long gloves. We had to dress very early in the afternoon and, after having the occasion recorded by Vandyke, the photographer, took our places in our car in the Mall by 5.30 to 'queue up' with all the other débutantes. It was one of the sights of the Season – to see the pretty girls in all their finery playing cards in their cars to while away the time, or eating sandwiches to keep themselves going. By 8.30 we had crawled down the Mall as far as the Palace and were herded into an anteroom known irreverently as 'The Ostrich Farm'. Here we had to wait, each débutante accompanied by an older woman who had herself been 'presented' and who was acting as sponsor. When our turn came, our names were called out. We had to form up in the queue and have our trains spread out by pages. Then we had to walk the length of the Throne Room, curtsey to the King, curtsey to the Queen, then make our way to seats at the far end of the room where we could watch the rest of the presentations. One had to keep a very straight back when curtseying and incline one's head gracefully without losing one's ostrich feathers. It was not easy, particularly with a train and a bouquet to manage as well. Afterwards, while watching the rest of the proceedings, we sat next to Field-Marshal Lord Allenby who had entertained us in 1921 on our way home from India. He let Christian hold his baton. It was rather nice – covered in velvet.

That same month, the World Guide Conference meeting at Foxlease elected me World Chief Guide. It was a staggering compliment – I hardly felt my stature in youth work compared with my husband's. It was also an enormous responsibility, though I have tried all these many years to show myself worthy of the honour.

The late twenties and early thirties really saw us reach the peak of our work together as husband and wife in the service of our brother and sister Movements. All too soon, Robin's advancing years would necessitate his withdrawal from active Scouting. For the present, however, he was full of energy and enthusiasm and ideas and fun. The closing 'engagement' of 1930, I think, symbolises what we were trying to do:

December 9th, 1930 – Both to London early, but delayed 40

minutes by fog. Rush to Euston and there we both 'unveil' name plates on two huge L.M.S. railway engines called 'The Girl Guide' and 'The Boy Scout' and each wearing the respective badges on their sides! We both make speeches and the railway officials do so also. We and the Scout and Guide Guards of Honour climb about on the engines. We are photographed and cinema'd and 'talkie'd' and then depart . . .

Those trains were like the Scout and Guide Movements—two powerful driving forces capable of taking millions of young people safely along the right lines.

CHAPTER SEVENTEEN

Mixed Fortunes

Years: 1931–1933

1931 was a year of mixed fortunes. On the one hand, Scouting and Guiding were having a quite phenomenal success all round the globe. We undertook a world tour from January to July, concentrating in particular on New Zealand and Australia. We were thrilled at the progress made in every country we visited. The Guide Movement received another generous gift from the American lady, Mrs. Storrow, (who had been our hostess in Boston in 1919) in the form of a chalet at Adelboden in Switzerland, to be used as an international skiing and training centre.

On the other hand, there were many family problems. Peter had left Charterhouse at Christmas having repeatedly failed his School Certificate examination. He was not academic and examinations were always an agony and a humiliation for him. Charterhouse was really too much a school for high-flyers; Peter would have done better somewhere less competitive but, like so many parents before and after us, we did not appreciate this and thought the high standard would be good for him. Now we were in a quandary. He needed School Certificate for entry to Sandhurst. After much heart-searching and anxious discussion we decided to send him to Chillon College in Switzerland, hoping that the complete change of atmosphere would stimulate more interest in matters academic.

Money was becoming an increasing worry. Our world tour had cost us personally £1,000 over and above what had been paid for officially. We financed it out of the proceeds of Robin's biography, *Lessons from the 'Varsity of Life*. He wrote it—or rather, dictated it to me—during the first part of our voyage. He had already planned the book before he left England and took his file of notes with him.

We had a nice cabin on the *Rangitata* and for a large part of each day of the five weeks between leaving Southampton on January 16th and arriving in Auckland on February 19th, he would pace up and down the cabin dictating his story.

In addition to the cost of travelling, our general expenses were enormous. What with our many tours and the vast amount of entertaining we undertook, I had to keep dipping into capital to make ends meet. Even so, the steady increase in the cost of living brought its strain. I tried to economise:

> October 5th, 1931 – Decided this week that, owing to increased big taxation, we must reduce expenditure. So I gave the little 'tweeny' notice – five maids ought to be enough really – and Brooker the third gardener will go when he can get a job elsewhere.

Mother had, back in 1929, somewhat rashly given up her home and gone to live with my brother Arthur. It had not worked out and she was very unhappy there. After the breach, she moved in with us and one evening in the middle of October 1931 I went up to her room to bid her goodnight and found her unconscious. She had had a slight stroke. She recovered, but was very ill and vague for some weeks afterwards. She and Arthur had not spoken to each other since their quarrel over a year before so I had the delicate and unenviable task of 'interviewing' my brother and persuading him to come and see her. What a change of role from the baby sister who used to attend so admiringly on big brother Boogie!

In the past he had always been Mother's favourite and I know that a lot of her antagonism to Guides was of his prompting. Now, in her frailty, mother clung to me pathetically. She was eighty that December and after the stroke could not dress herself unaided. She required a great deal of care and attention. It was some relief during the period of strain that she became more tolerant in her attitude towards Guiding and even brought herself to give grudging approval to my work.

In fact, I was doing very little Guiding that autumn for the care of mother was keeping me very much tied to Pax Hill. I note from my diary, however, that I escaped for two enjoyable outings with Robin: the State Opening of Parliament ('all very solemn and dignified and

the House crammed. The King's speech rather poor and very short!')
and the Degree Ceremony at Oxford when my husband received an
Honorary LL.D. That evening, back in London:

> We give ourselves a lovely treat of a grand theatre party of just
> us two! Saw the most splendid enthralling play — 'Cavalcade' by
> Noel Coward, beautifully acted and wonderfully staged. I have
> never seen anything finer. Most dramatic and clever and touched
> us both as it has scenes about Mafeking Relief. We loved it.

Chillon did not seem to have any more success with Peter than any
other school and during the twenty-four hours of January 12th, 1932,
first of all we learned that Peter had failed the School Certificate
examination yet again; then mother had another and more severe
stroke. To crown the misery of the day, both Robin and Peter took to
their beds with 'flu.

Mother lingered on another three weeks, growing gradually
weaker and more incoherent. At last, blessedly unconscious, she died
peacefully on February 5th and was buried at Parkstone, next to
Auriol. I went to the funeral service but could not face the burial.
It seemed so final, putting my beautiful and imperious mother under
the cold ground.

Her will was a shock and a dreadful blow to me. It must have been
made some years earlier for she had repeatedly assured me during
the past year that she was leaving me well endowed and that I was
not to worry at all about money. When I had felt so anxious about our
soaring expenses, the thought had comforted me that sooner or later I
should be quite a wealthy woman in my own right. When the will
was read, however, the cruel fact emerged that she had left everything
to Auriol's three daughters and nothing at all to me except her 'wearing
apparel'. I can only think that it was her way of hitting back at me for
wearing the Guide uniform she hated — for nothing of hers fitted me
except an old fur coat. I was very, very upset. Just as in childhood I
had always been the 'runty' one, left out by the mother, now even at
her death the same thing seemed to have happened. Brother Arthur
also became even more unpleasant after her death and the rift between
us, always of recent years a wide one, now became a chasm.

Fortunately I was not one to brood over slights, and money had never been to me more than a means to an end, so I quickly overcame my disappointment. After all, nothing could be a richer treasure to me than my beloved husband—only six years younger than my mother in age, yet a generation younger in spirit and vigour. Moreover, it was the 'Coming of Age' year for Guiding. There were celebrations up and down the land, culminating in a great and inspiring Service of Thanksgiving in St. Paul's Cathedral on May 28th where, in the presence of Princess Mary, a congregation of 5,300 Guides renewed their Promise. Even more moving and gratifying were the letters that reached Robin and me from all over the world, thanking us for the work we were doing, and paying tribute to what Guiding meant, and had meant over the years, to the writers of the letters. When one receives such touching tributes, one forgets the fatigue and disappointments inherent in any job. The radiant, eager faces of the young people we lead are sufficient reward.

I myself, though, was singled out for a special reward that year for, in the Birthday Honours, I received a G.B.E. When I 'Jam-Rolled' (our personal verb for travelling in the Jamboree Rolls-Royce) to the Palace for the Investiture, I took Annie (our cook) and three of the housemaids with me so that they could at least have the pleasure of driving up to the front door of Buckingham Palace, even if they could not go in. I wore Guide uniform for the Investiture. It was rather fun. One was put in a sort of pen when one arrived—a little pen for the K.B.E.s and the G.B.E.s and the D.B.E.s (I was in a pen with an Admiral); a larger pen for the C.B.E.s and a big one for the O.B.E.s. I was the third person that day to be decorated by King George V. I was very proud to receive the award; it was such a great honour for the Movement.

A month later I was abroad again on Guide business, without Robin this time. I visited Paris, then went on to Switzerland for the 'official' opening of the Guide Chalet, on again to Vienna and finally to Kattowice in Poland for the 7th World Guide Conference. I mention this Conference for two reasons.

The first is that in Poland 'Thinking Day' had its origins. A Belgian Guider at the Conference suggested that there should be one day set apart in each year when all of us should think of each other in terms of

love and friendship. It could have as vital a power as the Women's
World Day of Prayer. There was also a practical suggestion that on
'Thinking Day', each Guide throughout the world should contribute
'A Penny for Your Thoughts' towards the World Association funds.
The Conference paid Robin and me the compliment of choosing our
joint birthday, February 22nd, as Thinking Day. At first the idea hung
fire but, one by one, the nations began to promote the scheme. Money
began to pour in for the World Association and the totals have risen
steadily from £520 12s. 6d. in 1933 to £35,346 in 1970/71 – the last
year for which I have the complete figures. Far greater than the
financial success, however, is the spiritual impact of Thinking Day.
A special message I broadcast some years ago gives my assessment of
its value:

> During the twenty-four hours of February 22nd, these kindly,
> generous thoughts are being thrown out into the ether by Guides
> who care personally about the preaching of love and goodwill in
> the world, and these thoughts and prayers are concentrated thus as a
> live force for the developing of friendship and understanding, for
> which all peoples are longing.
>   Though you cannot visit sister Guides in France or Finland, in
> Austria or Australia, in Italy or Iceland, Canada or Chile, Ghana or
> Guatemala, U.S.A. or U.A.R., you *can* reach out to them there in
> your MIND. And in this unseen, spiritual way you can give them
> your uplifting sympathy and friendship.
>   Thus do we Guides, of all kinds and of all ages and of all nations,
> go with the highest and the best towards the spreading of true peace
> and goodwill on earth.

My second reason for mentioning the Conference in Poland is to
quote an extract from my diary illustrating the progress in flying over
the past forty years: 'August 17th, 1932 – Up at 7 and drive to Aerodrome. Fly to Berlin by 10.0 a.m. Then fly to Hanover. Then fly to
Amsterdam by 5.0 p.m. Then fly to Croydon by 8.50. Awfully tiring.'
Today, Warsaw to Heathrow takes only three and a quarter hours by
direct flight.
  As I said in the opening paragraphs of this story, my life has spanned

such a long period that I am continually being tugged one way by the marvels of the seventies and another by the claims of the past. This was happening all the time during my married life, especially as my husband's connections were with an even earlier age. Inevitably, Robin's Army career impinged constantly on our life together, particularly his famous exploits during the Boer War. One by one, however, the associations with Mafeking were growing less. Each year there were fewer faces at our regular Mafeking Lunch on May 17th; the precious silver model of the Mafeking gun had been stolen and never recovered; and on July 20th, 1932 Robin was pall-bearer at the funeral of his colleague of the Matabele Campaign of 1896, the man who led the Relief Column into Mafeking—Colonel (later Field-Marshal Lord) Plumer. Robin himself was now seventy-five and he must have wondered how soon he too would follow his old comrade.

In November, I see that we dined with the Cyril Maudes at their flat and then went on to see Cyril acting in a new comedy, *Once A Husband*. He was another connection with Mafeking. He was also an ardent old Carthusian and had been a friend of Robin's for many years. On that May evening of 1900, he had stopped his play in the middle of an act to announce that Mafeking had been relieved. All London had gone wild that night and the English language had received a new word, 'Mafficking'.

Cyril and his first wife, Winifred Emery, had been one of a number of husbands and wives in the actor/manager partnerships of that time— couples like Oscar Ashe and Lilian Braithwaite; Seymour Hicks and Ellaline Terriss; or the Beerbohm Trees (she was not a very good actress, but insisted on having a part in every play). Winifred died and some time later, when Cyril re-married, Robin was to be best man at the wedding. As we were leaving for the church, I said 'You had better take a ring with you in case Cyril forgets his.' I gave him my mother's ring and he put it in his pocket. Sure enough, when they were waiting for the bride to arrive, Robin checked with Cyril. 'Have you remembered the ring?' He *had* forgotten; he had left it behind in his flat.

On this November evening in 1932 we had the added pleasure of meeting Sir James Barrie. I had always wanted to meet him, particularly as his play, *Peter Pan*, had so many happy associations for

11

Robin and me. He was a sad disappointment—'a shy awkward uncouth little man'.

If Barrie was a disappointment, other things were not. Peter, who had had private coaching after leaving Chillon, at long last qualified for the Royal Military College, Sandhurst, and Heather 'came out'. She was 'launched' at the Hampshire Hunt Ball at Winchester but her 'season' had to wait until we had taken her on a Mediterranean cruise.

We left Southampton for Malta on February 15th, 1933 aboard the *Largs Bay*. We had a wonderful reception in Malta and I had an opportunity of going over a battleship in the naval dockyard there ('I do like new experiences'). After Malta, we toured Sicily, and finally reached Rome on February 28th.

We were to have a private audience with the Pope, Pius XI, on March 2nd so I had taken the precaution of borrowing a black lace veil from Marie Denaro, the Guide Commissioner in Malta. I knew that one wore black and had taken a short black dress with me for the occasion. Imagine my dismay when Mrs. Kirkpatrick, the wife of the British Chargé d'Affaires at the Vatican, told me that, to be correct, the dress had to reach the ground! We did some frantic improvisation with borrowed garments and I finally attended the audience swathed to the chin in Mrs. Kirkpatrick's black velvet evening coat and Marie's black veil. Only the purple ribbon of the G.B.E. was my own. I felt a perfect fool. Robin, of course, looked splendid in evening dress with all his medals and orders. It seemed an awful fuss for ten minutes' audience but the Pope was most gracious. He spoke no English but, through an interpreter, expressed his approval of Scouting and Guiding and the 'magnificent work' it was doing as 'a great family carrying out the ideal of unity'. Before we left, he blessed us both, and our work.

It was ironic that, following hard upon the Pope's endorsement of our work, Robin should go straight to an interview with Mussolini. The Italian leader had closed down all youth movements in the country (including Scouts) and had substituted his own organisation, the *Balilla*. Robin and the Duce had a cordial meeting but Robin could not agree with Mussolini's assertion that the *Balilla* was an improvement on Scouting. It was, Robin pointed out, compulsory instead of voluntary; super-nationalistic rather than international; that though it attached the same importance as Scouting to physical fitness, it omitted any spiritual emphasis. Moreover, instead of developing individual character, it turned out youngsters all to one mould. Robin deplored the emphasis laid on nationalism and militarism. Although he believed in service to one's country, that service, he felt, should never be used as an instrument of aggression.

The following day we took tea with the Marchese Marconi and his wife at their flat in the Via Condotti. He was the inventor of wireless. He sent and received the first signals across the English Channel in 1898 and across the Atlantic in 1901. Unlike His Holiness, Marconi spoke English perfectly at our tea-party with him. He was to die only four years later at the early age of sixty-three.

We visited Naples, Genoa, Marseilles, Gibraltar and Tangier, returning home by March 19th—in plenty of time to prepare for Heather's London season. It followed the traditional pattern of the period: endless débutante balls that went on until the small hours, exciting for the young people but boring for the parents! There was the traditional Queen Charlotte's Ball at Grosvenor House and we ourselves gave a reception in Heather's honour for over two hundred guests at the Mercers' Hall. May 12th was the day of Heather's 'presentation' at Court and once again we went through the ritual of sitting in the Jam-Roll for over two hours in the Palace courtyard awaiting our turn. It was much more enjoyable presenting one's own daughter. Our only disappointment was that the King was absent due to a bad attack of rheumatism and the curtseys had accordingly to be made to Queen Mary and the Prince of Wales.

My diary for this summer is full of chatter about family affairs. There seemed to be perpetual sunshine. I was absorbed and happy and oblivious of the clouds that were gathering over Europe; but the signs were already there for those who could read them.

At the 1929 Jamboree there had been both Italian and German Scouts camping alongside boys from all over the world. At the 1933 Jamboree at Godöllo in Hungary, there were no Italian Scouts at all. Robin (who was at Godöllo with Peter) was, however, expecting a contingent of over a thousand German Scouts. They did not come. Shortly before the Jamboree, Hitler appointed Baldur von Schirach as *Jugendführer des Deutschen Reiches* (Youth-Leader of Germany). His first action was to abolish all existing youth organisations, including

Boy Scouts, and to proclaim the *Hitler-Jugend* the official and only movement for young people in Germany. Scouting stayed suppressed in Germany until the war was over. The new German Scouts after the war were officially recognised by the World Conference in 1950.

Shortly after the Gödöllo Jamboree, my husband was approached by the German Ambassador, Joachim von Ribbentrop, to meet von Schirach with a view to establishing friendship between the *Hitler-Jugend* and British Scouts. Already there was doubt as to the way the *Hitler-Jugend* were going to develop and I am glad to say that my husband was cautious and far-seeing enough not to allow his Scouts to become embroiled. I myself did not pay much attention to what was happening in Germany. I was far more concerned with the arrangements for the first Guide and Scout cruise.

I consider the cruises one of my triumphs. They were my own idea entirely—another inspiration from the World Conference in Poland in 1932.

I was at a camp-fire there one evening. Some Polish Guides were performing—a very beautiful national dance, if I remember rightly after forty years. I do recall turning to Daisy Mander who had accompanied me from England.

'Oh Daisy!' I exclaimed. 'Isn't this wonderful. How I wish I could bring some of our little English Guiders here to see this, to see how the same game is being carried on in other countries.'

'Why don't you?' asked Daisy.

So I did.

As soon as I returned from Poland, I discussed my idea with Scout and Guide Headquarters. Then we approached the White Star Line and said 'If we supply the passengers, could you supply us with a ship?' They agreed willingly and offered us the *Calgaric*. We had no difficulty in filling our passenger list. As soon as the notice of the cruise went out in *The Guider* and *The Scouter* we were inundated with applications. When the *Calgaric* sailed from Southampton on August 12th, 1933, there were six hundred and fifty Guiders and Scouters on board.

Our cruise, christened 'The Argosy of Peace', called at Rotterdam, Gdynia in Poland, Klaipeda in Lithuania, Riga in Latvia, Tallin in Estonia, Helsinki, Stockholm and Oslo. Alas, many of those places have since been swallowed up by Russia but in 1933, each had a separate identity and in each of them we received the friendly welcome I had wanted our British Guiders and Scouters to experience.

It would be impossible to describe the cruise in detail but I can remember being pulled through the streets of Helsinki in an open carriage with Scouts between the shafts. The carriage was all bedecked with blue and white cornflowers, the Finnish national colours. We had the privilege of spending a day with Field-Marshal Mannerheim, the great saviour of Finland. He entertained all six hundred and fifty of us at a garden party in the *Brunnsparken*. In the middle of tea, a very small Finnish Wolf Cub marched smartly up to Robin, clicked his heels, saluted smartly and, presenting an open book and pen to him, said in English 'Chief Scout, please to write here.' Robin took the pen and book and asked jokingly 'But what if I don't know how to spell my name?' A look of dismay spread over the small boy's face and he gasped 'I can no more English!'

I can recall sitting sharing a rug with Queen Maud of Norway at a camp-fire at Frognarseteren, a skiing station high on a hillside above Oslo. We were in a sort of dell, jam-packed with Norwegian Scouts and Guides. Suddenly, it seemed as if someone had switched on a light for they had all taken their hats off at the same moment and the evening sun was gleaming on their pale, fair hair.

In Stockholm we dined with Count Folke Bernadotte who was later so tragically to be shot by Stern Gang terrorists when acting as United Nations mediator in the Middle East. His widow later became Chairman of the World Guide Association and his brother, Crown Prince Gustav Adolf was Chief Scout of Sweden and visited us at Pax Hill. I can still remember his visit. He came with his charming wife, Princess Sybilla. I went to London myself and collected them from Clarence House in Jam Roll and drove them down to Pax Hill. They were such a lovely couple. He was killed in an air crash just after the war.

The cruise was an enormous success and set the pattern for others that followed.

Altogether it had been a wonderful year, full of variety and interest and happiness both in home and public affairs. One of the last entries in my diary for 1933 echoes the gay note that had characterised the whole year: 'Tuesday, November 21st, 1933 – Dressed in my best evening dress plus my G.B.E. gold 'collar' for breakfast! — and then Jam-Rolled up to the House of Lords for the Opening of Parliament.'

I little realised that it would be the last public function Robin and I would attend together for many a long month.

CHAPTER EIGHTEEN

Many Journeys

Years: 1934—1937

On New Year's Day, 1934, Betty was rushed into hospital for an emergency appendix operation. Two days later in the King Edward VII Hospital for Officers, Robin underwent an operation for the removal of the prostate gland. We knew that any operation on a man of nearly seventy-seven was bound to be attended by some anxiety but we were not over-worried; Robin had a splendid constitution.

Something went wrong, however, necessitating a second operation. 'I go through hell', I wrote in my diary. I was frantic with anxiety. News of my brother's divorce, reported in the newspapers on January 7th, seemed unimportant. I was torn between visiting Betty who was recovering in one hospital and being on hand at the other where Robin hovered between life and death. He suffered a bad relapse and on January 25th had to have a blood transfusion. Thereafter I just stayed on at the hospital, sitting by his bedside hour after hour, weeping with anxiety and exhaustion, dozing a little, then waking and praying that he would pull through.

It was the first time in my life that I had really felt the need to pray and I clung to its comfort as the only thing I could do to help my darling. He was in dreadful pain, wandering in his mind, and his strength was at such a low ebb, one could only live from hour to hour. February 9th brought yet another relapse and another blood transfusion. He was still so desperately ill on February 23rd that I did not dare leave him to see Peter off from the East India Docks.

Peter was going out to join the British South African Police, having failed to make the grade at Sandhurst. I do not think he would ever have succeeded there, even had he not been slipping off to London to take out his girl-friend when he ought to have been studying. (We discovered too late that he had become unofficially 'engaged'.) With the benefit of hindsight, I can see that we should never have suggested Peter go to Sandhurst in the first place for the Army was not really to his taste, though he admired my husband's career tremendously; Peter was far too gentle by nature to be a soldier.

Gradually, Robin pulled round and by the middle of March I was able to have him transferred by ambulance to Pax Hill. He was still desperately frail but I had his bed moved to the window where he could lie happily, looking out on to the quiet garden and the birds and the soft loveliness of our view. By the end of the month, he had recovered sufficiently to be carried aboard the *Adriatic* for a cruise in the Mediterranean. Once again, our two Movements had taken over a whole vessel but on this occasion Robin was kept apart from them in case he should be subjected to too much strain. He did not leave the ship at any of the ports of call; instead he rested and relaxed in the sea air and healing sunshine.

The voyage did wonders for his health and a day or two after our return to England he was fit enough to attend the King's Scout St. George's Day Parade at Windsor Castle on Sunday, April 22nd, before H.M. King George V. The King and Queen Mary received us both and showed a most gracious interest in our two Movements. The Duke and Duchess of York were also present, with the two little Princesses, then eight and three years of age.

I was still anxiously watching Robin's health. I was constantly reminded of the gulf in years between us as one by one various members of his generation died. In May I went over to Sheffield Park to see Uncle Arthur Soames, my father's oldest and last surviving brother. He died shortly afterwards, on July 22nd. My brother Arthur inherited Sheffield Park and to my surprise, I learned that Uncle Arthur had left me a substantial legacy.

Robin continued to take things quietly throughout the summer and undertook no public engagements. I was, accordingly, alone when I went up to Leeds in September to give a lecture at the Institute of Science and Art on 'Scouting and Guiding and the Man who made them'. It was an easy topic for me to talk on for my admiration and love for Robin deepened with each precious year of our marriage. The

Earl of Harewood was in the chair for the lecture. He and Princess Mary graciously entertained me for three days at Harewood House. It was all very informal. We strolled through the gardens and round the lake to feed the ducks, and on the first evening sat like any ordinary family with the Princess doing her embroidery and me my knitting. The following day it poured with rain so the Princess took me on a tour of the great house, showing me their magnificent collection of furniture and paintings. Then, just as millions of others must have been doing up and down the country, we 'listened in' to the Queen 'launching the big new ship, *Queen Mary*'.

The long months of rest had built up Robin's strength and in October of 1934 we left Tilbury on the *Orama* for another world tour that was to keep us out of England for nine months. This time we took Heather and Betty as our secretaries, to have their now very capable assistance with all the 'hidden' work a tour involved and also to help Heather over a broken engagement. This time we circled the globe from west to east, taking in Colombo, Malaya, the East Indies and Thursday Island, North and East Australia, reaching Melbourne in time for the first Southern Hemisphere Jamboree in Melbourne over Christmas and New Year of 1935. We returned via New Zealand, Tahiti and the New World.

We had a special reason for wanting to revisit Canada. Always, wherever we had travelled, we had emphasised the ideal of 'One country, one Movement'. Occasionally it was impossible sufficiently to reconcile deeply opposed groups to make this possible. In France, for example, the Roman Catholics and Protestants have always kept to separate organisations. In Canada, there had been no trace of religious apartheid until the early thirties when, again, the Roman Catholics began breaking away from the national association and forming their own Scout and Guide organisations. It had been in anticipation of such a breakaway that we had sought our audience with Pope Pius XI two years before. Strengthened by the Pope's approval of our work and, in particular, of the 'ideal of unity', we were able to have a 'cheery talk' with Cardinal Villeneuve in Quebec, as a result of which the breakaway organisations agreed to become affiliated to the national bodies.

It was the twenty-fifth year of King George's reign and on May 6th,

1935, Robin lit a Scout bonfire in Winnipeg, starting a Jubilee chain of beacons right across Canada.

From Canada we went on to the United States where Franklin D. Roosevelt, the 'nice crippled Governor of New York' we had met in 1930, was now President. We had lunch with him at the White House and found him most charming and easy to talk to. He had a swivel chair at the table. He was so full of life, one completely forgot his affliction.

It is an indication of my husband's powers of resilience that, now seventy-eight, he could arrive back in England on July 28th after a nine months' tour and leave the very next day for a Rover Moot in Sweden! Nevertheless, he *was* seventy-eight, and at that age he found the English winter trying. Accordingly, we decided to let Pax Hill for a few months and, taking the girls with us, spent the winter in Africa.

We went first of all to Kenya to stay with Eric Walker. He had been the first secretary of the Scout Association, the one who had 'parked' his aircraft by Ewhurst Church that February morning in 1915 before returning to France and, subsequently, to the miseries of a German prisoner-of-war camp. After the war, he had married Lady Bettie Fielding and emigrated to Kenya. There, at Nyeri, after sundry enterprises from rum-running to coffee planting, he had founded the Outspan Hotel. He and Bettie used to write begging us to visit them and extolling the beauties of the Outspan. We came, we saw, and lost our hearts to the place.

The hotel was planned as a series of individual bungalows, each facing towards the magnificent view of Mount Kenya, some eighty miles away. It is an idea which has been widely adopted since in the planning of hotel accommodation but in 1935 it was unique. Another original idea of Eric's was the building of Treetops, a shelter in the branches of a huge forest tree by the side of a water-hole where one could watch in safety the wild creatures that came to drink—duicker and water-buck, forest hog, elephant, rhino and so on. Treetops became well known at the time of the accession of our present Queen for she was there the night her father, King George VI, died. Since that time, the original shack has been replaced by a bigger and more luxurious construction but in 1935 there was only the rather rickety little erection into which one climbed by ladder.

Kenya was everything Eric had promised. The climate was gentle, better suited to old bones than the damp of an English winter. The country was open and wild, yet with everything one needed readily to hand at Nyeri or Nairobi. There was a sense of peace and beauty, and everywhere the wild animals Robin loved to film and paint. He had, many many years before, given up any desire to shoot game with a gun. Now a ciné-camera was his delight. We went on safari with Eric and six of his 'boys'. My diary records that we 'saw giraffe, zebra, duicker, ostrich, oryx, dik-dik, baboon, hare, gerunuk, rabbit, ketate, guinea-fowl, greater bustard, jackal, stem buck, Grant's gazelle, Thompson's gazelle (Tommies), wild boar, vultures, secretary birds, storks' — but no elephants or lions on that particular trip.

All too soon we had to move on to carry out Scout engagements elsewhere: 'Zanzibar — Excellent Scout Rally. Rained a bit — but did not damp anybody's marvellous enthusiasm. Arabs, Africans, Goans and Indians all in it.'

On December 23rd, we called in at Beira where, to our delight, we found Peter waiting to meet us. He had managed a twenty-four hour pass. It was nearly two years since we had seen him and we had so much to talk about. This was a new Peter, no longer nervous and bedevilled by an inferiority complex. He had 'found' himself in Africa — or perhaps he had found himself when no longer living in the shadow of a famous father! It cannot, on reflection, have been easy for him to have us as his parents. And I, for my part, had always regarded him with something akin to impatience because he had not inherited the brilliance of his father. It was a joy now to find him relaxed and happy. We said goodbye to him, not knowing when we should see him again, and boarded the S.S. *Incomati* again to continue our voyage to Durban. The next day we were both shivering with fever and spent Christmas of 1935 confined to our cabins with malaria. I recovered fairly quickly but Robin was very much pulled down and continued to be ill throughout the remainder of our tour.

Despite this, he managed an intensive tour of South Africa and was able to attend a Jamboree at East London. For myself, I experienced on January 11th what I described as 'one of the most thrilling, history-making moments': the Wayfarers were accepted into the Guide Association of South Africa. 'One country, one Movement'. White had joined hands with black on equal terms. It was a giant stride forward for South Africa, even if it has taken several steps backwards since!

We were in Queenstown when we heard of the death of King George V. It seemed strange, all those thousands of miles away and surrounded by coloured faces, to hear over the radio King Edward VIII proclaimed King in London. To hear the rolling, dignified phrases that have been used down the centuries was strange and oddly stirring.

Other things were stirring, too—the first rumblings of the explosion that was soon to turn the world upside down.

March 31st, 1936—The newspapers here give bad accounts of things in other parts of the world—riots in Spain; rebellion in Japan; Italy crushing poor Abyssinia with poison gas and bombs; Germany defying the Peace Treaty and moving troops on to the Rhine; France suffering from her gold going away to America; etc. etc. The world does seem to have gone a bit mad just now.

We sailed back to England in May aboard the *Llandovery Castle*, calling among other places at the little island of St. Helena which was able to muster a Guard of Honour for us of sixty Scouts, a hundred and forty Guides, plus innumerable Cubs and Brownies. I think every boy and girl on the island must have belonged to one or other of our two Movements.

Voyages seem to have a special magic for our family. Just as Robin and I had met and fallen in love on the *Arcadian* in 1912, so on that return journey on the *Llandovery Castle* Betty met and fell in love with Gervas Clay, a young District Commissioner returning to England on leave from Barotseland in Northern Rhodesia. They were to be engaged, married and on their way back to Africa before the summer was out. The wedding took place on September 24th at Bentley Church and we had a reception for four hundred guests at Pax Hill. Betty wore the silver-embroidered train that Auriol had worn at her wedding in 1911 and I at my presentation at Court in 1913; and just as my mother provided the wedding-ring for my marriage to Robin, so I gave Betty and Gervas their wedding-ring. The following day, the young couple sailed from Tilbury to start their life together in Northern Rhodesia.

Weddings were very much the talk of the day.

September 30th, 1936 – There is the most amazing lot of gossip going on about our naughty little King and his behaviour over this ... American woman that never leaves him. It is talked of publicly and in papers in America, but only secretly here. But one meets it at every turn and he is lowering himself and our prestige quite terribly and one wonders what he is going to do next. It is a bad business.

Despite the painful, personal problems with which the King was wrestling, he still had time and thought to spare for other people. On Wednesday, November 4th, 1936 we were astounded and gratified to receive a letter saying that the King offered my husband for use during his lifetime 'The King's House' at Walton-on-Thames. The house was a Jubilee Gift to King George V by the Royal Warrant Holders, but he did not live to see it. Each warrant holder had contributed towards the furnishings and equipment of the house. Maples had given the beds, the Goldsmiths and Silversmiths Company had provided the plate, and so on. It was a lovely place, exquisitely appointed, filled with every conceivable labour-saving device and comfort. It was a terribly tempting offer and, as the house carried an endowment for repairs, we could have lived there at a fraction of what it cost us at Pax Hill. But Pax Hill was our *home*. We had found it, added to it, cherished it over nearly twenty years. We loved the open views of the rolling countryside. We had planted the trees and the roses, we had brought up our children there, we had played with the dogs in the house and the garden. The dogs! Shawgm! That really decided it for us. It was inconceivable that Shawgm would be allowed to sleep on the King's sofa – and Shawgm was so very dear to us. We decided to decline the King's most generous offer and, as events turned out, it was a right decision.

Still the rumours of the King's desire to marry Mrs. Simpson flew about from drawing-room to drawing-room and on December 3rd the news broke in the British press. My diary records my daily and mounting concern. On December 10th I wrote:

Stunning newspaper headlines about the King determining to abdicate. Ironically we had our Coronation Camp Committee and we went on with it—in a sort of dazed hesitant way—wondering what the news would be. At 4.0 it came—and the Prime Minister (Baldwin) made the momentous statement that he gives up the Throne. One feels quite stunned by this amazing happening.

The next day, December 11th, as everyone now knows, the King abdicated and spoke over the air for the last time to 'his people' before leaving for France. We ourselves were due in Paris that same day for the 25th anniversary of the founding of Scouts in France. We were uncertain whether we should go for we both had qualms as to what sort of reception we should have. In the event, we did go to Paris where we were amazed at the way the news of the abdication was received. 'You English are a wonderful nation,' we were told. 'You can change your king overnight without losing your *savoir faire*.'

We were both greatly grieved and slightly ashamed that King Edward had put his personal happiness before his duty to his country. We felt a great sympathy for the new king, George VI, whom we had met at Windsor two years before. Kingship brought a heavy burden of responsibility and one could not but admire the nobility with which the new King took it up.

In 1937 Robin and I paid another visit to India. Our journey out was made anxious by a letter we received from Peter just before we sailed. The regulations of the British South African Police forbade Troopers to marry. Despite this rule, he now broke the news to us that he had been married since January 3rd, 1936 and had a little son, Robert, born in October of that year. It hurt us that he had not told us of this before, though I realise now that he had not wanted to involve us in the deception. What worried us even more was the unwisdom of taking on the responsibility of a wife and family before he was really earning enough to maintain them; and the even greater unwisdom of risking his career by marrying without permission. In the event, both problems were solved by his resigning from the B.S.A.P. and joining the Department of Native Affairs in Southern Rhodesia.

The main purpose of our visit to India on this occasion was to attend the first all-India Jamboree at Delhi. I think, too, that Robin knew that at eighty, it would be his last opportunity of visiting a continent he loved very dearly. *And* his old regiment was stationed in India, too, on the North-West Frontier and he was thrilled to be able to attend their last mounted parade before mechanisation – before they were turned into what Robin called 'a kind of steam perambulator.' Lady Arthur was at the parade. She told me how he rode on to the parade ground and, although it was his eightieth birthday, addressed the regiment *à haute voix*. She was in Westminster Abbey on *my* eightieth birthday, thirty-two years later, and heard me reading the Lesson. Apart from Heather (who accompanied her father to the parade), Dorothy Arthur must surely be the only person who was present on both occasions.

Once again we were entertained by the Viceroy, now Lord Linlithgow, only on this visit we were housed in the splendour of the new Lutyens Palace in New Delhi. It was vast and 'terribly regal' with a staff of two thousand servants. The grounds were exquisite, laid out with paths and fountains, with pergolas and roses and a wealth of English flowers.

It was a tremendously interesting time to be in India, with all the ferment over change of government. Everywhere one went, the Indian people were talking, thinking, reading, dreaming of independence. There was a campaign of 'civil disobedience' in progress and many members of Congress served prison sentences rather than cooperate with the British administration. There was also a certain tension on account of terrorist activities. When we dined with the Governor of Calcutta, Sir John Anderson, fourteen armed police roamed around the house and the bodyguards had rifles in their hands instead of the traditional lances.

To some it may seem a madness that they are getting this large measure of self-government on April 1st (I wrote at the time). But I don't see how it could be withheld with justice any longer . . .

One is so apt to speak of India as if it were one country – but really of course it is practically more like a continent, with its vast mixture of races and religions and complex problems of peoples.

Despite the uncertainty attending Independence, of one thing I was

certain: that Guiding had a great deal to offer to the children of India
and to the women who were only just beginning to emerge from their
traditional secluded way of life. I left Robin in New Delhi to rest and
went off on a tour on my own, visiting Guides in Agra, Madras,
Hyderabad, Mysore, Bangalore, Nagpur, Calcutta, Patna, Lucknow,
Jaipur. Everywhere I went, I saw evidence of the growing strength and
influence of Guiding on the young women of India, and they were all
so friendly and so delighted to welcome me.

'Small lots of Guides waiting to greet me at about 4 other stations
down the line. I get out and shake hands with dozens of hot brown
paws, and we beam upon each other.' Altogether, the tour of India was
a wonderful experience and one felt one had gained considerable
advancement for the Movement by the contacts made.

We arrived back in England in time for yet another St. George's
Day Parade at Windsor, only before another King. On this occasion
we were entertained to lunch:

> Sunday, April 25th, 1937—Robin and I lunched with Their
> Majesties at Windsor Castle—a wonderful family party of Queens
> and Princesses. The King and Queen welcomed us in like any
> ordinary host and hostess, and were so easy to talk to. She is ab-
> solutely sweet. We all strolled in to lunch at a round table. R. sat
> on Queen Elizabeth's right and next to Queen Mary—I sat on her
> left and Princess Helena Victoria was on my other side. Princess
> Beatrice and Queen Ena of Spain and Princess Marie Louise were
> there too. Princess Elizabeth and Margaret Rose came in for dessert
> and sat by R. and me and ate and gave us bits of coffee sugar.

When we arrived home to Pax Hill after the parade, we found that
one of the dogs had been sick on the drawing-room carpet. No sooner
had I changed out of my finery than I was down on my knees clearing
up the mess. I love contrasts!

London was *en fête* that summer for the Coronation of King George
VI. I shall never forget the splendour of the State Banquet we attended
at Buckingham Palace two nights before the Coronation—a marvellous assemblage of people of note, the flower of the nation and
Commonwealth: royalties, Prime Ministers, Church dignitaries,

Maori greeting (above) at Hawkes Bay, New Zealand, 1935; (below left) receiving a monster cone full of icecream money saved by Australian Brownies, Guides and Rangers; (below right) another Australian welcome.

Olave in the United States
(top) on the roof of Girl
Scout H.Q., New York;
(left) at Boy Scout H.Q.,
Philadelphia and (below)
receiving an American
Express credit card from
the Boy Scouts of America.

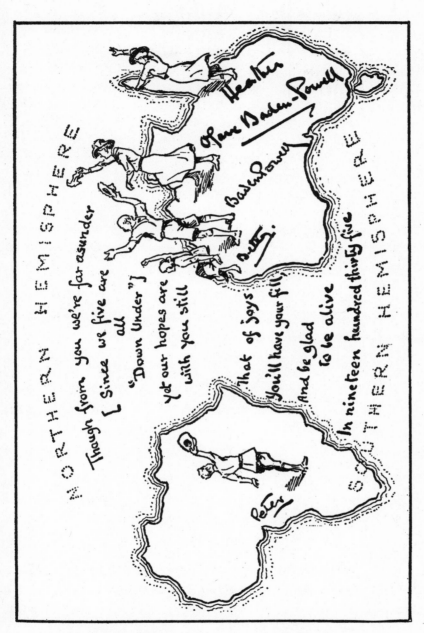

B.-P.'s design for our greeting card, Christmas 1934

Rajahs, Governors. The room was ablaze with the glitter of jewels and uniforms and medals and decorations.

May 12th was Coronation Day. In order to be in our places early, we slept in London the night before—Robin at Scout Headquarters and I at Guide Headquarters. Sir Philip Game, who was then Commissioner of Police, arranged for an escort to help us through the crowds to our seats in the House of Lords stand at Westminster. We walked through Horse Guards and down the middle of Whitehall which was, of course, cleared of traffic. Someone said 'There's B.-P.!' and everybody cheered. It was so exciting and heart-warming. Scouts were on duty selling programmes. They are called on quite a lot to help with State occasions; it is a great honour.

Robin received the Order of Merit in the Coronation Honours—perhaps of all his honours and decorations, the one of which he was most proud. It was a public recognition of what everybody felt about him.

Dindo—(he wrote following a radio broadcast that summer)

I've been overwhelmed with B.B.C. praisings from every Mercer!

Also—what touched me very much—the taxi driver who took my luggage . . . to Euston asked to shake hands as he wanted to thank me for my talk on Tuesday and the Scout training which had made a *man* of his boy. It is so good to hear a *genuine* tribute like that.

Now don't go and over work because I'm away: give those fat dogs a bit of exercise.

Your loving
Bin.

Betty's first child, Gillian, was born that summer. Betty was blissfully happy in her marriage. Peter wrote that he was settled into the D.N.A. in Southern Rhodesia. With his letter came our first from his wife, Carine. I noted with approval that 'she sounds as if she would pull Peter together'. Heather had found herself a congenial job as secretary to Lady Kennett, the former widow of Captain Scott of the Antarctic. (His ship, the *Discovery*, was, incidentally, given to the Scouts later that year). It looked as if, for the first time for years, Robin and I were going to have time for each other.

First of all, though, we had to attend the Fifth World Jamboree at Vogelenzang in Holland. It was going to be a problem to know how to protect Robin while he was there. He was such a beloved leader to the millions of Scouts around the world that he was mobbed wherever he went. In their eager enthusiasm to be near him and touch him, the boys did not realise the strain it was for a man of his age. I shall never forget his speech at the closing of the Jamboree. I think he knew he would not live to see another.

The time has come for me to say good-bye. You know that many of us will never meet again in this world. I am in my eighty-first year and am nearing the end of my life. Most of you are at the beginning, and I want your lives to be happy and successful. You can make them so by doing your best to carry out the Scout Law all your days, whatever your station and wherever you are.

I want you all to preserve the badge of the Jamboree on your uniform . . . It will be a reminder of the happy times you have had here in camp; it will remind you to take the ten points of the Scout Law as your guide in life; and it will remind you of the many friends to whom you have held out the hand of friendship and so helped through good will to bring about God's reign of peace among men.

Now good-bye. God bless you all!

We celebrated our silver wedding on October 30th, 1937 — a wonderfully exciting day with hundreds of cards and letters and telegrams, and gifts ranging from a silver tea-caddy from the Princess Royal to a handsome cheque from all the Scouts and Guides and Cubs and Brownies in the world 'to purchase some of those domestic wants that are always felt in a household, such as the provision of a toothbrush!'

Once again we planned to spend the winter in Africa and sailed from the East India Docks on November 25th aboard the *Llandaff Castle*. Perhaps when Robin made his farewell speech at the Jamboree he had guessed that it was not only his own life that was soon to pass away but the life of the whole world as we knew it and had enjoyed it over the years.

Genoa. 5th December, 1937 . . . into the town and we saw hundreds of the 'youth movement' *Balilla*—boys and girls—all dismissing after a big anniversary parade they had had in the town. The boys mostly carrying rifles and it seems all very 'belligerent', super national and a great danger for the future.

CHAPTER NINETEEN

Death of a Hero

Years: 1938–1941

We went straight to the Outspan after landing at Mombasa and Robin went down almost immediately with what I convinced myself was only bronchitis and lumbago. When the doctor examined him immediately after Christmas, however, he pronounced his heart 'very tired' and prescribed long and complete rest—for at least a year. We immediately cancelled the tours we had planned to make together in the Rhodesias and South Africa, and my own for the following summer in England, and settled down in our little bungalow at the Outspan for a 'silver honeymoon'. Robin was having awful heads, just as he had had when we were first married, only now there was additionally a pain around his heart and he could walk only very short distances without becoming distressed.

But we were happy together at the Outspan—so happy that we put up to Eric the idea that we should invest enough money in the hotel for him to build us a bungalow of our own. That way we could spend the six winter months in Kenya and he could let it like any other of the hotel bungalows during the summer months when we should be in England.

The weeks passed by, one quiet day following upon another. Migwe, our 'boy', would call us with early morning tea. The birds would be singing and there would be a divine early morning smell of fresh damp earth. After breakfast, I would deal with our correspondence and then, as Robin grew stronger, we would take a gentle walk to the top of the golf links. In the afternoon he would rest until tea-time while I sat doing mending or some other quiet occupation. Then Robin would go out on the verandah to paint or read or write and I would take a long, strenuous walk. I had been so used to having my days packed with activity that it was not easy to slow down.

Eric gave us a baby hyrax for our birthday on 22nd February and we christened him 'Two-Two' in honour of the day. He was an affectionate wee creature, rather like a squirrel, and would accompany me on my walks, sitting on my shoulder. He sat on my lap while I typed letters and was the nearest substitute we could find in Africa for our beloved Shawgm.

It was wonderful to see my husband gradually returning to health and by the end of February, I felt he was well enough to leave in the excellent care of Eric and his wife while I visited Peter and Betty.

First I flew to Salisbury and then up to Inyanga to visit Peter and to meet his wife, Carine, and our first grandchild, Robert—named after my husband. I found Carine 'quite splendid, good-looking, capable, alive, intelligent and very sweet' as I reported back to Robin, and I was quite captivated by little Robert. Normally I do not like babies very much but at sixteen months he was bright and always laughing, and clamoured to be with me all the time.

I flew on to Mankoya to visit Betty and Gervas and to inspect our second grandchild, Gillian. Gervas, as District Commissioner, 'ruled' over some 34,000 Barotse tribesmen. Their home was in a remote part of Northern Rhodesia, 350 miles from Lusaka and 40 miles from the nearest white person, a missionary in an equally isolated station. I had to charter a private plane to get me there. I was away four weeks in all and by the time I arrived back at Nyeri, Robin was completely his old self again.

We decided to return to England for the summer and sailed from Mombasa aboard the *Llangibby Castle* on April 13th. A week later, we met Peter, again at Beira as in 1935, only this time with his new family. It was wonderful that Robin had the opportunity to hold his grandson in his arms.

By May 21st we were back at our beloved Pax Hill where we spent the summer very quietly. Robin undertook no engagements at all and I only made brief appearances in public—on television for the first time from the Alexandra Palace on June 16th, and at Windsor on June 19th for a parade of First Class Guides before their Majesties. I was proud to see the two Princesses wearing our uniform in public on that occasion.

Another Cruise of Good Will had been arranged for August. This time it was to Iceland, Norway, Denmark and Belgium. Robin was determined to keep his promise and go. However, on the doctor's orders, the 700 Scouters and Guiders aboard the *Orduna* were not able to see much of him, although his very presence aboard was an inspiration to them; and he could wave to the enthusiastic Scouts and Guides gathered on the quayside at every port of call, even if he did not go ashore.

Robin spent the rest of the summer quietly winding up his affairs in England. I think he knew it was the last he would see of the country he had served in war and peace over so many, many years.

He gave many of his most interesting mementoes to Scout Headquarters for the 'Chief's Room'; he would not be showing visiting Scouts over Pax Hill again. 'Eccles', the caravan the Scouts of the World had given to us in 1929 was returned to the Association and given a place of honour at Gilwell Park. September 1938 was the first occasion since the Gilwell Reunion had been instituted that the beloved 'Chief' was not camping there. Dear Shawgm had to be put down on September 7th, deaf and blind and full of years. His going left an ache in our hearts for he had been such a devoted companion. My brother-in-law, Bob Davidson, died of sprue two weeks later. Europe was poised on the brink of war. It was an unhappy time.

There was to be a breathing-space. The Munich Agreement was signed and the flood-tide of violence held in check for another year. 'Friday, September 30th, 1938 — Peace definitely decided last night, and the relief is intense. We were apparently within 24 hours of war, and it has been a ghastly experience for the whole world.'

We heard from Eric Walker that our bungalow at the Outspan was completed so we selected such of our books and silver and personal effects as we felt we should need, put the remainder and our furniture in store, let Pax Hill and sailed on October 26th for Africa aboard the *Llandaff Castle*. Despite the Munich agreement, there was tension: 'November 1st, 1938 — We keep well down towards the coast of Africa, to be out of the zone where those brutal Spaniards have mines laid round their Spanish coast and even ten miles out to sea.' It was a peaceful voyage after that early alarm. Captain Brown allowed us the use of his private deck so that Robin would not be disturbed by other passengers. We reached our new home on November 24th.

We christened the bungalow 'Paxtu' — Pax the Second. 'Tu' in Swahili means 'altogether' or 'complete' so 'Paxtu' also meant 'Complete Peace' — and so it was for us.

The bungalow was all we had hoped. It had a wide stone verandah facing the magnificent view of Mount Kenya and soon we attracted to the verandah our 'bird club' of weaver birds, wax-bills and bul-buls. The garden was bright with the glowing reds and yellows of cannas and golden shower. We had a little lily pond with a fountain and while I gardened, Robin painted and wrote. He seemed wonderfully restored in health and produced some of his finest work at Paxtu. He was well enough to go fishing and to spend an occasional night at Treetops. He recorded his impressions of Kenya in the magnificent water-colours reproduced in his two books, *Birds and Beasts in Africa* and *More Sketches of Kenya*.

Migwe came again to look after us. Two-Two refused to come back so, in his place, we acquired another hyrax, 'Hyrie', who proved even more affectionate than his predecessor. He was quite a baby when I bought him (for 5d.) and was perfectly house-trained. He lived on a diet of rose petals and carrot tops.

I could not be idle. If we were to settle in Kenya for six months of each year and meet regularly the natives of that country, I must learn the language. I feel strongly about people knowing the language of the country in which they live. It is the least one can do as a courtesy to the country of one's adoption; it shows one has taken trouble. That was one mistake made by many British women in India in the days of the British Raj; they just could not be bothered with the language. Swahili was not easy but I managed to master enough to get by. I went to classes given by a Roman Catholic priest at the mission in Nyeri, along with the Swiss housekeeper and the manager of the Outspan Hotel.

> I feel very stumped by all the grammar and these awful prefixes of ni's and tu's and wa's and things! . . . I find it all most difficult to memorise. I never could learn by heart even when young, and when 50 it is even worse!

I was taking no active part in Guiding apart from 'doing Brownies' with Eric Walker's two little girls but occasionally I would go the ninety-five miles to Nairobi and discuss Guide affairs there or attend meetings of the East African Women's League.

My niece Christian joined us in March of 1939. She had had to have a serious operation on her back and, still far from well, came to the warmth of Kenya to recuperate. Betty arrived with little Gillian from Rhodesia to be with me for the birth of her second baby, who arrived on April 16th. Heather flew out from England for a short visit. At the same time, to my dismay, Robin began to be ill again, with his heart troublesome, and itching all over his arms, back, legs and head. If I ever thought time would hang heavily on my hands at Paxtu, the illusion was soon dispelled! I was on the run all the time between my three patients.

Robin was very frail, hardly eating anything at all. I had to coax him to take spoonfuls of arrowroot or Brand's Essence. Fortunately, we had an excellent doctor only ten miles away. He would turn out at any hour if needed and often slept the night at Paxtu if he was called out late. We had to dress Robin's arms and legs with ointment three times a day. The irritation never left him and nothing we tried seemed to bring relief. His temperature varied wildly, leaving him limp and weak, though wonderfully patient and long-suffering. However, once again he made a fair recovery and felt strong enough to go on a short safari expedition on which he was to base one of his finest paintings.

August 1st, 1939 — After longish tour round returning to camp about 8.0 (a.m.) we suddenly saw a rhino come walking out of the bush. Watched him coming and when he saw us his head went down and his tail went up and he rushed towards us. Capt. Gethin 'stepped on the gas' and we fled off! He trotted off at 18 m.p.h. and we escorted him for a little. It was a real thrill! Went back again to Namanga; and in the evening went out again looking for elephants and had a grand sight of one by the road and he 'saw us off' too — at only 9 yards' distance — all most exciting and lovely. A real good day!

This elephant was the subject of Robin's painting. It now hangs in the International Centre at Gilwell Park.

Robin had been too ill to return to England for the summer of 1939 but we had tentatively booked our passages on the *Klipfontein* sailing for England on March 23rd, 1940. It was not to be.

Sunday, September 3rd, 1939 — Listen in anxiously many times in the day and then — in the evening — the awful news comes through of war having been declared by France and us on Germany.

Robin's first reaction, old and frail though he might be, was to feel he should be in England, but the Deputy Chief Scout, Lord Somers, assured him that the Scouts were rising splendidly to the needs of the occasion; he was to stay where he was in Kenya. It was hard for him to resign himself to inactivity at such a time of crisis for Britain. I busied myself stitching at surgeons' caps and masks for the Red Cross. It was the only form of war-work I could find to do. I felt idle and useless and positively guilty when I played squash or tennis. Some salve to my conscience came a month later. The Governor of Kenya, Air-Marshal Sir Robert Brooke-Popham, was returning to active service in England. His wife, Opal, was naturally returning with him. She asked me to take over her work as Colony Commissioner of Guides in Kenya. I threw all my pent-up energies into the work. I knew there were many prejudices of colour and race in Kenya which cut clean across the Scout and Guide principle of brother- and sister-hood with 'every colour and creed'. I had the satisfaction soon of seeing the Guides of Kenya agree to multi-racial camps, despite strong anti-Indian feeling in the colony generally.

It was frustrating not being able to receive detailed news from England. Letters arrived infrequently and those we had were the short 'airgraphs' with no room for more than the briefest of messages. We heard that Pax Hill had been commandeered by the Army but no more than that.

Still the pleasant, relatively undisturbed life carried on, as unreal as the 'phoney' war in Europe at that time. I still played tennis every day on the Outspan courts. Robin was still well enough to come with me on a four-day safari at the end of January 1940 and to make another splendid painting out of the experience.

. . . Muhori spotted buffalo and we saw a herd disappearing into thick bush—lots of big black hind quarters! Further on we stopped and got out (of the truck) and crept near an ant heap and then saw and watched at close range 124 buffalo come up out of the river and wander along quietly grazing—oblivious of our presence! It was marvellous and most thrilling. In some ways it was most unsafe and a real risk as 'buffs' turn nasty easily. But the wind was the right way and they did not see us.

In February of 1940 we had a wonderful family reunion. Peter and Gervas were able to obtain leave at the same time and were able to bring their respective families to the Outspan. It was the last time Robin would have all his family around him and the only time he would see all his grandchildren. Out of all our family, only Heather was missing. She was in the A.T.S. 'driving her general all over the Eastern command.'

The 'phoney' war ended in the spring of 1940 and we heard with growing dismay the quite dreadful war news: Norway and Denmark invaded, the Germans sweeping through Holland and Belgium. Was it only three years since Robin had escorted Queen Wilhelmina round the Vogelenzang Jamboree? Now she had had to seek sanctuary in England. —

May 21st, 1940—We listen in twice a day to terrible news of ruthless destruction of towns, bombing and machine-gunning of helpless fleeing civilians and refugees pouring over to England. And England—our England—is even endangered too.

May 26th, 1940—To Church . . . Somehow though one tries to believe in a God Almighty and right and truth and goodness and all the things that matter, this war and the way it is going simply shakes one to the core . . .

France was over-run and sued for peace. The Allied armies retreated to Dunkirk and their fortunes sank lower and lower. The only cheerful note in my diary for this period is on June 24th when Heather married Squadron-Leader John King, R.A.F., at Bentley Church.

It seemed as if my own darling Robin's health was reflecting the grim combat taking place so far away from the peaceful plains around Nyeri. He was 'up and down' for no apparent reason at all—more often 'down' than 'up'. His temperature was constantly above normal making him feel sick and feeble. Always there was the itching to his legs and arms. The doctor and I tried one ointment after another but always with the same negative result. He would obtain momentary relief and our hopes of a cure would rise, but soon the itching was as trying as ever. It made him peevish and irritable which seemed to me incredible, for always he had been so patient and loving and good-tempered. I found it hard myself to be patient for the strain of caring for him was telling on me too, and then if I had been irritable with him, I would be full of self-reproach.

In September, Dr. Doig warned me that his heart was 'awfully tired'. I was in despair—how much longer had we together—weeks? months? —certainly not years. Yet his voice was as strong as ever and his mind clear. He was keenly interested in everything that went on around him, listened to the wireless, dictated his regular article for *The Scouter* and even, in October, drew our Christmas card. But the end could not be far away.

Betty drove up from Northern Rhodesia for a week at the beginning of November, bringing Christian back to us. She had been with Betty for the past six months. Now she became a tower of strength, for by the middle of the month Robin had to have someone in attendance night and day. I do not know how I should have managed without her and a Dr. Piokowski, a Polish/Jewish refugee doctor who was staying at the Outspan and who called in frequently to give Robin injections of morphia to soothe him.

Wednesday, November 13th, 1940—A horrid night, and he slept badly, coughed a lot and felt very ill, the poor lamb. Got up to fuss round him almost every hour, and it is dreadful to see him suffering—so breathless and gasping and groaning—so tired out.

Life seemed so unreal. If I moved outside Paxtu, I found life going on in the usual way. I met people and talked and exchanged news. The guests at the Outspan came and went, played tennis, squash and went on safari. Back in the bungalow, Robin's tired old heart ticked more and more slowly. He just lay there with his eyes shut, unable to move himself, not wishing to talk. At intervals we fed him with a little jelly or soup or egg flip. At the end of November he rallied slightly and was able to lie out on the verandah. Occasionally, I would read to him but he would fall asleep almost at once. I think I feared most the times when he was out of pain for then he seemed to lack the will to fight back.

December 4th, 1940 – A rather bad day, as his back aches, and he feels miserable and everything is wrong. But in a way that is a good sign, that he is strong enough to be grumpy!

By the middle of December I really thought he was going to pull through. He sat out in an armchair, read the papers for the first time in five weeks and 'actually smiled again'. He was able to sit out and hear the King's Speech to the Empire on Christmas Day but he was depressed at the monotony of his daily existence – one could not call it 'life'. I was in despair. I wanted Robin to live, but not like this.

We had a nurse, Sister Ray, to help look after him. On the 6th of January he was fearfully weak but understood when I gave him the news that the Italians had been beaten at Bardia. He did not have too bad a night and the next day we had morning tea together at 6.0 and I sat beside him talking till breakfast time. He slept most of the day and I felt sufficiently hopeful to play tennis up at the hotel. That night, however, he was suddenly much worse. At 2.30 in the morning of January 8th, Sister Ray woke me and said 'He is going.'

I went into his room and just sat by his bed, watching that dear, darling life ebbing away. He was so white and thin, quite unconscious and still, breathing very slowly in gusts. Sister Ray sat on the other side of the bed holding his pulse. It was only flickering, she said. By 5 o'clock, I thought he would still live the day through and went back to bed to get warm for I was chilled – with anxiety as much as by the night air. I kissed his dear forehead and left Sister Ray sitting by him. I lay wide awake and shivering in my bed, listening. At 5.45, Sister Ray said quietly 'He's gone.'

He looked so sweet and perfect in death, just as he had been in life – utterly noble and good and dear and wonderful and great and faultless.

CHAPTER TWENTY

Alone

Years: 1941 – 1942

I could not bear to go to Robin's funeral; I wanted to remember him in life, not death. It was, I have been told, a simple, dignified and moving military ceremony. He was laid to rest in the little cemetery at Nyeri, only a few hundred yards from Paxtu, in sight of the mountain he loved and used to watch in all its moods from the verandah of our bungalow. The Governor was there, and soldiers and sailors, and Scouts and Guides — African, Asian and European. Christian took the tribute of flowers I had myself picked and arranged. I stayed with friends twenty-five miles away and spent the day of the funeral walking and walking, weeping and weeping in agonised grief.

I had known when I married him that, with thirty-two years between us, I might well have to face an early widowhood but it was a thought I had pushed to the back of my mind as nearly thirty years of happy marriage went by and still we were together. Nothing prepared me for the anguish I felt at his going. I felt only half alive, dazed with grief and loss.

I went back to Nyeri the day after the funeral and forced myself to go to the cemetery to see his grave. It was covered with Flanders poppies and as I sat and wept beside it, I felt suddenly comforted, as if he were near me and understood. It was a feeling I was to experience many times over the next few months. However great my unhappiness, no matter how often and suddenly and embarrassingly the tears would flow, always at his graveside I was to find peace.

Meantime, I had to force myself to start living again. I was fifty-one and though I did not wish to live without my darling Robin beside me, I could not count on dying.

There were over four hundred letters and cables awaiting me on my return to Paxtu, including one from the King and Queen. It was good discipline to have to sit down and make myself reply to them all. I forced myself to sort out Robin's clothes, giving some to Migwe and packing up the remainder for evacuees in England. I put away his watch and his painting things, as I had done so many times when we had gone on journeys together; only this time I could not go with him. At night in bed, I clutched little Hyrie to me for comfort and wept into my pillow.

I found he had left me four letters. They had been written at various periods of his life when he had felt the future was uncertain. Instead of throwing away the early ones, he had simply added another to the envelope over the years. The first was written in France when we were both on active service there during the First World War.

> Etaples, 21 January 1916
>
> Dindo darling, I look on it this way if you were to get killed before me: I feel that one must always pay for what you get in this world and if it is something very good you must naturally expect to pay the more heavily for it. The question comes — is the good worth the cost?
>
> That question has often occurred to me when I have found myself more and more in love with you — more and more bound to you. I have realised, only in part perhaps, how awful will be the break when it comes (as some day it has to come for one of us). I have asked myself, would it be better to live as some couples do, on easy terms of friendship so that when the parting comes it is not so knock-down a blow to the survivor? My answer has been No — this glorious love between us is worth any shock that can come later. It is such absolute and continuous happiness, so long as it lasts, that it gives life a different character altogether: and to have had the few years of it that we have had is well worth any temporary pang of sorrow that may (and has got to) come at the end. So if the blow has to fall on me, I feel that by Being Prepared for it in this way I shall be able to bear it in looking on it as the price I have naturally got to pay for having had the best and happiest life that any man ever had. And I shall still have part of you with me in the dear children — and they will help to fill the empty place.

But if all this happens you won't see this note — you will only get it if the converse happens — that is if I go first. But it applies equally to you. Will you see it in the same light? . . .

The second letter, undated, and with no address, refers to the above:

Dindo,

I wrote you a long screed on the day that you and I went to Bingley's funeral and took charge of Mrs. Bingley at Etaples during the war. It had brought home to me the point that some day we two would be parted and I wanted to leave you a little word of farewell . . . I do want you to know that I *am* thankful to you, my darling, for all that you have done to make life a heaven on earth for me.

If you had never done all the other good deeds that you have done (for our children, for Auriol's children, for the G.G. etc.), you would still have the satisfaction of knowing that you did for me what no other person in the world could or would have done. You have not wasted your life and opportunities in selfishness but have spent them in giving out kindness. And that is where I feel hope in leaving you, sweetheart. I know the parting will have to be bitter. It is bound to be: we have to pay something for the good time we have had, and it is the one who stays that has to pay. But if it were me to stay I should pay it gladly — to me our life together has been worth any temporary pain that could be inflicted.

I expect you see it in that light too — don't you, dear? But, as I say, what comforts me most is the knowledge that your pluck and sensible way of looking at things will carry you through the first strain, and that your power and habit of doing good for others will give you the occupation that will bring back the sunshine in your life after this shadow of the cloud has passed over.

You have our children to work for and to bring out and you have the G.G.

I hope I shall see you and hear you saying 'Yes, dear, it is all right. Don't you worry. I shall be all right directly' — and then you would get to work with brave heart and tackle your work afresh

Olave's eightieth birthday party, February 22nd, 1969.

With H.M. the Queen and H.R.H. Princess Margaret, receiving Diamond Jubilee mugs, 19th May, 1970.

Sitting for a portrait bust by sculptor David Wynne, 1971.

The World Chief Guide, still at her desk.

to make it the biggest success that ever was seen for the good of others.

If there is a hereafter, I shall be watching – and waiting.

Your

Bin.

The Third letter was written at Pax Hill some time after his recovery from the serious prostate operation:

Pax Hill, Bentley, Hampshire.
28 Nov. 36

My Dindo D.

I have seen so many men of my age die quite unexpectedly and in case this should happen to me I want to leave you a little word of farewell. I wrote you a note to that effect years ago and left it – and another – in the envelope where you will find this. I was going to tear them up as being out of date but I have glanced through them, and though they were written so long ago they still exactly reflect what I feel today and shall feel to the end – that our love and happiness through the past quarter of a century has been well worth the price that you or one of us will have to pay in losing your mate.

Thank God you are not going to mope over it, for you have plenty of good work before you yet to do with the Girl Guides. So, darling, buckle to, with brave heart and do it.

If there is a Beyond, I shall be there, watching and waiting.

Bin.

The last letter was written at the Outspan only a few months earlier:

1940

Dindo darling:

I don't know whether my increasing and unaccountable weakness of the last few weeks may mean the beginning of the end for me, but if so I don't mind *personally* – it is only the natural thing. I have arrived at the time of life for passing on.

I have (had) a most extraordinarily happy life, most especially in these last 27 years of it which you have made so heavenly and

13

successful for me. I don't think I have frittered away much of my time while alive. It is good to think that in addition to my keen soldiering our efforts for the boys and girls have been successful beyond all expectations.

It is good too to feel that our own youngsters are all happily married and established in life. The world has been awfully good to me and in a way I am sorry to leave it and all its interests, but I have reached the stage where I can be of no more use other than a looker-on so it is right that I should go.

But what is more to me than all the world is *you*, my darling. The fact of having to leave you is the one pang that haunts me—not only on my own account but more especially because it will mean a terrible break in your own life. One thing that comforts me is that you are so sensible that you will see it in its right proportion as a natural thing that had to come, and you will face the ordeal with courage during its short spell, till time heals the wound.

I am glad to think that you have the best form of consolation before you in the shape of plenty of work with the Guides. Also you have the great love of your children and their children to help you. I hope that Christian will join you and be another daughter and right hand to you.

I do hope too that so soon as I go you will be off *at once* to stay with Betty and so to soften the first shock of loneliness . . .

Your sorrow would be the only regret I should have in dying: if I know that you will not let it grieve you unduly, I shall die all the happier, my D.

Your
Bin.

I make no apology for quoting those letters in full. Their tenderness and their message were frequently in my mind during the weeks that followed as I struggled to master my almost overwhelming grief, as I tended his grave, as I endeavoured to cope with the hundreds of letters that reached me from all over the world. *How* he was loved! I could know and take comfort from the thought that my own sense of loss was shared by hundreds of thousands—no, millions—who knew him. I walked, and wrote, and thought, and tried to count my blessings.

'Thinking Day'—our birthday—brought a renewed sense of loss but I knew from his letters that it would grieve him if I surrendered easily to my sorrow. Others in this dreadful war were suffering the same, and greater, loss than I. Robin had told me that I had 'plenty of good work before me'. I decided to get on with it.

The East Africa Women's League was my salvation at this time. They asked me to become their President and I flung myself into the work with an energy born of a desperate need to find oblivion in hard work.

The E.A.W.L. was a sort of Kenyan equivalent of the Women's Institute in Britain. At that time it was only made up of European women; now it is, nominally at any rate, inter-racial. We did general welfare work among local inhabitants, organised various schemes for the education of African women, raised funds for local hospitals and churches—all the activities that women usually take on themselves in the service of the community. We even had a scheme for receiving 'bombed babies' from England and evacuee children from Greece but neither of these schemes came to anything. There was much work to do. I offered to do a tour for them, combining it with Robin's instruction to visit Betty as soon as possible after his death.

First of all, though, I had to see that the 'God's Acre' where my beloved husband was buried was all in order. I arranged for a simple headstone and a small walled garden around the grave. This put in hand, I bought an old car—a Dodge, which was virtually tied together with string but was all I could for the moment afford—and set off with Christian for a three months' tour.

It was really quite incredible. We had no thought of danger, no anxiety about animals and bandits. If we stopped to worry at all, it was about whether we should get stuck in the mud anywhere en route. One could not undertake such a journey today. We christened the car TURCK as we were to visit Tanganyika, Uganda, Rhodesia, Congo and Kenya. We took our two 'boys', Migwe and Muhori, with us, and little Hyrie in a special two-storey travelling house I had made for him. The boys did not speak any English but I had learned enough Swahili by now to ask for what we wanted.

The first part of our trip, as far as Mombasa, we were escorted by a South African Army car with two mechanics on board. Colonel Trevitt arranged this—I think he thought it was quite mad, two women going off on their own in such a ramshackle car. We had various Army escorts during our long trek across Tanganyika. We visited the Crater Lake, passing round Mount Kilimanjaro; we watched a lioness at her kill a few miles out of Arusha and eventually crossed the border into Northern Rhodesia at Isoka, where Gervas was in charge of the District. We stayed with him and Betty for two weeks, then put the car aboard the S.S. *Liemba* and spent six days crossing Lake Tanganyika

> . . . anchoring every few hours, to pick up rice, etc. from minute native huts clustered on the shore, the people coming out in dugouts . . .
>
> We dawdle along by day . . . but hear news over the wireless of the fall of Crete — ghastly fighting and evacuation of Crete, revolt in Iraq, etc.

Even in Central Africa, one could not escape the war. We reached Ujiji, the end of the old slave route, where Livingstone was found by Stanley in 1871. We were watching an exhibition of drumming and dancing by forty pygmies on the Congo border when 'we hear amazing news of Russia having declared war on Germany and thus being allies of ours'. We visited the National Park Albert and Lake Edward in the Congo but there was an epidemic of yellow fever in the country so we headed back to the Uganda border.

Then we broke down. Christian's back trouble became aggravated with driving so each day after lunch she would lie down for a while. I would walk ahead and eventually she would catch me up in the car and we would carry on together. On this particular day, I set off to walk as usual. I walked and walked. There was still no sign of Christian. I began to feel a bit uneasy and kept looking back. Eventually I saw Migwe panting towards me. The car had broken down, he said. Nothing they tried would make it go. I went back to the car and Christian. It was just as Migwe had indicated; the car had died on us completely. At this juncture we were more than a little worried, for one cannot just phone up the nearest garage in the middle of Africa! By some miracle a lorry came along and gave us a tow as far as the Uganda border. It was all of ninety miles.

The Customs were horrified. We could not come into Uganda from Congo without being inoculated against yellow fever. We must go back.

'How are we going to manage that?' we asked. 'The car won't go so we *can't* go back.'

In the end, they let us through on condition that we stayed two weeks in quarantine there at Fort Portal. It was a most enjoyable fortnight. We met lots of Guiders in the town, including the Roman Catholic Mother Superior, and a German Guider who had been to Foxlease.

After our period of quarantine had expired, we toured all over Uganda, visiting Scouts and Guides in Mission Schools and leper colonies, attending meetings of the E.A.W.L. and seeing the beauties of the country, such as Thomsons Falls. We arrived back at Paxtu on August 13th having been travelling for over three months.

But the long trip had not cured my unhappiness. Back in Nyeri the sense of loss crowded in on me again. 'August 24th, 1941 — Frightfully depressed and hate being alive, and the dreadful war goes on and on and on.' I planted grass and roses round 'my' grave but I had not enough to fill my time so in November I made another tour of E.A.W.L. branches in Kenya, travelling 1,158 miles in three weeks.

Japan entered the war in December and peace seemed further away than ever. I kept thinking of the work my darling had left to me to do. I kept receiving letters from England telling me thrilling stories of the heroism of Scouts and Guides in Britain and in the occupied countries of Europe. Then I had one letter in particular that challenged me. It was from Miss Tennyson, the Editor of *The Guider*, and she wrote: 'Come home and see what Guides are doing in the war. You will never forgive yourself if you don't see it.' That settled my decision; I would return to England just as soon as I could get a passage.

There was much to see to. I had to retire from being President of the E.A.W.L.; I had to appoint a new Colony Commissioner for the Guides; I had to find a home for my adorable Hyrie; I had to say goodbye to Paxtu and Robin's grave and all the things that had become so dear to me.

May 6th, 1942 — I just loathe this coming away. It seems stupid to do it, when I hate it so. But I know I must. Cried horribly over leaving Hyrie and everything. *When* shall I get back I wonder.

I flew down the coast to Durban to spend a few days with Betty who was on leave there with her husband. The plane was blacked out and one could not see anything. I still had to wait for a ship so I did a brisk tour of South African Guides ('being idle doesn't suit me', I wrote sternly in my diary). I hung about Cape Town waiting for a passage. I phoned the shipping company every day, and every day they said the same thing: 'Nothing at the moment but stay on the end of a telephone.' I hardly dared go out in case I missed the call. At last, on July 22nd, 1942 the telephone rang with the message 'Be on board tomorrow.' The ship was the *City of Marseilles* homeward bound from Australia to Liverpool. I went on board the next day and at 6.0 a.m. on Friday, July 24th, 1942 set sail for an England I had not seen since October 1938.

CHAPTER TWENTY-ONE

A New Challenge

Years: 1942 – 1945

It seemed strange and sad to be steaming out of Table Bay without Robin beside me. The voyage was strangely unreal, too. There was an ever-present danger of attack by submarine and we had to carry our life-belts all the time. Portholes were blacked out and had to be kept shut at night. But the sunny days followed each other and nothing happened. I made friends with Mrs. Hepburn, the lame and elderly widow of a Methodist minister, who occupied the cabin opposite mine. She was lonely and frightened and needed friendship. I began to read my Bible but '... All this living time is a sort of dull hollow passing of time without any real spark of life in it – all empty.'

We reached Freetown without incident and had to spend several days there waiting for a convoy to assemble. At last we set sail for Liverpool. There were constant alerts.

> Continuous ringing of the siren means 'subs' are about and we go aloft: the intermittent ringing means danger from the air, and we must go below.
>
> August 25th, 1942 – carry our life-belts always with us now – to the bath and all – as well as a haversack of money, passports etc. in case we suddenly have to take to the boats.
>
> August 26th, 1942 – News came through of the Duke of Kent being killed in an air-crash in Scotland.
>
> Friday, August 28th, 1942 – Frequent alarms – ships on either side torpedoed. Sloops rushing round dropping depth charges. U-boat attack lasted 2 hours. All slept in our clothes. Carry coats and bags everywhere.

I was not frightened; I was still in a state of numb unhappiness. When the two ships went down on either side of us, I wished I could have gone down with them; it would have been a quick and easy way out. But we steamed on without being hit. The next day, Saturday, there was only one alarm but on the Sunday the convoy was again attacked by U-boats. Depth charges shook our big ship. There were three more alarms of submarine attacks that day, and the following day an aircraft alarm. On the Tuesday we were attacked three times from the air but on each occasion our attacker was 'seen off' by a protecting Sunderland. The real danger was from U-boats and the atmosphere aboard grew steadily more tense as we approached England. There were to be no more attacks, however, and on Saturday, September 5th, on a rough, cold, grey, wet and windy day, the convoy entered the Mersey.

It was evening by the time we had got ashore. I did not fancy scrambling for a late train to London so I shepherded old Mrs. Hepburn to the Adelphi Hotel, booked in myself and then went out to go for my first walk in wartime England. I was shocked. There had been a raid the night before so that I came immediately upon the stark horror of bombing. It was a revelation to me; I was not prepared for it to be so bad.

The following day Mrs. Hepburn and I travelled to London on one of the slow, crowded trains that I was to come to know so well. I handed over my elderly charge to her sisters at Euston and then I was on my own.

First of all, I had to have a bed. No one in London knew I had come home. I booked in at the Grosvenor at Victoria. I had not stayed there since 1912 when I came up to London from Lilliput with mother to buy my trousseau.

It was Sunday so I thought I had better find a church and say 'thank you' for my safe voyage to England — I could not say 'home' for I had no home any more. I walked down Victoria Street to Westminster Abbey but it was closed, so I went on past the Houses of Parliament and on to Westminster Bridge. I stopped in the middle and leaned over the parapet, staring at the water. I was tempted to jump in; it would be one way out of my loneliness. But I didn't. The thought came into my mind that if, after so many dangers, I had been spared to reach England safely, it must be for some reason; and I remembered Robin's charge to me in his letters. I must carry on the work he had started. So I turned round and walked back to the hotel.

The next day I telephoned to Heather and Eileen Wade and Annie, our old cook, and told them I was home. I had to get an Identity Card and a Ration Book. There was so much to learn and understand about wartime England. In the afternoon, I decided I must take the plunge and offer my services to Guide Headquarters again. I remember walking along Buckingham Palace Road on the opposite side from Headquarters and thinking 'I can't do it, I can't take up the reins again.' Eventually I forced myself to cross the road and go in, and everyone was so pleased and welcoming that for the first time for months, I felt life could be worth living again.

The problem was where and how to live. I had no home in England any more for Pax Hill was occupied by Canadian troops and, anyway, I could not have afforded to go back there. Money was going to be quite a problem. Robin's Army pension had died with him for he had retired many years before he married me. So I had nothing to live on except the income from my marriage settlement and any small bits and pieces that came in from Robin's books. I moved in temporarily with Eileen Wade at the International Scout Office. I slept on a camp bed and kept my few possessions in a suitcase. It was horrible—the most miserable of times. However, one day in Buckingham Palace Road, I ran into Verena Clarendon who was County Commissioner for Guides for London. Her husband was the then Lord Chamberlain.

'Where are you living?' she asked.

'Nowhere,' I replied, and told her about my camp bed and suitcase.

She must have told her husband for he wrote and told me to phone Sir Ulick Alexander, Keeper of H. M. Privy Purse, to see if there was a 'Grace and Favour' Apartment vacant at Hampton Court Palace. I was astounded; I had never dreamed of such a privilege being accorded to me; but when God wants one to do something, He smooths away the difficulties in one's way.

I went down to Hampton Court and was shown the apartment I now occupy. It was a bit dilapidated owing to wartime shortages of labour and materials but it would be *home*. I was so thrilled and grateful, particularly when the Warrant arrived, signed by Lord

Clarendon, which stated in beautiful flowing script: 'I hereby authorise The Lady Baden-Powell by The Grace and Favour of the King to hold the Keys and Possession of the Apartments in His Majesty's Palace of Hampton Court previously in the occupation of . . .' and so on, setting out the conditions for occupation. It was too wonderful, solving at once the problem of a home and also, in a large measure, the problem of money. I managed to get some of my furniture out of store and moved in on December 21st, 1942. I have been here, on and off, ever since.

However, those four months between arriving in England and settling in to Hampton Court were not spent idly. There was much to do.

There were Scout and Guide folk from the occupied countries who had managed to escape to England. They were grateful for any friendship we could extend to them. I went on a tour of Kent towns battered by air-raids to meet Guides and Scouts who worked with such courage in any emergency. I still remember a service in windowless Canterbury Cathedral. I went to the bombed cities of Hull and Portsmouth, Plymouth and Exeter, wherever I felt my presence could give encouragement. The avalanche of letters and wires of welcome when it became known I had arrived back in England had touched me deeply. And I went to see yet another grandchild—Heather's son, Michael, born that autumn.

I had much to be grateful for: another beautiful home, where I soon settled comfortably with dear Annie and Scofield our former cook and gardener; useful work to do and the strength to do it; my children happily married, and grandchildren whose development I could follow; wonderful friends; and even more wonderful, memories of thirty years with a man who had been all in the world to me.

I did not confine my attention only to Guiding; I also founded a Branch of the E.A.W.L. in London. At this time, there were women going out to Kenya either to serve themselves or with their Service husbands. They welcomed advice on what to expect out there. Kenyans on leave in England were always sure of a welcome from us. Of course, over the thirty years since I founded the Branch, the *raison d'être* of the E.A.W.L. has changed with the changing conditions in Africa. Since the Africanisation of Kenya, the Branch has devoted its energies increasingly to assisting repatriates, many of whom found it difficult to adjust to conditions in England. Today the Branch is still very much a going concern.

It was not easy for me to adjust to conditions in wartime England. Rationing was a particular problem. I still found myself issuing invitations on the same scale as at pre-war Pax Hill and soon discovered that, not only had I no longer a staff of eleven to call on, but that a weekly ration of 2-ozs. butter will not go round afternoon tea for fifty! However, I discovered a good caterer, Nutthalls, next door to The Mitre Hotel at East Molesey and, enlisting the help of other 'Palace Ladies' (as I call my fellow-residents at Hampton Court), I would entertain large parties of ex-Scout servicemen from overseas, Canadians and Americans in particular. They loved to visit my apartment and examine Robin's treasures. I still managed to entertain the now considerably reduced staff from Guide and Scout Head-quarters but, alas, there was no country-dancing on the lawn any more as at Pax Hill.

Petrol was rationed, too, nor had I any car so I had to travel every-where by train. I soon got used to (even if I did not enjoy) the slow, frequently stopping, crowded wartime trains when one sat for hours in the corridor on one's suitcase. For travelling around the Palace grounds and into East Molesey for shopping, I took to bicycling again as I had done at Pax Hill when the children were small. I went on using the bicycle, christened 'Tifling', till I was well over seventy.

About this time, the Scout Association launched its Baden-Powell Memorial Fund Appeal with a view to raising enough money to erect in London a meeting-place and hostel for British and Overseas Scouts as a permanent memorial to my husband. Now, in wartime England, the first efforts were being made to raise the necessary money.

On April 9th, 1943, Joan Marsham (the then Chairman of the Girl Guides H.Q. Executive Committee) drove me to Windsor Castle for a Grand Concert in aid of the Fund. I regret to say that we arrived late and the King and Queen were waiting for us! The concert was given by the 1st Buckingham Palace Company of Girl Guides and H.M.S. President III Company of Sea Rangers. The Guides presented most of the items and the 'star' actor was, undoubtedly, Patrol Leader the Princess Margaret. She, as 'Officer in Command', took 'The Royal Salute of the Little Wooden Soldiers'; she played 'The Colonel'

in a riotous sketch entitled 'The Tin Gee-Gee' and also appeared as 'A
Hiker' in a typical Guide item entitled 'The First-Class Hike'. Princess
Elizabeth was one of a group of Sea Rangers who closed the concert
with a selection of Rounds, Sea Shanties and Negro Spirituals. 'What
a charming family they are!' was my diary comment that evening.

I, too, was once again finding myself part of a family. Being near
to London, I was a useful dumping ground for my grandchildren
when Heather came up to Town!

January 28, 1944 — Heather went off to London and left Annie
and me to cope with Michael — but I do *not* like babies!! Oh! the
bother of endless feeding and washings! . . . Give me a HYRAX for
cleanliness! — so nicely house-trained compared to a human baby.

The War dragged on. There were bombs dropped in the park at
Hampton Court. The whole Palace shook and a lot of windows
were broken in the front. I went briefly to Pax Hill to pick some goose-
berries from the kitchen garden and was dismayed to find how
battered and dishevelled it was after being occupied by the Army for
four and a half years. I went down to Sussex on Guide business and
called in at Sheffield Park. There were army huts clustered among the
specimen trees in the arboretum. How old Uncle Arthur would have
hated it!

Gradually, however, there began to be a glimmer of hope that the
tide was turning our way. At Guide Headquarters, as the Scouts also
were doing, we began to organise and train relief teams to go into the
worst devastated areas of Europe as soon as they were liberated. The
Guide and Scout World Bureaux discussed plans as to making the
best use of the services of the two Movements in what we knew would
be an extremely complex post-war world. I flung myself whole-
heartedly into the work of planning and also toured the country,
seeking to keep the spirits high and the ideals bright of the young
people who would lead our country into the future.

More and more, now that my own children were grown-up and
off my hands, I felt I had a duty to all my other 'children' up and
down this country and all round the world.

I heard constantly, of course, from Guide friends in the Americas and in all the British Dominions and Colonies. But there were no letters from our dear Scout and Guide friends in Europe. They were cut off completely. How my heart ached for them and wondered how they were faring – the young Finns who had pulled our carriage through the streets of Helsinki; the Polish Guides who had performed their national dances for us in 1932; the boys and girls, men and women we had met in Denmark, in Norway, in Greece, in Belgium, in Holland, in Austria, in France – all countries now oppressed and 'occupied'. Just occasionally, I would hear a little news from some prisoner who had escaped or from one of the many courageous agents who went backwards and forwards between Britain and occupied Europe. I knew that Scouts and Guides were carrying on their work in secret, that many of them were showing dauntless bravery of spirit but there were so few details. I was longing to be able to see them again, to talk to them, to tell them how proud I was of them and how proud the Founder would have been.

When 'D-Day' came and the Allied landings in Normandy, the opportunity of visiting them began at long last to appear a possibility. First of all, however, we had to endure the enemy's 'last fling' against this country – the VI Flying Bombs and the V2 Rockets. Hampton Court seemed to be directly underneath one of their regular routes across southern England and sometimes they seemed to skim our beautiful Tudor chimney-pots. I used to stand by the window watching them – though with a cushion in my hands to bury my face in should the engine cut out anywhere near us. It seemed inconceivable that the Palace, which had stood unspoiled ever since the sixteenth century, should ever be destroyed. Providentially it remained almost intact and was only shaken by nearby bombs, one of which brought down my ceiling in the summer of 1944.

I arrived back home to find the damage after a tour in the Midlands. During the tour I had spent one night with the Duke and Duchess of Gloucester at Barnwell Manor, near Peterborough. I walked up from the station, I remember, and they both very kindly strolled down to meet me. I cannot recall much about the visit except that they invited me to watch Prince William being bathed and put to bed. He would be about two and a half then. They obviously did not know my feelings towards babies!

The Allied offensive in Europe gathered momentum. On August 23rd Paris was freed; on August 31st Rumania joined the Allies; on September 3rd our Armies reached the Belgian border; the next day they were in Holland; Finland came over to the Allies as well. I decided it was time to start making my own preparations.

By the end of October 1944 I was able to send official messages to Guides in France and Switzerland. At the same time I started in on an intensive course of French lessons. If I was going into Europe, I wanted to be able to talk to people in their own language.

As early as January of 1945 I learned from a friend in the Diplomatic Service on leave from Italy of the renaissance of Scouting there where it had been suppressed for the past fifteen years. Guides also were starting up in Italy. It was not until April, however, that I was able myself to get permission to set foot on the continent.

I went to France first, landing at Dieppe. In one way it was just like old times, with Scouts and Guides waving and singing and cheering on the jetty as our boat drew alongside. But evidence of the long and bitter struggle of the war was all around in the shell-pocked buildings and debris of bombing.

The very first official ceremony after landing—and it was to be repeated all over France, wherever I went on this tour—was at the town War Memorial. Scout Patrol-Leaders broke the Union Jack and the French Tricolour from two flagstaffs that had been erected for the occasion; we sang our two National Anthems; I laid a wreath on the War Memorial, and we were all silent for a moment, some of us thinking back to those we had known and lost in the First World War; all of us thinking of this even greater conflict, still not concluded. It was a solemn moment.

But after that, it was all joy in Dieppe. They all wanted to say 'Thank you' to Britain for the way she had helped them during the war, and because I was British they heaped their appreciation on me. It was all most embarrassing and thrilling and wonderful. I remember in particular one tiny little incident that made me feel very humble.

For years, France had been short of milk. The little that there was was reserved for babies and small children. Many people had not tasted milk for years. In spite of this, in their determination to show me the best hospitality possible, two Guides had gone off early that morning calling at several farms outside the town until they had managed to obtain a tiny jug of milk for my tea. I felt ashamed to be depriving a baby of its ration but it would have hurt the Guides more had I refused to drink it.

In Paris I found Scouts and Guides responding to the demands of a new situation that had arisen as the Allied armies drove deeper into Germany. Every train from the north brought its pitiful cargo: of political prisoners released from concentration camps, of slave labourers who had been deported from France to Germany, now freed to return to their families. They arrived at the rate of ten thousand a day. Many were sick and under-nourished, all were confused and tired, wanting to get in touch with relatives from whom they had been parted for years.

The Scouts and Guides helped day and night to man the *centres d'accueil*—'Welcome Centres'—at the main railway stations in Paris. They would feed these men, escort them from one part of Paris to another, would put them in touch with the various Relief agencies. One day an urgent request for volunteers was made over the radio to cope with the sudden arrival of a much larger contingent of repatriates than usual. Fifteen hundred Scouts and Guides turned up to offer their services.

St. George is the Patron Saint of Scouts. On his day, April 23rd, we held a wonderful 'Scouts' Own' (our special name for an act of worship) in the Bois de Boulogne. This was followed by the laying of a wreath on the tomb of the Unknown Warrior at the Arc de Triomphe and a *défilé* of over 40,000 Scouts and Guides down the Champs Elysées. It is impossible to describe the enthusiasm, the wonderful feeling of thanksgiving that after five years of oppression they were free to wear openly the uniforms they had only been able to wear in secret over the past four years, free to express their loyalty to their God and their country and to their neighbours. As I stood on the saluting base with General Lafont, the Chief Scout of France, and the other Scout and Guide leaders, watching this seemingly endless procession of youngsters march past, I heard someone in the crowd shout out: 'It's nearly over. We're in Berlin!'

I had the privilege of a private interview with General de Gaulle the following day. I had already met him in England in January of 1943 when we had entertained Scout and Guide leaders who had escaped from France. On that occasion he had come as 'Président d'Honneur'. Now he was the saviour of France – a very tired man, but still with the time and the courtesy to spare to discuss the future of Scouting and Guiding in France and the possibility of holding the first post-war Jamboree in his country, in the Forest of Moissons.

I toured a good deal in France. I went first of all to Normandy where, despite the damage that war had done to so many places and despite the weather that made travelling cold and wet and unpleasant, I received a wonderful welcome everywhere. Then came one of the most stirring experiences of my life for, as the first civilian English woman visitor since D-Day, I went to see the Landing Beaches out on the Normandy coast.

Driving down a rough country lane, we came to the tiny hamlet of Asnelles, and found a string of flags draped across the road and a group of children dressed in their national costume, standing waiting, each holding a Union Jack. Their parents in their rough clothes came from their cottages and grouped themselves round me and shook me by the hand. The fact of my being 'World Chief Guide' meant nothing to them. They only knew that I had come across from England to see them and they came out to greet me because I was British, and they knew better than anyone about the landing on their very doorsteps on D-Day, and what France owed to the Allies. What a pity that spirit of friendship, so warm in 1945, has cooled so markedly over the years that have followed!

I went up to Alsace and Lorraine and to the Rhine, driving at times through minefields where only our road had been cleared. I actually crossed into Germany over the pontoon bridge at Strasbourg, the 'Pont de Kehl', which had been under enemy shellfire three weeks before.

Wherever I travelled I heard of the wonderful courage Scouts and Guides had shown during the occupation – helping escaping prisoners, distributing Underground literature, taking down in secret the B.B.C. broadcasts to occupied Europe and, in many cases, still gathering in secret to hold their meetings where they could renew together the spirit of loyalty and the dedication to right principles that they needed to sustain them through their anxious ordeal.

I was in Colmar when peace came. There was a crowd in front of the

Mairie in the town square. A loud-speaker relayed General de Gaulle's speech from Paris – rather hurriedly spoken, with no flowery phrases, just the bare statement that hostilities had ceased and an armistice had been signed. The confused noise of the sirens in Paris sounded next, and the 'All Clear' was taken up by the local hooters and sirens, all over the little Alsatian town. And then the bells pealed out from the church on the other side of the square, and the old white-haired Mayor of Colmar stood, very quiet, with the tears streaming down his face. The war was over.

In the afternoon of VE Day I crossed from France into Switzerland, so beautiful and undamaged after the battle-scarred areas I had been touring during the past month. I was able to visit 'Our Chalet' at Adelboden and meet again the Swiss Guider-in-Charge, Ida von Herrenschwand. ('Falk' was the 'totem-name' by which she was known to us.) She was one of the people who used to pass news to and from Guide people in different parts of Europe during the war years. In Switzerland, as elsewhere, the young people in the Scout and Guide Movements had played a valuable role, assisting the Red Cross in its work of mercy towards prisoners-of-war and helping with camps for refugee children.

Wherever I went in Switzerland, I received small tokens of affection that touched me deeply – bunches of flowers, quaint little drawings, simple poems, home-made sweets and so on. Sometimes they were accompanied by notes from the donors, more often they were left anonymously in my hotel room or even in my railway carriage on leaving stations. One of the more original offerings took the form of a V-sign made out of fresh bananas on the seat of my carriage!

Back into France I journeyed, visiting Lyons and touring Provence, always with the feeling that doorways of friendship were opening again that had been locked for years. Nowhere did I feel this more strongly than in Italy whither I flew from Marseilles at the beginning of June. I was housed in a poor and rather unpleasant hotel 'in a filthy part of this disgusting dirty town' (Naples). The people seemed dejected and cowed. One had a sense of great pain endured for no great purpose and towards no great end. The Italians seemed still numb with the shock of betrayal by the leaders in whom they had put too much trust, and by the loss of prestige and power.

14

Some Italians, however, had recovered from the shock. Scout flags and uniforms, hidden since the early thirties in cupboards and cellars, even sewn inside mattresses for safety when Scouting was forbidden, were now brought to light. Men who remembered Scouting were anxious to start it up again and were helped in this by Scout members of the Allied forces in Italy. This was the 'renaissance' my Diplomatic friend had told me about. Guiding had been started up in Rome as early as December 1943, before the whole of Italy was freed. The Guides had met in secret in the catacombs, like the early Christians nearly two thousand years before.

When I myself reached Rome, I was once again received in audience by the Pope—this time Pius XII. On this occasion I wore World Guide uniform and it was accepted without question. No full-length black dress and veil this time.

After Italy, Luxembourg—a tiny state and one that had suffered out of all proportion to its size. There I was privileged to meet not just the Grand-Duchess and her Guide daughters, but one of the great Scouts of the country: Robert Schaffner, later to become Prime Minister of Luxembourg. He had been captured early in the war, working for the Resistance, and was now newly repatriated from the dreaded Buchenwald Camp. It was the Scout spirit, he told me, that had given him the inner strength to endure the torture and privation and horror of his years in prison camps.

Similar tales of incredible fortitude greeted me in Belgium. I had a long talk with the Queen Mother at the Royal Palace of Laaken. She paid tribute to the way in which the Movements had served the country; even more, she admired the international aspect of Scouting and Guiding where, as she expressed it, 'there are no frontiers of the mind'.

On VJ Day, August 15th, I was in Sweden and a week later had dinner at the British Embassy in Stockholm with the Minister, Mr. Jerram (later Sir Bertrand Jerram, K.C.M.G.) who was the man actually to receive and hand on to Britain Japan's message of capitulation.

This was the start of a tour of Scandinavian countries where, again, doors long closed to official Scouting and Guiding now stood wide open. I heard of the dogged work that went on in Finland, of the quiet courage shown in Denmark, of the self-sacrificing heroism of so many Norwegian Scouts. It was all wonderful and heart-warming and moving. Had I not been challenged by Miss Tennyson's letter to me in Kenya three years before, I might have missed all this. Now I could see, dramatically illustrated, all those qualities my husband had sought to inspire in young men and women: loyalty, courage, self-reliance and fortitude.

But Kenya! Would I ever see that again?

In the middle of September 1945 I returned to England and to an accumulation of post. I had travelled some thousands of miles during the past six months, I had seen and heard some terrible things—and when I thought I had my emotions completely under control, a letter from Kenya made me break down again. Hyrie was dead—my dear sweet precious cuddly little hyrax that had been such a comfort to me when my darling Robin died. I sat at my desk and wept.

CHAPTER TWENTY-TWO

Ambassadress-at-Large

Years: 1945–1956

My bedroom at Hampton Court adjoins the Great Hall. Sometimes during the daytime I can hear through the wall the buzz of tourists' chatter. I have been told that Shakespeare and his players performed in the Great Hall in the days of the first Queen Elizabeth and that the room I now sleep in was then the players' changing room. So I never know whether Shakespeare dresses in my bedroom or whether I sleep in his dressing-room!

Whatever the truth of the Shakespeare story, I do know that psychic people have found my apartment peopled by ghosts. I see an interesting entry to this effect in my diary for October 1st, 1945:

> Lord Dowding comes to tea and brings 'L.L.' with him (Mrs. Hunt). She at once feels my own Darling's presence, and also Queen Anne Boleyn!! She finds that this unhappy Queen had used my little 'turret room' at the end of my bedroom as her secret praying room . . . She 'sees' the Queen, who is beautiful, in the room.

There were other, more sinister ghosts to lay in 1945. We were hoping that Guiding could start up again in Germany but it would need very careful handling. If it started up too soon and too vigorously, it could be viewed by some as a carefully camouflaged revival of the *Bund Deutsches Madel*, the girls' side of the Nazi *Hitler Jugend*. For such a suspicion to be attached to Guiding would be disastrous. In fact, Guiding was not resumed in Germany until 1948.

Meantime, the way was now clear for me to carry on with the work my husband had left for me to do. He had bidden me in the letters he left behind to 'make Guiding the biggest success that ever was for the good of others.' This I have endeavoured ceaselessly to do for the past thirty years, seeking to establish Guiding in every country under the wing and care of the World Association. I have travelled continually from one part of the country to another, from one county to another, from one country to another.' Since 1942, I have been round the world five times and have flown 653 flights totalling well over half a million miles in all types of aircraft. It was as well that I was not put off flying by that fatal crash I witnessed in 1910, for I should not have been able to meet even a fraction of the many thousands of brother and sister Scouts and Guides throughout the world without this wonderful and efficient means of transport.

Immediately after the war, of course, one had to travel as best one might. In January 1946, for example, I set off on a six-and-a-half-month tour of Canada, U.S.A. and the West Indies as one of only fourteen passengers on a small cargo ship. Wherever I went on that tour, the fund-raising events undertaken by Guides were to enable them to send food to the hungry and war-weary people of Europe. It was thrilling for me to be able to go 'shopping' on such a large scale for people in Holland and Poland, as well as Britain, and to be able to tell the Canadian and American Guides and Brownies exactly what foodstuffs I had bought with their generous contributions and had despatched to Europe.

I met Winston Churchill during that tour at a reception in Havana given by the British Minister in Cuba. I little thought at the time that I should meet him again, and quite soon, at a purely family gathering.

That autumn of 1946, I am happy to say, my brother Arthur and I managed to establish a friendly relationship with each other for the first time, really, since my mother's death in 1932. The new peace was 'ratified' by Arthur kindly presenting me with the fine portrait of my mother by Hugh Rivière that now hangs in my hall at Hampton Court. A month later, Arthur told me with delight of the engagement of his son, Christopher, to Winston Churchill's youngest daughter, Mary. She had been in the A.T.S. stationed in Paris; Christopher had been Military Attaché to the then British Ambassador to France, Duff Cooper. Christopher himself (now Sir Christopher Soames) has since held that high office. I had not seen Christopher since he was a small boy at prep school!

Early in December my brother gave a dinner party at Claridges to celebrate the engagement. I wish I could remember details of the occasion, for Winston Churchill was there and his eldest daughter, Mrs. Duncan Sandys, deputising for her mother who was ill. I am sure the great man must have produced at least one *bon mot* during the evening! However, after a quarter of a century, my recollection of the party is hazy and my diary merely records that it was 'a very good dinner' and that it was a 'rather historic family gathering'. I met Mrs. Churchill some six weeks later at brother Arthur's flat but, unfortunately, when the wedding itself took place the following year, I was abroad.

In July 1947, I left on a world tour that lasted twelve months. Most of the time was spent in Australia and New Zealand, where, as has happened so fortunately on most of my tours, I was usually given hospitality by the Governor of whatever state I happened to be in. In May of 1948 I was the guest of General and Lady Freyburg at Government House, Auckland. I still remember our V.C. host's hilarious description of his attempt to swim the Channel in 1926.

He had always been a strong swimmer and had trained hard for this, the toughest 'swim' anyone could tackle. At last the day arrived when the tide and the weather conditions were right. He entered the sea at Cap Griz Nez and set out strongly for England. He swam for hours and hours, sustained at intervals by drinks of hot Bovril dispensed by his wife who, along with his trainer, was following in a small boat. The hours passed, the wind freshened, the sea grew rough. By the time the cliffs of Dover were in sight, Freyburg was looking cold and tired and unlikely to succeed in his bid. His wife was as anxious as he was for him to succeed, so, in the hope that it would stiffen his resolve and put him in better heart, she laced his Bovril generously with brandy. Alas! The brandy had the reverse effect of that desired! (Here the General rose from his seat to demonstrate his faltering stroke). He grew more and more sleepy, his strokes became more and more feeble until at last he had to be fished ignominiously out of the water almost in a state of oblivion!

So many countries, so many people to meet. I must have shaken hands with millions over the years, for my tours take me not just to the big, important centres but to small towns and villages as well, where I can meet and have fellowship with ordinary people in their home setting. Every tour is made up of such contrasts: sometimes a tiny chat at a wayside halt with half a dozen girls gathered on the platform to greet me for the five minutes the train pauses there; at other times, all the pageantry of a civic reception. I have been privileged to meet most Heads of State, so many, alas, now gone: Dr. Benes of Czechoslovakia who fought so hard for his country's independence and died, over-thrown by the Communists, a broken-hearted man in 1948; Eamonn de Valera, Prime Minister and later President of Eire; Queen Wil-helmina of the Netherlands; Prime Minister Huggins of Northern Rhodesia; King George and Queen Frederika of Greece; the late and unlamented King Farouk of Egypt. I was even entertained in Omdur-man to a grand dinner party given by Sir Abdel Rahman, the Mahdi. He was the posthumous son of the 'Mad Mahdi' who led the Holy War in the days of General Gordon of Khartoum.

This last meeting was in December 1949 — my first visit to Africa since I left it in 1942. Having landed once more on that continent, I plucked up courage to go to Kenya again — alone. I arrived there in heart-thumping trepidation and drove up to Nyeri to spend Christmas in my own little cottage of Paxtu. Once I arrived in that beloved place, all my anxiety fell from me and I was once more enfolded in the magic of the home where we had been so happy. All the agony had sloughed away and now I felt only thankfulness for the great happiness we had shared together.

One tour has tended to lead on to another. I was in the West Indies during the early months of 1951. I had visited Guadeloupe, Martinique, Barbados, Trinidad, Tobago, Grenada, British Guiana, St. Vincent, St. Lucia, Dominica, Montserrat, Antigua, St. Kitts, Bermuda and the Bahamas. Now I was in Jamaica, waiting for the ship that was to carry me on the last leg of my tour, to Puerto Rico and Haiti. I was spending the day with some friends in Brownstown on the north coast of the island. It was hot and the water looked inviting.

'Let's go for a swim,' suggested my friends.

'But I haven't a swimsuit,' I replied.

'We'll borrow one,' they said.

Later, I was on the beach—in the borrowed swimsuit—when the lender of it came down to join us with one of *her* visitors, a Mr. Harold Peat. We started to talk.

'Have you ever been to the United States?' he asked me.

'I was there in 1948,' I replied.

'And are you coming again?'

'I don't suppose so. No one has invited me.'

'I'll invite you,' he said. 'Come and do a lecture tour for me. I'm a lecture agent.'

So there and then, on the beach in Jamaica in a borrowed swimsuit, I agreed to undertake a lecture tour under his auspices the following winter.

It was a gruelling, if profitable, tour. Admittedly I travelled to and from the States in great luxury. The then Chairman of Cunard kindly gave me a free passage both ways in a de luxe cabin as a token of his appreciation of what Guiding stood for. In between, I worked extremely hard, giving lectures all over the States in cities as far apart as Chicago and New Orleans. I had just arrived in New York when I heard the sad news of the death of King George VI. I heard the funeral broadcast in Saginaw (Michigan) and saw a newsreel of the funeral service in Chicago a week later. It felt all wrong not to be in London at such a time of national sorrow.

The lecture tour was an enormous success, not only from the point of stimulating interest in Scouting and Guiding throughout the United States, but also financially. Indeed, I earned enough in fees to extend my tour for a further two months visiting Guide people in Canada and still to take home a modest profit. I wondered, just for a moment, whether I was ever going to reach home safely for our vessel, the S.S. *Scythia*, collided with another ship in thick fog in the St. Lawrence River and we had to return to Quebec for repairs.

I had had a faint hope that I might be able to return to Kenya for the winter of 1952 but the Mau-Mau troubles were at their height, particularly in the Nyeri area. It would have been dangerous and unwise to return so I spent the cold months of 1952/53 mostly at Hampton Court Palace. I was on my own there now for Annie, who had been in my employment since 1912 and had been resident at Hampton Court since 1942, became very ill and had to retire from my service. She and her husband settled in the West Country. In many ways it was pleasant to be on my own there for I had great plans for using my apartment to the full during 1953.

Coronation Year! What a busy and interesting year it was.

With the feverish interest there now was in everything to do with the monarchy, palaces became 'news'. The B.B.C. decided to film Hampton Court for television. They asked if I would appear briefly in the film to give it 'human interest'. On an appointed day in April, when the grounds of this old palace were brilliant with daffodils and wallflowers, the film team arrived and set up their cameras in the Sunken Garden. There were wires and cables all over the place, snaking across the paths and flowerbeds, dangling over the outside walls. The producer gave me my instructions. I was to walk into the garden where I would be met by Mr. Richard Dimbleby. He would say, with startling originality:

'How very nice to meet you, Lady Baden-Powell. Do you live here?'

I was to reply: 'Yes, I have a Grace and Favour Residence in the Palace,' and then we were to walk a little way together in the somewhat restricted space of the Sunken Garden, making polite conversation.

We greeted each other as planned, and walked and talked – but a plane went over and spoiled the sound. We shot the scene again. This time there was something wrong with the light. In the end, it took over two hours to record a tiny sequence that only ran for about two minutes.

I would much rather they had taken pictures of my 'Appendix' that summer. 'The Appendix' was the name I gave to my annexe. I have eight rooms in my main apartment and a charming roof garden outside. On the other side of the roof garden and, incidentally, over the Great Kitchen of the palace, I have an annexe of a further eight rooms. This wing is completely self-contained, with its own kitchen and bathroom. Up to 1952, these rooms had been used by Annie and Scofield. Now they were empty.

Pax Hill had recently been sold, as the Guide Association could no longer afford to run it as a Domestic Science College, so there was now available a large amount of the furniture which I had allowed the Association to use after the place had been de-requisitioned by the Army and taken over by the Guides. This furniture was moved into the redecorated rooms of the annexe so that I could accommodate up to twelve visitors at a time. I made the rooms available for use by overseas Guides visiting Britain for Coronation Year. The first visitors were two Guiders from Grenada who arrived on May 19th. Between that date and the middle of August, I accommodated a hundred and twenty visitors from twenty-five different countries.

I shall never forget Queen Elizabeth's Coronation Day. My son, Peter, had of course inherited the title on Robin's death so he and Carine were inside the Abbey in all their glory of velvet and ermine. (Peter had come back to England from Africa for good in 1949). I was fortunate enough to have a splendid seat outside the Abbey in the Peers' Stand opposite the Great West Door.

We had to be in our seats early. There was a 'Peers' Special' train at half past eight in the morning from Kensington High Street underground station to Westminster. There was a flat fare of, I think, a shilling for the journey. We all queued up in our finery – some of the peers fully-robed, clutching their coronets and lunch-bags in one hand and their shilling in the other. Unlike those trapped with their sandwiches inside the Abbey, I was able to have a much more comfortable lunch on the terrace of the House of Lords, until the rain poured down and spoiled everything.

By September of 1953, I was off again on another lecture tour of the States for the Peat Agency – 42,000 miles in six months, fifty-seven cities, twenty-five states, a hundred and fifty-eight talks!

In between the long tours, I had to fit in all the other visits – around Europe, around Britain. It was all very exhilarating but exhausting. The trouble is that I can never say 'No' to a request for my help if I feel it is going to benefit Guiding in some way. By 1955 I was beginning to feel my years. I was, after all, sixty-six and I had been growing increasingly deaf in one ear ever since I had damaged it some years before, flying when I had a heavy cold. In addition, I had taken in my sister-in-law, Hilda Baden-Powell, to live with me at Hampton Court. She was now eighty-seven and very frail following a fall.

January 1st, 1955 – And now I begin another year in 'my' Palace – with my old Hilda, and all her attendants – and I am more or less like a sheep-dog, running round in circles keeping them all on the move ... all seven of us apparently needed, and all kept busy too, our lives revolving round keeping hers going!

The poor dear was finally released from her suffering in May 1955, almost a year to the day from moving in to live with me. She was yet another link gone with the old pre-war days.

Her going left the way clear for yet another prolonged lecture tour in North America—for eight months this time, through Canada, U.S.A. and Mexico. First of all on the programme, however, was the great Niagara Falls World Scout Jamboree of August 1955. As I moved about from one sub-camp to another, shaking hands, meeting old friends from a dozen countries, making new friends from a dozen more, I knew that the work my husband started was as valid as ever in its power and potential to establish peace and friendship between nations. I tried to echo that thought in my closing speech, in which I told them: 'You will take away with you the thunder of Niagara in your ears—symbolic of power, and symbolic of *our* power to do good in the world through Scouting.'

After the Jamboree, I set out on my longest tour yet of the North American continent. I gave eighty-six talks in Canada at places as far apart as Toronto, Medicine Hat and Vancouver. I drove all over the United States, giving another one hundred and eighty-six major talks and seeing wonderful, wonderful sights—millions of big Red Monarch butterflies in the trees outside Monterey; hundreds of seals basking on a rocky islet off the Pacific coast; a blaze of azaleas in Mobile, Alabama; fantastically-shaped Joshua trees in the desert near La Jolla—and wherever I went, hundreds and thousands of eager, happy faces of Guides and Brownies, Scouts and Cubs.

No sooner was I home from the States in April of 1956 than I was invited to make a long tour of Africa the following autumn and winter. It was planned that I should pay short official visits to Malta, Cairo and Khartoum before setting out on the more leisurely and extended tour of Kenya, the Rhodesias and South and West Africa. All travelling arrangements and appointments had been completed when the Suez crisis blew up. There were frenzied writings and telephonings and cablings between me and the Foreign Office and Mrs. Abdel Nabi, the Chief of the Egyptian Guides, as to whether my visit to Cairo was 'on' or 'off'. When I left London Airport on October 28th, the visit was still 'on'.

I arrived safely in Malta and had the delightful surprise of being met by my grandson Robert, in white sailor rig. He was doing his National Service in the Navy and his ship had put in to Valletta. Two days later, Egypt and Israel were at war, British troops were moving into the Canal zone, the Security Council was in session in New York and the British and French Parliaments were anxiously discussing their position over the Suez Canal. The world was again on the brink of disaster but in the meantime, Cairo Airport was closed and I still had, somehow or other, to get myself to Khartoum to fulfil engagements on November 1st.

I managed, after some delay, to obtain a visa for Libya and arrived in Tripoli on October 31st. I drove confidently into the town from the airport to enquire at the B.O.A.C. office what to do next. Of course, with Cairo being closed, all flights were being re-routed, with all the attendant complications of too many passengers for too few planes. My confidence ebbed as the hours passed by. At 6.30 in the evening, to my great relief, the manager of B.O.A.C. kindly drove me out to the airport to catch the plane for Khartoum. Alas for my hopes! I sat and sat, and waited and waited, and after nine hours in a now crowded airport lounge, at 4.15 in the morning two Khartoum-bound planes touched down to refuel and left again, already full! I bundled back into Tripoli by taxi, found a hotel and went to bed.

It was impossible to get any proper news. There were rumours of awful 'acts of war' in Egypt, but nothing definite. Tension mounted. Europeans were advised to stay off the streets. I phoned B.O.A.C. repeatedly and was promised a seat on a plane at 4.0 p.m. – though even with that, I should be late for my first appointments in Khartoum. An hour later, they phoned me to say there would be no plane after all. At 7.0 p.m. they told me my only hope was to take the 6.30 a.m. plane the following morning back to Sicily and from there another flight to Rome and start out for Khartoum afresh! So I went to bed again to try to catch up on sleep, only to be awakened by the telephone in the small hours. Could I get myself to the Airport immediately. The plane for Sicily was leaving at 3.30 a.m., not 6.30 as advised!

I could and I did, and eventually, having paid out vast sums in additional fares for flying in the opposite direction from where I wanted to go, I arrived in Sicily and hung around for hours watching plane after plane leave for Rome but all too full to take me. I eventually reached Rome at 6.30 p.m. on November 3rd—already two days late for my first appointments in Khartoum!

More delays in Rome. There is a seat. There is not a seat. Have I a visa for the Sudan? I obtain a visa. Yes, they now have a seat but my ticket says London/Khartoum via Malta and Cairo, not via Rome. More arguments and delays. I cannot think now why I did not just give up and go home to England. At long last I board a plane for Khartoum and we taxi out on to the runway—but that is as far as we go. There is trouble with the engine! We all disembark again and hang around for four hours until the trouble is located and repaired. At last, at 10.0 p.m. on November 4th, we take off and fly through the night to Africa, arriving at Khartoum at six in the morning.

Despite the lack of sleep, despite the frustrations of the past six days and regardless of my sixty-seven years, I had immediately to face the following programme:

(1) Call on President of the Republic
(2) Call on Prime Minister
(3) Luncheon Party for Guiders at Government Guest House
(4) Give talk over the Radio
(5) Tea Party with Rangers and Guides at Guide Headquarters
(6) Call on Scout Commissioner's wife
(7) Call on Sir Abdel Rahman el Mahdi
(8) Dinner Party for 40 people at Government Guest House

I finally managed to slip away to bed at midnight and had to be up again by 5.0 a.m. to catch a flight to Entebbe! It is a good thing I have a strong constitution. No wonder I wrote in my diary: 'I am getting tired, and too old for much more of this work.'

How much longer would be required of me before I could say I had finished the work my husband had left me? On the closing day of 1956 I sat beside his grave at Nyeri. It was peaceful and beautiful there, the plot lovingly tended by the local Scouts, the hedge of Christ's Thorn I had planted now all in full bloom.

'So little time, so little done,' Cecil Rhodes had said of Africa. 'And so much still to do,' I might have added, thinking of the crying need of young people all round the world.

But for the moment I was at peace, in that hallowed acre that held all in the world that was most dear to me.

CHAPTER TWENTY-THREE

Autumn Years

Years: 1957–1962

February 22nd, 1957 was the centenary of Robin's birth and the summer of 1957 was just fifty years since his first experimental Scout Camp on Brownsea Island. Both events were celebrated on a big scale. There were articles about Robin in the newspapers, programmes on radio and television, special beds in the parks spelling out his name and achievements in flowers. There was even a commemorative postage stamp.

It was a source of great pride to see these tributes to my husband but on no occasion was I more moved and touched than during the Great Service of Thanksgiving for his life and work held in Westminster Abbey on our joint birthday. I had flown back to England from Kenya in time for the service. It was Thinking Day and it made me feel very humble to reflect that on that day in cathedrals and churches all over Britain, indeed throughout the world, there would be similar services of thanksgiving and rededication. What a privilege it had been to be part of so great a work, what a joy to have been married to one who was at once so great and noble and yet so tender and loving. How very richly God had blessed us both in giving us our work and each other.

My Thinking Day post, always an enormous one, was this year phenomenal. Letters arrived by the sackful, bringing me lovely glimpses into the past; telling me of happy meetings with my husband; speaking so lovingly of him and of what he did in inventing Scouting and Guiding. In the middle of all the excitement, I received a surprise cable from the Prime Minister of the Gold Coast, inviting me the following week to the celebrations in Accra marking the elevation of the Gold Coast to Dominion status as Ghana. It was too exciting an invitation to miss.

On Sunday, March 3rd, I flew from London Airport to Kano in

Northern Nigeria. The plane had been specially chartered by the new Ghana Government and was full of V.I.P.s from various parts of Europe as well as from Britain. We drove to Accra for the celebrations. There were displays of marching and dancing and wild drumming, all very impressive. There was a grand State Dinner. There was a reception at 'The Castle', the Governor's ornate Victorian residence in Accra where I had last stayed in 1950 when the Gold Coast was a colony. I always enjoy meeting old friends and acquaintances and there were many such present at the Castle. I wore Guide uniform so that people could 'place' me among such a big throng and had the pleasure of talking to Vice-President Nixon (as he then was), with delegates from Turkey, Iran, Chile and a host of other countries where I had toured either on my own or with my husband. There was also an interesting conversation, conducted through an interpreter, with a Russian delegate who insisted that their 'Red Pioneers' were 'something like Scouts'. I forbore to ask why, in that case, Scouting was forbidden in Russia!

After the reception, everyone surged into the town to see a parade of decorated floats. Princess Marina, Duchess of Kent, representing the Queen, pressed a button that started the illuminations. The sky exploded with fireworks and a huge arch spelled out in letters of fire the words 'Freedom and Justice'. Ghana was born, a self-governing Dominion within the Commonwealth.

The following day I attended the State Opening of the Ghana Parliament. I had been present on several occasions to witness the same ritual in our own House of Lords. The Accra ceremony was every bit as impressive, with the Duchess of Kent reading the speech from the Throne with the same dignity that invests the Queen. There were the same be-wigged and red-robed judges as at Westminster, except that the faces beneath the wigs were black; and instead of peers in velvet and ermine, there were ministers and the President, Kwame Nkruma, in native dress of cloth of gold.

The celebrations concluded with a most thrilling sort of 'Durbar' at Achimota. The Duchess, who had throughout played her part with royal grace and charm, received the Chiefs. It was an unforgettable sight. Although it was daytime, she was in full evening dress and diamonds. The Chiefs were gorgeously robed, walking with slow dignity across the arena, each beneath a ceremonial umbrella of brilliant hue, each attended by a retinue of up to a hundred, all arrayed in colourful garments. The heat was intense. The dry earth shimmered. All around the vast arena, excited crowds swayed and stamped in time to the insistent, ceaseless beat of the drums. It was the most thrilling ceremony I have ever attended, a new 'stage' in the development of Africa — yet I could not but recall that only sixty years before, in 1896, my husband had been sent to the Gold Coast on a punitive expedition to stop human sacrifices! It is a tribute to his personal magnetism that Scouting was accepted in those parts of Africa (and India) where he personally had fought against the native inhabitants during his military career.

The other memorable event of 1957 was the great Jubilee Jamboree at Sutton Park where 35,000 Scouts from ninety different countries gathered together for two weeks' fellowship.

The British contingent, for their arena show, put on a pageant depicting scenes from my husband's life. My grandson, Michael King (Heather's elder boy) played B.-P. as a boy at Charterhouse, sloping off to trap rabbits in the woods. Our own Peter played B.-P. at Mafeking and at Brownsea Island. There was quite a gasp of surprise from those who had known my husband; Peter looked so exactly like him. By a strange coincidence, Peter in August 1947 was 43, exactly the age his father was at the Siege of Mafeking. All twelve of our children and grand-children were present on that occasion, plus their husbands and wives, so it was a unique family gathering.

Anyone who attended the Sutton Park Jamboree will remember the mini-tornado that flooded the camp on Bank Holiday Monday. There were still muddy pools around the site even on the last day and, of course, I, taking a short cut through a wood, *had* to fall flat on my face in one such boggy patch! I was on my way to visit the German camp and was then to go straight to the arena to make the closing speech of the Jamboree, and here was I with my best uniform plastered in mud, to say nothing of my knees and hands. My Scouter escort 'saved my face' by enveloping me in a groundsheet and I was whisked back to my hotel to change without anyone knowing who the 'criminal' was with her head covered! I was back, in clean uniform, in time to give a farewell message, parts of which I reproduce here for they epitomise much of the creed by which I regulate my life:

15

In this lovely county of Warwickshire, in the green heart of England, we are all gathered together tonight for the last time in Sutton Park . . . At the time this Park was founded, a tragic Queen was facing her death. Having faith in a merciful God who would give her a new life in the Great Beyond, she said: 'My end is only my beginning . . .'

I don't think I could give you a better text to take away from this joyous Jamboree than those same words: 'The end is only the beginning.'

. . . For these two weeks, you—Scouters and Scouts of so many different lands and so many different languages—have lived in harmony together, forgetting the differences which *separate* and thinking only of the ties which *unite* you all in the great world brotherhood of Scouting . . . During all these days together, we have been *taking in*, in order that we may *give out* . . .

Now you go back to your everyday life in the world outside . . . taking with you some of the happiness and helpfulness and the spirit of friendship you have imbibed here, taking it away not just for yourself but in order that you may give it and spread it around you, whoever and wherever you may be.

. . . So may the end of this Jamboree be but the beginning of a new '*reaching out*' of left hands everywhere, and a carrying to the world outside some of the Jamboree spirit of fun and friendship.

Your Founder was one of the happiest of men because he knew the great truth that happiness comes not from what we have but from what we *give* and what we *share*.

You do not need me to tell you this, for you are preparing as Scouts to live lives . . . of giving, out of the best that is in you, and of self-sacrificing duty to God and to your fellows. Then when your time comes to go hence, you too will be able to say: 'The end was only the beginning.'

Less than five months later, I was to learn just how much the friendship of Scouts and Guides could mean. I was midway through a long tour of Australia and the East Indies, just about as far away from my family as I could be, when I became ill—an unheard of state of affairs for me. I was whisked into Portland Hospital on New Year's Day, 1958 and operated on for gall-stones.

Apparently Reuters reported the emergency operation and, fleetingly, I had the novelty of being 'world news'! That was when I became aware of the strong ties of friendship that Scouting and Guiding had made around the world. Cables, messages and gifts poured into the hospital. It was gratifying to receive an enquiry from H.M. The Queen, from Heads of State and Governors. What touched me more were the moving little messages from youngsters in all parts of the world. I was quite overwhelmed to discover how many friends I had.

Perhaps, also, this is why I continued my overseas tours for several years longer. I recovered splendidly from the operation and was fitter, if anything, than before. I felt that as long as I had the strength and had something to contribute, and as long as people wanted to see me, I had a duty to go to them and to give them encouragement. I have never had much patience with committees and sitting round a table discussing rules and red tape. I like to be out 'in the field' where I feel I can use my own peculiar gifts.

The duties of a Chief Guide have never been defined. I once wrote:

Roughly you are expected to work all day and all night, to be completely at everyone's beck and call, to have the wits and intelligence of a University professor, the pen of a ready writer, to toss off messages, articles, broadcasts and even books as easily and quickly as you would a meal, to travel hither and thither the whole year round doing Conferences, Rallies, Meetings, be 'at home' to those who wish to meet you there. Visit Camps all over the world and also at the same time be available at home for 'quiet talks when you have a free day' and so on!

It is not just a case of engendering interest and enthusiasm, either. Each tour highlights some particular problem which I try to solve. For example, in 1959 I spent three months touring South America. During that time, through meetings with Bishops, Archbishops, even with a Papal Nuncio (who produced photographs of himself as a boy in Scout uniform!) I was able to persuade the breakaway Catholic Scout and Guide Associations to be reunited with the national Associations.

'One country, one Movement.' It is a constant struggle to achieve this ideal. If I have not much time for sectarian Christianity, it is because I have seen all over the world what a divisive influence it can be.

Another result of the South American tour was the help it gave towards improving the status of women. For example, in Lima, it was quite an 'occasion' for the President's wife to give a reception for women Guide leaders – indeed, for women to be 'noticed' officially at all. I was quite overcome by the welcome I received in these Latin American countries. The girls almost mobbed me, so thrilled were they to be having their own celebrations. They would press close to kiss me, to touch my hands and clothes. It is at times almost frightening to find oneself the subject of such overwhelming adulation; it is such a responsibility.

But if there is one great lesson to be learned from world travel, it is that there is no part of the world which has not something to give as well as something to gain. It is a two-way traffic. Whether we are camping in some other country or hostessing in our own, we are getting as well as giving, carrying something away as well as leaving something of ourselves behind – not material things, but the intangible qualities of friendship and understanding and respect for each other's way of life.

Inevitably, of course, there have been tangible 'rewards'. Throughout my tours, I have received many decorations and 'freedoms' but none gave me greater pleasure I think, than the Freedom of the City of Panama which was bestowed on me on July 6th, 1959. It was forty-seven years since I had first set foot in Panama during the *Arcadian* cruise of 1912 – a happy girl of twenty-three with her beloved 'Lieut.-General Baden-Powell' as companion! Little did I dream then of what the future would hold.

I went on to Mexico to open 'Our Cabaña', a Guide training and holiday centre in sight of Mount Popocatepetl, which had been acquired through generous gifts from friends in the U.S.A. From there I continued on a tour of the States, gathering up several more 'Freedoms' en route, including the Freedom of Reno! I wrote: 'How everybody will chortle over my having the Freedom of this ghastly city of divorces and gambling. The centre of it really looks hellish with crowds milling round the gambling "shops".'

In 1960, I was invited to attend more 'Independence' celebrations in Africa, when Nigeria obtained Dominion status. On this occasion, Princess Alexandra was deputising for the Queen, with all the grace her mother had shown in Ghana three years before. The Nigerian Guides took part in the celebrations and I had the unique experience in Kano of attending a rally *inside* the Emir's mud-walled palace. I had an interview with the Emir himself and was introduced to his chief wife who was in Guide uniform. The walled city of Kano is quite amazing in its contrasts. It has a teeming population of thousands of poor, extremely dirty people. Donkeys, goats, fowl and naked children wander around the streets and the whole place looks positively 'biblical' — yet the city boasts of electric light and cinemas.

Later in 1960, I returned to the Indian sub-continent for the first time since 1937, and the first time since Partition. As I have mentioned earlier in this account of my life, I had felt that Guiding had much to offer the women of this teeming land. Now I was to see its results, clearly demonstrated. Both in India and in Pakistan I was able to see the Guide 'Literacy Project' at work. Guides were patiently teaching the illiterate to read. 'Each one, teach one,' was the slogan. They were running classes to teach their mothers and grandmothers to write. One would see old ladies sitting on the floor with pencils and copy-books learning skills we take for granted in six-year-olds in the West. In Lahore and Karachi, I saw Rangers staffing Community Centres in the middle of the most ghastly slums. Knowing the fatalistic attitude of the average Indian towards any kind of disaster, it made me feel very proud that the Guides' concern for their fellows had led them to undertake such a plucky form of service. In other places, Guides in their 'Garden Project' were reclaiming patches of waste ground and turning them to productive use — another form of practical service in a country where starvation is endemic.

But, oh dear, partition! It seemed dreadful to me that there should be a barbed wire fence and guards between peoples who had worked together twenty years before. It was as bad as the Berlin Wall. At least, I thought, let there be no 'partition' in Guiding! On Christmas Day, 1960 I was due to cross from Pakistan to India at the Wagga Customs post. My Pakistani friends drove me to the wire. My Indian friends were waiting to receive me on the other side. Despite the armed guards and customs officials, I brought the two groups of Guides together, took the Pakistani Guides on to Indian soil and put one left hand into another left hand. The pent-up longings of years of separation burst their bonds. Indian and Pakistani clasped each other affectionately and wept with joy at the reunion—and the armed guards looked the other way and did nothing at all to stop it. They couldn't!

A compartment had been reserved for us on 'The Flying Mail' from Amritsar to Delhi. It was a grubby old train dating surely from the great days of the Queen Empress Victoria. My travelling companion and I were locked into a First Class compartment and travelled in splendid isolation. We felt dreadful. The rest of the train was packed to capacity and at every station more passengers sought to fight their way into or even just *on* to the train.

'We *must* share our compartment,' I insisted. 'It's too selfish to be sitting in comfort with all those poor people herded like cattle.'

At Umballa we prevailed upon a station attendant to unlock our compartment so that a woman with two children could get in. In the end, it was not just *one* woman with children; it was *twelve*, all pushing and jostling! We travelled on for ten hours like that and by the time we arrived in Delhi we felt like herded cattle ourselves.

It was the occasion of the Queen's state visit to India and I found myself 'presented' to her three times in one day at different functions! I also had the privilege of breakfasting at his lovely home with Mr. Nehru and his daughter and grandsons. Unfortunately, I cannot recount any sparkling conversation for the Prime Minister had only that morning heard news of the death of one of his greatest friends, the Chief Minister of Bihar. In consequence, he was plunged in grief and hardly spoke a word. Other incidents of that tour stand out in my memory: walking barefooted to lay a wreath at the place where Mahatma Gandhi was cremated; watching the ethereal beauty of the Taj Mahal as its colour changed from golden to lilac to pink and then to ghostly white as the daylight faded; a 'Thinking Day' service in Pachmarhi, with prayers by Parsee, Muslim, Hindu and Christian Guides and Scouts.

I was back in England by the middle of March 1961 and had a busy summer. In July, H.M. the Queen opened Baden-Powell House in Queen's Gate, Kensington as a memorial to my dear husband. It was nearly twenty years since she, as a Ranger Guide, had taken part in the concert at Windsor Castle I described earlier, a concert put on to raise funds for this very project. It is a constant joy to me that my darling's memory is preserved in this practical and lively way, in a hostel where Scouts and Guides from all over the world can find comfortable accommodation and can meet and talk together in the very heart of London.

That other meeting place, 'Hampers Hotel' (as I was coming to call my apartment at Hampton Court) was constantly filled to overflowing. My grandchildren were all growing up and found me a useful 'base' on their trips to London. In addition, I found myself opening my home to visitors on the same scale as I had done at Pax Hill before the war. I had twelve beds almost constantly in use. I had forgotten that the Pax Hill days were twenty years and more ago, that I was younger then, that I had a large staff to call upon. Even though I was now over seventy, I still felt as full of energy, as eager to play my part as before.

I was helped by Mrs. Searle as my housekeeper for fifteen years. When she had been told of the vacancy at the Employment Exchange, the clerk had said 'It won't be a very difficult job. It's only one old lady. I expect she will only want an egg on a tray.'

In September I set off on yet another tour of the States and Canada. It was planned to take six months and had the usual packed schedule. I had only been one month into the tour when I was forcibly reminded of my years.

I was attending an official luncheon on Prince Edward Island. I felt hot and swimmy, and suddenly, without any warning, fainted clean away in front of everyone. I was rushed into hospital and told I had had a heart attack. My engagements for the next two months were cancelled and I was told to rest. It was a bitter blow. I had never yet failed to keep an engagement I had undertaken. Now I was forced to let people down on a large scale. I protested in my diary: '*Maddening* and *unnecessary*. I would be eager to risk another attack—which is not likely to happen after this prolonged rest! *Bother*!!'

One can go on for years and years without illness touching one's family in any way, then suddenly troubles seem to be heaped up, one on another.

I myself returned to England in the middle of April 1962. The heart attack had been a shock to me but I had made a complete recovery. Two other members of my family were ill and would not recover. My brother Arthur, who had been failing for several years, died in July—a merciful release for the poor man. I went to see him a few days before he died. He was in an oxygen tent and it was painful to see him struggling for existence.

More tragically (for Arthur was, after all, nearly seventy-six) my own Peter was dying. News had reached me while I was in America that he was in hospital with Multiple Myelomotosis—I think it is a form of leukemia. In the early summer he seemed to be recovering. He was allowed home and everyone hoped he was going to pull through. However, by October he was back in hospital, having massive blood transfusions. I saw him last on November 11th, 1962. He was very seedy, coughing a lot, and his doctor told me he was going downhill rapidly. His two boys, Robert and David, were with him and we all had tea together and pretended to be cheerful, but I guessed when I left him that day that I should not see him again.

I had to fly to Tokyo two days later to begin a tour of the Far East. I travelled through Japan, Korea, Okinawa, Taiwan, Hong Kong and Thailand to Malaya. I reached Kuala Lumpur on December 11th and found a telegram from Eileen Wade telling me that Peter had passed on the previous day. One could not but be grateful that he had been spared further suffering for he had no hope of any cure for his disease, but it was going to be a big ordeal for his family. He was only forty-nine.

Poor Peter. I wish I had understood him better. I had been so completely devoted to and admiring of my brilliant husband that I did not make sufficient allowance for our son. He had always been such a disappointment to me, yet he could not help it that he had delicate health, that he was not athletic or clever in anything except shooting (he was a brilliant shot and won competitions at Bisley). It was almost as if I was impatient with him for not being as outstanding as his father—and how could he possibly be so when men of as many parts as Robin come but once in a generation.

After Peter died, however, I began to realise—too late—that he was not so *un*like my husband as I had thought. Letter after letter, tribute after tribute, spoke of his capacity for friendship, his gentleness, his love and concern for other people—and that was always the burden of my husband's teaching: 'Be happy. Make other people happy.' Too late I realised that, in the things that really matter, Peter *was* his father's son after all.

I did not return to England. There was nothing I could do. So after completing my schedule of engagements in Singapore and Bombay, I flew to Kenya and the one place where I could be at peace—Paxtu.

CHAPTER TWENTY-FOUR

'My End is My Beginning...'

Years: 1963 to date

Since that time, I have gradually been slipping 'out of harness', taking a less active part in affairs. I still undertook engagements and tours, but not so many or so prolonged as before. As long as I had the strength and as long as I felt I had anything to contribute, I was prepared to play my part, but the years of maximum effort were over.

I was proud to attend, on May 15th, 1963, a ceremony when Brownsea Island, the site of that first 'pilot' Scout camp in 1907, was handed over to the National Trust.

My eldest grandson, Robert (now the third Baron Baden-Powell of Gilwell) was married in August of that year.

I went to the West Indies for the winter and undertook many Guiding engagements but was also grateful to escape the cold weather.

There was a 'wind of change' blowing across the islands and Central America. For one thing, there was much more tolerance on the part of the Catholic Church which was now allowing its Guides to join in *all* activities. For another, some of the big companies with interests in that part of the world had also become aware of the value of Scouting and Guiding and were encouraging its development in the new townships they had built for their employees. For example, in Venezuela, the Orinoco River Mining Company flew me up-country in one of their private planes to meet Guides and Scouts and their supporters at the settlement near their iron ore mines at Puerto Ordaz.

It was all interesting and stimulating and rewarding, but I found myself wanting to spend more and more time with my family. Betty and Gervas had returned to England for good during 1964. Robert and his wife came and stayed in my annexe when they were looking for a house in the London area. And each January, if possible, I liked to be at

Paxtu, not far from my niece Christian and her husband, and at 'my' grave for the anniversary of my darling's death. There was no grief any more. It was all too long ago to upset me. Rather did I feel peace and a quiet certainty that we should be together again. I only hoped it might be soon. 'If there is a hereafter, I shall be watching – and waiting,' he had written in his last letter to me.

When I arrived at the Outspan in January of 1965 I found that my bungalow was already occupied and I had to stay in the hotel for the first time since 1938. The new tenant of Paxtu was Mrs. Jaffe, wife of the producer of the film *Born Free*. The film itself was being shot at what used to be Eric Walker's home (he himself now lived in Majorca). Mildred Jaffe drove me over to the 'location' where I met Virginia McKenna who was playing the part of Joy Adamson. It emerged in conversation that she herself had been a Guide in her earlier years. It was quite fascinating to see what was involved in the making of a big feature film. A whole village had been set up to accommodate the 130 Africans involved; and there were eighteen wild lions and cubs in the caste!

In March 1965, Guiding suffered a grievous blow in the death of our beloved President, H.R.H. The Princess Royal. She had had a heart attack and had died suddenly while walking in the garden at Harewood House. I went to her Memorial Service in Westminster Abbey. She had been such an active President and a real friend. I remembered enrolling her as a Guide at Buckingham Palace; I remembered her wedding in that same Abbey where now we mourned her passing; I recalled with affection her gaiety at our own Silver Wedding celebrations, the many times she had joined us at Foxlease. So many old friends were going, but still I continued. How much more was there for me to do?

My niece Christian wrote to me from Kenya in July of that year, urging me to retire from active Guiding.

Better to stop on the crest of the wave and let everybody miss you *frightfully*, and by keeping your memory alive with deep affection, keep the Movement alive too. If you get *too* old before you retire, the Movement might feel a sense of relief when you finally did so, and your memory would not have the same inspiring

effect as if you had stopped when still at your peak. Is that sense or
not?

Wise words indeed, and very tempting—but I still felt there were
some things still to do. There would be one more world tour, one more
visit to India, one more to the States, one more to Central America
before I finally withdrew into private life. There was as yet no diminu-
tion in the flow of requests and invitations for my presence. As long
as people wanted me, I must go to them. Surely there would be a
'sign' telling me when to stop. My life had been so 'guided' that I had
complete confidence that God would let me know when my work was
finished.

I am not one to *demand* ceremony when I arrive anywhere but over
the years I have become used to having a reception party to meet me
wherever I travel and I was surprised, to say the least, when I arrived
on that last visit to San Salvador in February 1966 to find only one very
small Scout at the airport to greet me! I phoned through to Mr.
Stadler who had made the arrangements for my visit. Consternation!
I had arrived two hours earlier than expected! Within minutes he had
collected me from the airport and whisked me to his home for breakfast. Just before the time I was 'expected', we drove furtively into the
airport by a back entrance. As soon as the plane on which I was supposed to be travelling touched down, I joined the disembarking
passengers and 'arrived'—to find the Mayor, the Mayor's Band, rows
of Guides and Scouts and the usual posse of photographers all waiting
to give me a grand reception!

This was the public image. There has to be one. Whatever the personal unhappiness, whatever doubts and divisions exist, one must
always present a consistent 'image'. In 1966, there were doubts and
there were divisions in both Scouting and Guiding.

Both Associations had set up working parties to discuss how to
bring the two Movements 'up-to-date' to meet the needs of the much
more sophisticated rising generation. I was anxious that both Movements should keep to my husband's constant stipulation that Scouting
and Guiding should be *simple*, that they should be *for* the boys and girls,
and that they should be *fun*. Provided these qualities were retained and
provided the basic principles of Scouting and Guiding were not altered,

I saw no harm in changes. If a Movement is to live up to its name, it must *move* with the times. I know I am old, but I would never oppose change simply because it is change, particularly if the times demand a 'new look'.

What hurt me grievously, however, was the insistence of the Scout 'Advance Party' on reducing the Scout 'Laws' to seven from the ten my husband had devised. The Advance Party assured me that the *content* was unaltered in which case, I argued, why bother to change them? I begged them to reconsider their decision. The Laws, like the Scout Promise, have always been the same all over the world and I felt passionately that the proposed change would put Britain 'out of step' with the rest of World Scouting. Alas, my protests met with no success and the Advance Party proposals were accepted in full. I was deeply distressed and, for the first and only time in my long association with Scouting, felt tempted to resign from my position as its Vice-President. In the event, I did not do so; I could not bring myself to do anything which might be misconstrued outside and which might harm the Movement my husband had founded, but it was a very unhappy period and for a long time my relations with Scout Headquarters were strained.

Scouting, of course, has proved strong enough to cope with any change. It is now a bigger Movement than ever and, I consider, offering as fine a training as boys and young men will find anywhere. I still find it hard to accept the Laws in their condensed form but the heat has gone out of my opposition. I still look back with nostalgia to the old uniform — though I admit it is because the broad-brimmed hat and the shorts are so inextricably intertwined with precious memories of my husband. But these are minor things. I have sought always to keep the two Movements *pure* as my husband devised them. Thankfully I can testify that the 'Scout spirit' goes on unchanged, spreading its message of friendship and self-reliance and consideration for others. That, in the last reckoning, is what matters.

1966 closed tragically. I was having my breakfast in bed one morning in December when the telephone at my bedside rang. I lifted the receiver and a man's voice said 'Mum . . .' The voice was so strangled that for a moment I did not recognise John King, my Heather's husband. He broke the terrible news that Michael had been drowned —

the red-haired boy who at the Sutton Park Jamboree had played the part of his grandfather as a schoolboy at Charterhouse.

Michael had been on holiday in Crete and was returning to Piraeus in the car ferry *Iraklion*. They were overtaken by a violent storm and, apparently, a van being carried on the ferry broke loose. The violent pitching of the vessel caused the van to batter repeatedly against the sea-doors until these gave way and the sea rushed in. The vessel sank quickly with great loss of life. Michael was a good swimmer and could probably have survived but we heard later that he delayed getting clear of the sinking ship to help an elderly man on to a life-raft. His action cost him his life for, as the same man told John later, Michael was sucked down as the vessel went under and he was never seen again. It seemed such a waste of a young life, full of such bright promise. Why did he have to go? Why did I survive?

A prayer which I use frequently runs: 'God give me work till my life shall end; God give me life till my work is done.' I was still alive, presumably my work was not yet done.

My role in Guiding was changing. No longer was it necessary to watch over young and tender growth. The Movement was strong and wide-spread throughout the world. Rather now was I able to point out the needs of its weaker sections to the stronger, to obtain financial support, to endeavour to ensure that the public should not take the Movement for granted. Over the years, Scouting and Guiding have become so much part of the daily scene that people tend to forget that they still need financial support—perhaps even more today, with millions of young people involved, than they did in the pioneering days when they were numbered in thousands. Moreover, whereas in the early years, the Movements were novel and exciting and the recipients of considerable charitable monies, today those gifts go to help the more immediately urgent needs of famine and flood relief, the rescue of refugees and so on. The need in our organisations is still there, however, and still important. 'Feed The Minds' may seek to bring Christian literature to black Africa, but I feel it is of equal importance for struggling Scout and Guide leaders in some of, say, the backward South American countries to have training manuals in their own language. Scouting and Guiding are all sharing in the battle against illiteracy, ignorance and depression.

In this battle, I have been able to act as intermediary between the wealthy countries and those less well endowed. I am always being offered gifts—flowers, souvenirs and so on. Flowers, I tell the would-be donors, do not go with Guide uniform. Souvenirs, I tell them, are an embarrassment to carry around when one is 'travelling light' and hurrying from city to city by car or train or plane for weeks and months on end. I prefer the would-be donors to give the value of their gifts to some more worthy cause. On one of my tours of Australia, the Guides there offered to give me an ice-cream apiece as a way of saying 'Thank you' for my visit. Just one ice-cream per Guide. As they could hardly send thousands of sticky, melting cornets through the post, they sent the cost of each ice-cream to a central 'Ice-Cream Fund' which I have disbursed for the benefit of Guiding in other parts of the world. It was supposed to be a 'once and for all gift' but, somehow, the money has kept coming in and I have received hundreds of pounds each year. In this way I have been enabled to provide the books so urgently needed in South America. I have also presented doors for any Headquarters I have opened or where I have laid the foundation stone. As the Ice-Cream Fund has dwindled, I have had to give windows instead of doors, but they have been nonetheless appreciated and in each case a small plaque pays tribute to the generosity of the Guides of Australia.

In 1968, the Boy Scouts of America generously gave me a Credit Card for unlimited travel by air, train or car. This enabled me to make many short tours that I might otherwise not have been able to afford to undertake, and since 1970 when, for health reasons, I have given up overseas travelling altogether, they have graciously allowed me to use the credit card for other means of 'keeping in touch.' For example, my Christmas card always costs me many hundreds of pounds in printing and postage for there are 2,000 names on the list and those all people I call by their Christian names. For the past two years it has been financed in this way.

Instead of going out to other countries, I took to doing more entertaining of overseas visitors here at home. I had always entertained a lot, even in the days of rationing. Now, with the help of my 'Home Office' staff, as I called my good team of helpers here at Hampton Court, I gave regular 'finger lunches', once or twice a week, for up to as many as forty people at a time. They would be a 'mixed bunch'

from home and overseas, some in Scouting and Guiding, others from
the E.A.W.L., some people who had expressed a desire to help our
work, others, people I had met on my travels who were 'passing
through' London. It was truly amazing how often these strangely assorted
groups would find points of common interest, would discover they had
been at the same school, had mutual friends or some other connection.
I made a point of running through the guest list and outlining for the
benefit of the party some details about each guest, and at least twice
during the two or three hours of each occasion, I would ask everyone
to change around and talk to someone they had not met before.

Sometimes the guests would linger and luncheon would merge into
afternoon tea. There are many things still in my apartment to interest
a visitor. I have dozens of 'scrap-books' of my own and my husband's
journeyings, kept carefully ever since our marriage and brought
regularly up-to-date. It is a real thrill for visitors to be able to turn up a
certain year and find cuttings or photographs relating to their own
particular town or country. The apartment is full of reminders of my
husband. The walls are hung with his exquisite water-colours; a life-
sized sculptured head by him, called 'The Blind Slave', stands beneath
his portrait in the hallway. There are cases containing his ceremonial
swords and many souvenirs of his exploits—although I have returned
most of these to their donors for safe-keeping, as also I have given to
the Army Museum most of the relics of his Army career.

I love my home at 'Hampers' almost as much as my beloved Pax
Hill. I have been here for thirty years now and feel almost part of the
structure of the Palace. Once, as I mingled among the throngs of
tourists on my way to garden in my allotment in the Home Park, I
used frequently to be recognised. Now, as I grow older and drop more
out of the public eye, it happens less often. I remember—not so long
ago—returning from shopping in East Molesey. At the foot of my
stairs, a small boy was spelling out my name on the name-plate.
His mother yanked him impatiently away. 'Come along', she said.
'It's no good reading that. She's been dead for years.'

Of course, people in Scouting and Guiding know I am not dead. It is
nothing to have a whole company of Guides arrive for tea at Hampton
Court, or for my bell to ring and some overseas Scouter to say 'I saw
your name at the foot of the stairs . . .' What can I do? I do not like to

send them away – but I *do* wish they would telephone first so that I can change into uniform. They expect to see me in uniform.

I do not want to go on and on until everyone has forgotten about me or until I become a burden to my family. I am quite ready to die and quite unafraid. But I was glad I was spared to take part in our own Guide Diamond Jubilee celebrations, or 'Jubilations', as we called them.

They started with a wonderful Service of Thanksgiving in Westminster Abbey on Thinking Day 1969. It was my eightieth birthday and I had the rare privilege for a woman of being asked to read the Lesson. It was a most moving service, the Abbey almost bursting at the seams with Guides and Brownies who were packed two to a stall in the choir, were seated on hassocks down the aisles. I looked out over the sea of eager young faces, so full of warmth and promise. How humble it made me feel to think that my darling Robin and I had been privileged to create these two vast, world-wide Movements, to have influenced – I trust for good – generation after generation of boys and girls. Imagine the potential benefit to mankind if even half of those millions of youngsters who have passed through the two Movements remember their Scout and Guide Promise throughout their life.

> On my honour I promise that I will do my best to do my Duty to God, and to the Queen, to help other people . . .

So simple an idea, so far-reaching in its implications!

The Jubilations continued. I flew to Finland and to Belgium; I attended celebrations in Nigeria where General Gowon in Scout uniform opened the proceedings. I flew to East Africa again and stayed with President Nyerere. In Kenya I enrolled Jomo Kenyatta's wife, Mama Ngina, as a Guide. I went on down to South Africa where I was given a £1,000 Jubilee diamond to sell on behalf of the Association, I travelled to the United States, to Denmark. Everywhere I met with warmth and kindness. The welcome was heart-warming and enthusiastic. Despite my eighty years – or perhaps because of them – people seemed eager to see and hear me. The best part of any tour is the bliss of feeling one has done something of *use*, to have helped people, to have given them pleasure and encouragement. That way, one feels that neither the money nor the effort involved in the tour have been wasted.

16

I wish I could have 'lasted out' for the whole Jubilee Year but it was not to be. Towards the end of July 1970 I became very ill, very exhausted, endlessly sleepy. The hospital diagnosed acute diabetes and ordered a strict regimen to be observed in the future. No more foreign tours, no more jetting around the world. The demands of a strict diet and regular insulin injections made these impossible. The 'sign' for which I had looked to tell me when I should retire was now plain to see. It took a great deal of mental adjustment after almost sixty years of public service but I am reconciled now to spending month after month in one place after so many years of constant travelling.

Even the illness had its amusing side. I gather that I was very ill indeed, though I myself was unaware of this. Anticipating the worst, or rather 'Being Prepared' for it, the Guide Association had made plans for my Memorial Service. Whoever at Headquarters put up the post was used to popping into my envelope any circular addressed 'To All Commissioners'. Imagine my delighted surprise when I received details of my own Memorial Service!

I have been to every World Jamboree except one since they started at Olympia in 1920 so I was exceedingly disappointed when my doctors forbade my attending the most recent one in Japan in the summer of 1971. Those who organised it told me later that it was obvious that I just could not keep away: a hurricane coincidentally named 'Olive' struck the camp on the opening day!

I was allowed to go to Gilwell in September 1971 to unveil the magnificent head of my husband sculpted by David Wynne which was being placed in the International Centre there, but otherwise public engagements have been kept to a minimum.

So now I pass my days quietly in my palace, still meeting old friends, still tending the roses and rhubarb in my allotment. The big jets still stream out overhead, one every two minutes from Heathrow, flying to all parts of the world—my world. I shall not travel by air again but I still sit for many hours each day at my typewriter keeping in touch by letter with the thousands of people, young and old, whom I can no longer travel to visit; and their letters continue to flow in to Hampton Court from all over the world.

But surely this quiet mode of existence cannot be for much longer. God gave me a great work to do, and gave me the health and the vigour to carry it through until it was firmly established. Now there is no more I can contribute. Guiding and Scouting are strong. They have grown up and can carry on without my support, just as my own children and grandchildren have also grown and built lives and careers of their own. I have been called 'The Mother of Millions' and it is one of the sadnesses, as well as the joys of motherhood, that children outgrow their mother. Nonetheless, I hold fast in my mind the eager look in many children's eyes and the sweet friendly grip of outstretched hands.

If I have any message to leave, it is this: Believe in God. He guides and protects you all through life, as I trust this account of my life has demonstrated. Discipline yourself daily by having a plan—not just vague, wishful thinking. Commit yourself daily to doing something, however small, for somebody else, for by making other people happy you will find true happiness yourself.

I give thanks daily—for my good night's sleep, for the dawn of each new day with its opportunities of service.

I have so much to be thankful for—a lifetime of enjoyable and absorbing work, millions of 'my' children all over the world, but above all the precious and ever-fresh memory of nearly thirty years with my beloved Robin.

I can hear his voice speaking to me now through his last letter, and I long soon to 'go across' to be reunited with him.

'Dindo darling . . . I shall be waiting . . .'

List of Countries Visited

List of Countries where I have stayed and shared events with Guides and Scouts, their Leaders, Parents and Supporters.

1 Algeria, 1913, 1929, 1934
2 Antigua, 1951, 1964
3 Argentine, 1959
4 Australia, 1931, 1934/5, 1947/8, 1957/8, 1967/8
5 Austria, 1928, 1932, 1951
6 Bahamas, 1946, 1951, 1953, 1963, 1964
7 Barbados, 1912, 1930, 1946, 1951, 1964
8 Basutoland (Lesotho), 1927, 1942
9 Belgium, 1919, 1938, 1945, 1949, 1951, 1958, 1965, 1969
10 Bermuda, 1930, 1951, 1954, 1963
11 Brazil, 1959
12 British Guiana, 1946, 1951, 1964
13 British Honduras, 1959, 1966
14 Burma, 1921
15 Canada, 1919, 1923, 1926, 1935, 1946, 1952, 1953, 1955, 1959, 1961, 1965, 1967, 1969, 1970
16 Canary Islands, 1926/7, 1929
17 Ceylon, 1921, 1934, 1958, 1961, 1968
18 Chile, 1959
19 Colombia, 1959
20 Congo (Zaire), 1941, 1950, 1956
21 Costa Rica, 1959
22 Cuba, 1946
23 Curacao, 1948, 1964

24 Cyprus, 1949

25 Czechoslovakia, 1949

26 Denmark, 1924, 1933, 1936, 1938, 1945, 1949, 1952, 1957, 1960,
1962, 1963, 1970

27 Dominica, 1951, 1964

28 East Indies, 1934

29 Ecuador, 1959

30 Egypt, 1921, 1937, 1949, 1965

31 El Salvador, 1959

32 Estonia, 1933

33 Fiji, 1958

34 Finland, 1933, 1950, 1960, 1969, 1970

35 France 1901, 1910, 1915/6, 1921, 1922, 1925, 1931, 1932, 1933,
1934, 1936, 1945, 1946, 1947, 1948, 1953, 1955, 1965

36 French Guyana, 1964

37 Galapagos Islands, 1948

38 Gambia, 1950

39 Germany, 1919, 1932, 1945, 1956, 1960, 1964

40 Ghana (Gold Coast), 1950, 1957

41 Gibraltar, 1913, 1921, 1932, 1933, 1934, 1937, 1960

42 Greece, 1948, 1949, 1960, 1963

43 Grenada, 1951, 1964

44 Guadeloupe, 1951, 1964

45 Guatemala, 1959, 1964, 1966

46 Haiti, 1951

47 Holland, 1933, 1937, 1946, 1949, 1954, 1962, 1966

48 Hong Kong, 1958, 1962, 1966

49 Hungary, 1928

50 Iceland, 1938, 1956, 1962

51 India, 1921, 1937, 1960/61, 1962, 1966, 1968

52 Indonesia, 1935, 1957

53 Ireland, 1915, 1944, 1946, 1949, 1950, 1959

54 Israel, 1921, 1964

55 Italy, 1913, 1932, 1933, 1937, 1945, 1948, 1956, 1961, 1965, 1967,
1968

56 Jamaica, 1912, 1930, 1946, 1951, 1964

57 Japan, 1962, 1966

58　Kenya, 1935, 1937, 1938/42, 1949/50, 1956, 1957, 1959, 1962/3,
　　　1964/5, 1967/8, 1968/9, 1970
59　Korea, 1962, 1966
60　Latvia, 1933
61　Lebanon, 1960
62　Leichtenstein, 1945, 1966
63　Libya, 1956
64　Lithuania, 1933
65　Luxembourg, 1945, 1965
66　Madeira, 1927, 1929
67　Malaya, 1934, 1935, 1938, 1961, 1962
68　Malta, 1913, 1932, 1933, 1934, 1937, 1948, 1956, 1967, 1968
69　Martinique, 1951, 1964
70　Mauritius, 1965
71　Mexico, 1946, 1956, 1959, 1962, 1964, 1966, 1967
72　Montserrat, 1951
73　Newfoundland, 1923, 1935, 1946, 1961
74　New Zealand, 1931, 1935, 1948, 1967
75　Nicaragua, 1950, 1959, 1969
76　Nigeria, 1950, 1960, 1969
77　Norway, 1909, 1924, 1932, 1933, 1938, 1945, 1946, 1949, 1952,
　　　1965
78　Nyasaland (Malawi), 1950, 1956
79　Pakistan, 1937, 1960
80　Panama, 1912, 1930, 1931, 1948, 1959, 1965
81　Peru, 1959
82　Philippines, 1958, 1966
83　Pitcairn Island, 1948
84　Poland, 1932, 1933
85　Portugal, 1934, 1960
86　Puerto Rico, 1951
87　Sierra Leone, 1929, 1942, 1950
88　South Africa, 1926/7, 1931, 1936, 1942, 1950, 1970
89　St. Helena, 1936
90　St. Kitts, 1951, 1964
91　St. Lucia, 1951
92　St. Vincent, 1951, 1964

93 Sudan, 1949, 1956, 1965
94 Surinam, 1964
95 Swaziland, 1942, 1950
96 Sweden, 1924, 1933, 1935, 1936, 1945, 1949, 1950, 1954, 1955, 1957, 1962, 1965
97 Switzerland, 1922, 1931, 1932, 1934, 1938, 1945, 1946, 1949, 1951, 1952, 1954, 1955, 1956, 1958, 1962, 1966
98 Tahiti, 1935
99 Tangier, 1913, 1929, 1933, 1950, 1960
100 Tanzania (Tanganyika) 1935, 1941, 1950, 1957, 1963, 1970
101 Thailand, 1962, 1966
102 Thursday Island, 1934
103 Tobago, 1946, 1951, 1964
104 Trinidad, 1912, 1930, 1946, 1951, 1964
105 Uganda, 1935, 1941, 1950, 1956, 1963, 1965, 1967, 1968
106 United States of America, 1919, 1923, 1926, 1930, 1935, 1946, 1948, 1952, 1953/4, 1955/6, 1959, 1961/2, 1963/4, 1965/6, 1967, 1969, 1970
107 Uruguay, 1959
108 Venezuela, 1964
109 Windward Islands, 1951, 1964
110 Zambia (Rhodesia), 1926, 1936, 1938, 1941, 1950. 1956, 1963
111 Zanzibar, 1935, 1950, 1957

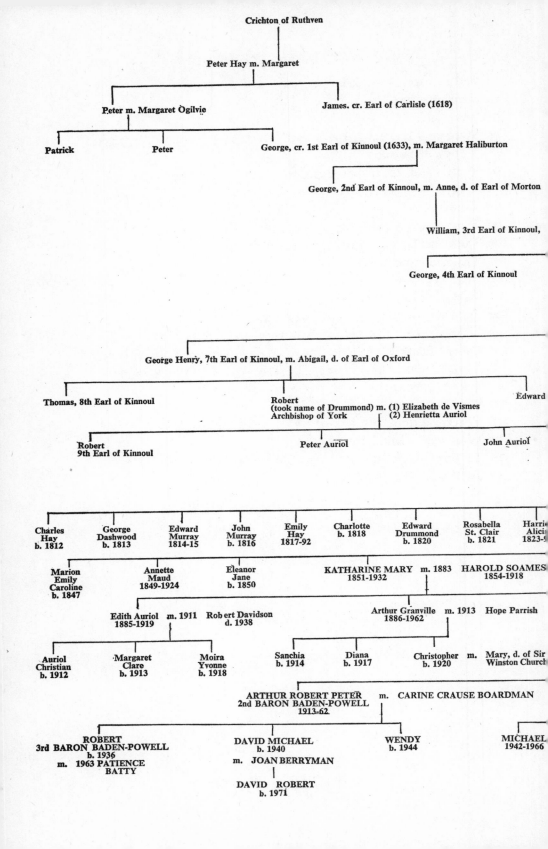

Crichton of Ruthven

Peter Hay m. Margaret

Peter m. Margaret Ogilvie

James. cr. Earl of Carlisle (1618)

Patrick

Peter

George, cr. 1st Earl of Kinnoul (1633), m. Margaret Haliburton

George, 2nd Earl of Kinnoul, m. Anne, d. of Earl of Morton

William, 3rd Earl of Kinnoul,

George, 4th Earl of Kinnoul

George Henry, 7th Earl of Kinnoul, m. Abigail, d. of Earl of Oxford

Thomas, 8th Earl of Kinnoul

Robert
(took name of Drummond) m. (1) Elizabeth de Vismes
Archbishop of York   (2) Henrietta Auriol

Edward

Robert
9th Earl of Kinnoul

Peter Auriol

John Auriol

Charles
Hay
b. 1812

George
Dashwood
b. 1813

Edward
Murray
1814-15

John
Murray
b. 1816

Emily
Hay
1817-92

Charlotte
b. 1818

Edward
Drummond
b. 1820

Rosabella
St. Clair
b. 1821

Harrie
Alicia
1823-9

Marion
Emily
Caroline
b. 1847

Annette
Maud
1849-1924

Eleanor
Jane
b. 1850

KATHARINE MARY   m. 1883   HAROLD SOAMES
1851-1932   1854-1918

Edith Auriol   m. 1911   Robert Davidson
1885-1919   d. 1938

Arthur Granville   m. 1913   Hope Parrish
1886-1962

Auriol
Christian
b. 1912

Margaret
Clare
b. 1913

Moira
Yvonne
b. 1918

Sanchia
b. 1914

Diana
b. 1917

Christopher   m.   Mary, d. of Sir
b. 1920   Winston Church

ARTHUR ROBERT PETER   m.   CARINE CRAUSE BOARDMAN
2nd BARON BADEN-POWELL
1913-62

ROBERT
3rd BARON BADEN-POWELL
b. 1936
m. 1963 PATIENCE
BATTY

DAVID MICHAEL
b. 1940
m. JOAN BERRYMAN

WENDY
b. 1944

MICHAEL
1942-1966

DAVID ROBERT
b. 1971

THE FAMILY TREE OF OLAVE, LADY BADEN-POWELL, G.B.E.

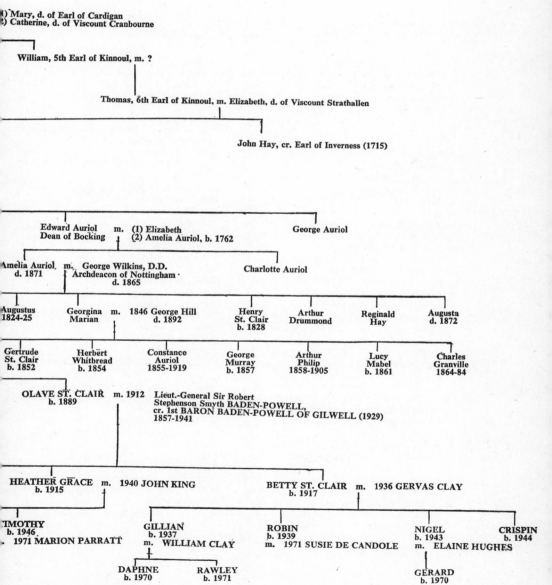

(1) Mary, d. of Earl of Cardigan
(2) Catherine, d. of Viscount Cranbourne

William, 5th Earl of Kinnoul, m. ?

Thomas, 6th Earl of Kinnoul, m. Elizabeth, d. of Viscount Strathallen

John Hay, cr. Earl of Inverness (1715)

Edward Auriol   m. (1) Elizabeth   George Auriol
Dean of Bocking   (2) Amelia Auriol, b. 1762

Amelia Auriol   m.   George Wilkins, D.D.   Charlotte Auriol
d. 1871   Archdeacon of Nottingham ·
                     d. 1865

Augustus   Georgina m.   1846 George Hill   Henry   Arthur   Reginald   Augusta
1824-25   Marian   d. 1892   St. Clair   Drummond   Hay   d. 1872
                                                  b. 1828

Gertrude   Herbert   Constance   George   Arthur   Lucy   Charles
St. Clair   Whitbread   Auriol   Murray   Philip   Mabel   Granville
b. 1852   b. 1854   1855-1919   b. 1857   1858-1905   b. 1861   1864-84

OLAVE ST. CLAIR   m. 1912   Lieut.-General Sir Robert
b. 1889   Stephenson Smyth BADEN-POWELL,
                            cr. 1st BARON BADEN-POWELL OF GILWELL (1929)
                            1857-1941

HEATHER GRACE   m.   1940 JOHN KING   BETTY ST. CLAIR   m.   1936 GERVAS CLAY
b. 1915   b. 1917

TIMOTHY   GILLIAN   ROBIN   NIGEL   CRISPIN
b. 1946   b. 1937   b. 1939   b. 1943   b. 1944
. 1971 MARION PARRATT   m. WILLIAM CLAY   m. 1971 SUSIE DE CANDOLE   m. ELAINE HUGHES

              DAPHNE   RAWLEY   GERARD
              b. 1970   b. 1971   b. 1970

Index

Index